A Peoples Education Skillbook for

AP*/Honors

English Language and Composition

Analysis, Argument, and Synthesis

John Brassil

Sandra Coker

Carl Glover, Ph.D.

Peoples Education™
Your partner in student success™

The Authors

John Brassil is English department chair at Mt. Ararat High School in Topsham, Maine, where he has taught Advanced Placement* English Language and Composition since 1983. He is a question leader and former table leader at the AP English Language reading, and has conducted AP summer institutes and other workshops throughout New England, in Canada, at the AP Annual Conference, and at conferences of the National Council of Teachers of English. A National Board Certified Teacher, John is a mentor to new AP English Language and Composition teachers in Maine. He also has contributed to College Board professional development publications.

Sandra Coker, an experienced teacher of AP English Language and Composition, currently teaches at Westlake High School in Austin, Texas. A table leader at the AP English Language and Composition reading, she also conducts AP summer institutes and teacher development workshops nationally and internationally. Sandra is also a contributing writer for **AP Strategies:** *Laying the Foundation*, a curriculum guide for Pre-AP teachers. She has created a curriculum document for the Texas Education Agency that aligns English Language Arts objectives with AP English goals.

Carl W. Glover, Ph. D., is associate professor of communication studies at Mount St. Mary's University, where he teaches courses in classical rhetoric, argument, public relations, and public speaking. For five years, he directed the freshman seminar program and now directs the University Writing Center. He has published articles and book chapters in the history of rhetoric, writing centers, and written composition. He has also served as a reader and table leader for the AP English Language and Composition Exam. In his free time, Carl is the lead singer of the Fire City Jazz Band.

Dedication
To Donald M. Murray, teacher of us all

Author Acknowledgements
We wish to thank Claudette Brassil, James and Stephen Coker, Sally Glover, and Richard Lynn Campbell for their steadfast support. We also thank the staff at Peoples Education.

Executive Editor: Doug Falk

Supervising Copy Editor: Lee Laddy

Editorial Services: Words and Numbers

Vice President of Production and Manufacturing: Doreen Smith

Senior Production Manager: Jason Grasso

Assistant Production Manager: Steven Genzano

Marketing Manager: Brian Moore

Permissions Manager: Kristine Liebman

*AP is a registered trademark of the College Board, which was not involved in the production of, and does not endorse, this book.

Your partner in student success™   ISBN   978-1-4138-4878-6

Copyright © 2008
Peoples Education, Inc.
299 Market Street
Saddle Brook, New Jersey 07663

Printed in the United States of America.

10   9   8   7   6   5   4   3   2   1

Table of Contents

Modern Applications of Ancient Rhetoric

Successful students in an advanced course such as Advanced Placement English Language and Composition should be able to perform three tasks:

1. Analysis. A close examination of texts, with the awareness of a writer's purpose and the techniques the writer uses to achieve it.

2. Argument. A discourse intended to persuade an audience through reasons and/or evidence.

3. Synthesis. A bringing together of several texts, both written and visual, to form a coherent essay.

To do these tasks effectively, you should understand the rhetorical techniques of ancient Greece and Rome, as well as have insight into modern perspectives on rhetoric and argument. This chapter focuses on using ancient rhetorical techniques for analysis. Chapter 2 covers modern approaches to argument and synthesis.

In this chapter, you will learn some tools of rhetoric as you analyze a modern piece of persuasive writing, "Letter from Birmingham Jail," by Dr. Martin Luther King, Jr. This powerful essay demonstrates King's masterful application of rhetorical techniques.

About "Letter from Birmingham Jail"

In April 1963, the civil rights leader and clergyman Dr. Martin Luther King, Jr., was jailed in Birmingham, Alabama, for leading anti-segregation protests. His "Letter from Birmingham Jail," dated April 16, is an open letter to eight white clergymen from Alabama. In it, King responds to a statement by these clergymen that expressed their belief that the battle against segregation should be fought in the courts and not in the streets. The letter was published in *The Christian Century* on June 12, 1963. For the full text, see http://www.thekingcenter.org/prog/non/Letter.pdf

The Five Canons of Rhetoric

The basic outline of classical rhetoric is composed of five categories, or "canons":

- invention
- arrangement
- style
- memory
- delivery

Memory and delivery are concerned primarily with oral or spoken rhetoric and will not be treated in this chapter. Invention, arrangement, and style, however, are relevant to both oral and written rhetoric. You will examine these three canons in depth.

Invention

Invention is the process of coming up with ideas for speaking or writing. According to Aristotle, the great rhetorician of ancient Greece, under the heading of invention are three "proofs" or appeals: ethos, logos, and pathos.

Ethos is the character or credibility of the speaker/writer.

Logos is the content of the written or spoken message.

Pathos is the emotional appeal to the audience by the speaker or writer.

Aristotle calls these proofs "artistic" because they are under the control of the speaker or writer, who creates them in the minds of the audience.

Aristotle points out that these three *artistic proofs* need to work together in balance for the speaker or writer to achieve maximum persuasive effect. People use their hearts as well as their minds in making decisions, and these three proofs are tools for both analyzing and creating effective arguments.

Ethos

Ethos is an appeal based on the character or credibility of the speaker/writer. In "Letter from Birmingham Jail," how does King establish his credibility, his character? Instead of beginning the letter with the impersonal "Dear Sir," or "To Whom it May Concern," King opens with "My Dear Fellow Clergymen." The greeting is warm, but it is also more than that. By addressing his audience as fellow clergymen, he is reminding them that they are in fact equals, that they all work in the same profession, and that they all share a common ground.

King says he seldom takes the time to respond to criticism, but he makes an exception in this case because these are "men of genuine good will" and their "criticisms are sincerely set forth." The clergymen have accused King of being an outsider coming in to stir up trouble, and King uses the ethos appeal in three ways to respond to this accusation:

1. He points out that he is acting not as an individual but as president of the Southern Christian Leadership Conference, which has an affiliate organization in Birmingham. The local chapter invited him to "engage in a nonviolent direct-action program if such were deemed necessary."

2. King says that, like the prophets of the Old Testament and the New Testament, he goes wherever there is injustice. By citing scripture, he is appealing to the religious background and shared values of the clergymen, his audience.

3. King observes that it no longer makes sense to talk about an "outside agitator," because

   > "We are caught in an inescapable network of mutuality, tied in a single garment of destiny."

These three points establish that King is one of them, not an outsider, and therefore his words should be credible. King goes on to establish his character for his audience by pointing out the four basic steps of his nonviolent campaign. He is trying to convince his readers that he did not take these actions impulsively; but that they were the result of a four-step process. The steps, in King's words are

1. "collection of facts to determine whether injustice exists"

2. "negotiation"

3. "self-purification"

4. "direct action"

He wants his audience to see him as a person who carefully weighs all options before taking action.

As King concludes his letter, he makes further use of ethos. He apologizes for having taken so much of the audience's precious time, ironically noting that he has lots of time in jail. He goes on to beg forgiveness for any overstatement and hopes the letter finds the clergymen "strong in the faith." In his conclusion, he is again establishing that his character is the same as theirs because they share the same profession and have a shared common ground.

Logos

King's ethos is further established through his use of logical argumentation, logos. In Greek, *logos* means "word," the content of the argument. King answers each of the clergymen's arguments pragmatically and ethically. To illustrate King's response, it is useful to reduce the clergymen's arguments into a logical structure. Their objections can be restated in the following manner:

- "Outsiders" should not be leading local protests (major premise).
- King is an "outsider" (minor premise).
- Therefore, King should not be protesting (conclusion).

Syllogism

Arranged this way, those three statements are an example of a logical **syllogism**, which is a chain of reasoning moving from general, universal principles to specific instances.

While King is establishing his credibility, his ethos, he also responds to the clergymen's argument pragmatically, by countering their minor premise, that King is an outsider. He points out that he was invited by local leaders to assist in the protest and he is president of the Southern Christian Leadership Conference. Therefore he is not an outsider.

Next King addresses the major premise ("Outsiders" should not be leading local protests) from an ethical point of view. He states that the Apostle Paul and the Old Testament prophets went wherever there was a need, wherever God sent them. He further writes that all communities in the modern world are interrelated:

"Whatever affects one directly affects all indirectly. Never again can we afford to live with the narrow, provincial 'outside agitator' idea."

Enthymemes

Aristotle states that under logos, or the content of the message, the two most powerful tools are the enthymeme and the example. Everyone knows what an example is, but the enthymeme, while used by all of us every day, is a little-known concept outside the realm of rhetorical studies. The **enthymeme** is a shortened syllogism that serves the purpose of a more practical and expedient way to argue. A well-known example of a syllogism turned into an enthymeme is the following:

- All people are mortal (major premise).
- Aristotle was a person (minor premise).
- Therefore Aristotle was mortal (conclusion).

Aristotle's syllogism, restructured as an enthymeme, would be the following:

Aristotle was mortal because he was a person.

Left out of the enthymeme is the major premise, or the universal principle that *All people are mortal*.

In an argument, the speaker or writer can leave out the universal principle because everyone would agree that all people are mortal. This principle does not need to be stated. It is an assumption shared by everyone. Therefore, enthymemes have great practical value in argumentation. However, an argument might be vulnerable if the audience does not accept the unstated principle that supports the argument.

The clergymen's syllogism, containing a major premise, a minor premise, and a conclusion, can be restated as an enthymeme in this way:

King should not be leading local protests, because he is an outsider.

This enthymeme leaves out the major premise that "outsiders" should not be leading local protests. The clergymen assume that this is a universal principle that supports their argument. King does not accept their unstated principle and thus finds a weakness in their argument. Addressing it effectively, he writes,

> "Never again can we afford to live with the narrow, provincial 'outside agitator' idea. Anyone who lives inside the United States can never be considered an outsider anywhere within its bounds."

Using Syllogisms and Enthymemes in Arguments

Syllogisms are used primarily in a logic course, but are rarely used in real-world argumentation. They are cumbersome and impractical, and, if we had to lay everything out in a syllogistic pattern, we would complete very few arguments. On the other hand, the enthymeme, a kind of shortened syllogism, has great practical value, and writers use them every day.

When you analyze arguments, an important step is finding the enthymemes and the unstated principles that support the enthymemes. An argument's vulnerable point is often that unstated principle. An argument's acceptability to an audience hinges on the audience's acceptance of that unstated principle, and a sympathetic audience is willing to accept unstated principles because they hold those principles in common with the speaker or writer. With a neutral or hostile audience, however, the speaker/writer must work harder to gain the audience's acceptance of unstated principles. Therefore, the writer, like King, must understand the audience's values, beliefs, and priorities in order to use enthymemes successfully.

Combining Enthymeme and Logos

King next uses logos in the letter to address the issue of breaking the law. King did break the law, a court-ordered injunction against demonstrations, and he writes of this irony:

> "Since we so diligently urge people to obey the Supreme Court's decision of 1954 outlawing segregation in public schools, it is rather strange and paradoxical to find us consciously breaking laws."

This argument is the crux of the letter, and King devotes eight paragraphs to justifying his position. The clergymen's argument runs as follows:

- It is always wrong to break the law (major premise).

- King broke the law (minor premise).

- Therefore, King is wrong (conclusion).

As an enthymeme, this syllogism could be restated as follows:

King is wrong because he broke the law.

In this instance, King cannot dispute the minor premise that he broke the law. He did break the law, and he admits it. Changing his tactics, he addresses the unstated principle of the clergymen's position that it is always wrong to break the law. King claims that there are just laws and unjust laws and that we have a "legal" and a "moral responsibility to obey just laws" and "a moral responsibility to disobey unjust laws."

King next distinguishes between just and unjust laws. He makes three points:

> "A just law is a man-made code that squares with the moral law or the law of God. An unjust law is a code that is out of harmony with the moral law."

"An unjust law is a code that… a majority group compels a minority group to obey but does not make binding on itself."

"A law is unjust if it is inflicted on a minority that… had no part in enacting or devising the law."

Because of the three distinctions that King draws between just and unjust laws, he concludes that the segregation laws, and specifically laws against his public demonstrations, are unjust.

King then bolsters his argument by citing both biblical and historical figures who broke unjust laws. For example, the early Christians were fed to the lions or burned as candles for refusing to obey the unjust Roman law that required them to renounce their Christian faith. He also mentions Socrates, the patriots of the Boston Tea Party, and the Germans who disobeyed Hitler as examples of individuals who broke unjust laws. By using both biblical and historical references here, King appeals specifically to the clergymen and more broadly to the general public. He continues to establish his ethos as a traditionalist, not as an "extremist."

The clergymen, however, characterize King's "activity in Birmingham as extreme." To turn the clergymen's accusation into an enthymeme, it would read:

> *King is wrong because his actions are those of an extremist.*

The unstated principle behind this enthymeme is *Extremism is wrong*.

King first responds directly to the accusation that he is an extremist. He points out that his voice is a moderate one in the civil rights movement, between the radical voice of Elijah Muhammad and the conservative voices of older African Americans who have "adjusted to segregation." King states,

"…we need emulate neither the 'do-nothingism' of the complacent nor the hatred and despair of the black nationalists. For there is the more excellent way of love and nonviolent protest."

King then addresses the unstated principle supporting the enthymeme: "extremism is wrong." He lists some of the great, often revered extremists of history—Jesus, Amos, the apostle Paul, Martin Luther, Lincoln, and Thomas Jefferson. This is good company to keep if you are an extremist, and he uses the rhetorical technique of identification in aligning himself with such highly respected leaders.

Pathos

Logos appeals to the intellect. Pathos is an appeal to the emotions of the audience. People tend to follow their hearts more so than they do their minds, and King could have provided a display of emotional fireworks in his discussion of the evils of segregation. Instead, he spoke more from a logical and ethical perspective. Yet he presented this with passion:

But when you have seen vicious mobs lynch your mothers and fathers at will and drown your sisters and brothers at whim; when you have seen hate-filled policemen curse, kick, brutalize, and even kill your black brothers and sisters with impunity; when you see the vast majority of your 20 million Negro broth-
5　ers smothering in an airtight cage of poverty in the midst of an affluent society; when you suddenly find your tongue twisted and your speech stammering as you seek to explain to your six-year-old daughter why she can't go to the public amusement park that has just been advertised on television, and see the tears welling up in her little eyes when she is told that Funtown is closed to colored
10　children, and see the depressing clouds of inferiority begin to form in her little mental sky, and see her begin to distort her little personality by unconsciously developing a bitterness toward white people; when you have to concoct an an-

swer for a five-year-old son who is asking in agonizing pathos: "Daddy, why do white people treat colored people so mean?"; when you take a cross country

15 drive and find it necessary to sleep night after night in the uncomfortable corners of your automobile because no motel will accept you; when you are humiliated day in and day out by nagging signs reading "white" men and "colored"; when your first name becomes "nigger" and your middle name becomes "boy" (however old you are) and your last name becomes "John," and when your wife and

20 mother are never given the respected title of "Mrs."; when you are harried by day and haunted by night by the fact that you are a Negro, living constantly at tip-toe stance, never quite knowing what to expect next, and plagued with inner fears and outer resentments; when you are forever fighting a degenerating sense of "nobodiness"—then you will understand why we find it difficult to wait.

King could have filled his letter with emotion-packed examples of civil rights abuse, but he writes the majority of the letter as a more reasoned and principled argument. In the preceding paragraph, he uses the rhetorical appeal of pathos by piling emotional example upon emotional example in a concentrated way.

We will return to this paragraph in our discussion of style.

Arrangement

Invention, or the process of coming up with ideas to speak or write about, is the first step in forming an argument. Once you know what you are going to say, you must next decide in what order to present your ideas. This process is known as **arrangement**.

King's letter follows nicely the arrangement of the traditional classical oration, a form most commonly associated with the great Roman orator Cicero. These are the parts:

- **Exordium**: Introduction. The writer gains the audience's attention.
- **Narratio**: Background information. The writer gives the facts of the case.
- **Propositio**: The proposition. The writer presents his or her thesis, or main idea.
- **Partitio**: The main headings or topics. The writer outlines what will follow.
- **Confirmatio**: Arguments supporting the proposition. The writer gives evidence to prop up the thesis or main idea.
- **Refutatio**: The anticipation and refutation of counter-arguments. The writer answers in advance any objections that opponents may raise.
- **Peroratio**: Conclusion. The writer summarizes the chief arguments, calls for a specific response, and makes a final emotional appeal.

In classical oratory, not all parts are used in every speech. Often, the partitio is not stated directly because it is implicit in the document. Let's look at the King letter in terms of its classical structure.

Exordium

King opens with the *exordium*, or introduction, "My Dear Fellow Clergymen." As you already know, King uses this introduction to establish his ethos, build common ground, set a warm tone, and gain the acceptance of his ideas by his audience.

Narratio

The *narratio*, or background, is next. In this section, King addresses the current situation in Birmingham and attempts to explain why he is writing now. He is responding to an opportunity created by the letter from the clergymen, and he continues to build his ethos, or character, in this section of the letter by pointing out the following:

> "If I sought to answer all the criticisms that cross my desk, my secretaries would have little time for anything other than such correspondence ... and I would have no time for constructive work. But since I feel that you are men of genuine good will and that your criticisms are sincerely set forth, I want to try to answer your statement in what I hope will be patient and reasonable terms."

Even in providing background information, he uses the narratio to convince the clergymen to view him as a patient and reasonable man.

Propositio

The *propositio* is King's main idea or thesis. Having gone through the four steps of preparation for nonviolent protest (collection of facts, negotiation, self-purification, direct action), King asserts, "We had no alternative except to prepare for direct action."

Confirmatio/Refutatio

King combines the *confirmatio* and *refutatio*, the main argument and the counter-argument, by listing the clergymen's objections to his activities and showing how they are wrong. This is the longest section of the letter and presents the logos of King's argument. He discusses just and unjust laws, justifies his actions on moral and ethical grounds, and responds to accusations that he is an extremist. Anticipating his audience's arguments and addressing them both demonstrates his perception and deals with their arguments before they have raised them.

Peroratio

The *peroratio* is the conclusion. In his conclusion, King expresses confidence in the future because the destinies of black and white people are tied together in striving for the common goal of freedom for all people. Then he adds a personal touch. He comes full circle, starting out with the personal "My Dear Fellow Clergymen" and ending with his hope that the letter finds the clergymen "strong in the faith" and his desire to meet them one day as "fellow clergymen."

Style

Invention is the process of coming up with ideas, and arrangement is putting those ideas in order. In using **style**, a writer must decide how to express those ideas. Stylistic choices can contribute to the writer's ethos, or character, make the content, or logos, of the message more memorable and artistic, and enhance pathos, or the emotional appeal of the writer's message.

King was a master of style. One could write a book just on the stylistic choices he made in his writing. In the following discussion of style, we analyze only the passage quoted previously from "Letter from Birmingham Jail" to demonstrate pathos. For our purposes, we focus on two of King's most commonly used tools:

- the periodic sentence
- figurative language

The Periodic Sentence

While King makes use of both short and long sentences in his "Letter from Birmingham Jail," the long passage about the evils of segregation is only one sentence, consisting of 331 words. Commonly used in the ancient world, this is called a *periodic*, or very long, sentence that is not grammatically complete until the end of the sentence.

There are two types of periodic sentence:

- one that delays the predicate until the end of the sentence
- one that delays both the subject and the predicate until the end

This delaying tactic in a periodic sentence builds anticipation, suspense, and excitement as the reader finally reaches the climax upon reading the end of the sentence.

King's pathos-packed periodic sentence delays both the subject and the predicate. After the first clause, "But when you have seen vicious mobs lynch your mothers and fathers at will," King then provides a long list of dependent clauses that end with the delayed subject and predicate in the main clause, "then you will understand why we find it difficult to wait."

But **when** you have seen vicious mobs lynch your mothers and fathers at will and drown your sisters and brothers at whim;

when you have seen hate-filled policemen curse, kick, brutalize, and even kill your black brothers and sisters with impunity;

5 **when** you see the vast majority of your 20 million Negro brothers smothering in an airtight cage of poverty in the midst of an affluent society;

when you suddenly find your tongue twisted and your speech stammering as you seek to explain to your six-year-old daughter why she can't go to the public amusement park that has just been advertised on television, and see the tears
10 welling up in her little eyes when she is told that Funtown is closed to colored children, and see the depressing clouds of inferiority begin to form in her little mental sky, and see her begin to distort her little personality by unconsciously developing a bitterness toward white people;

when you have to concoct an answer for a five-year-old son who is asking in ag-
15 onizing pathos: "Daddy, why do white people treat colored people so mean?;

when you take a cross country drive and find it necessary to sleep night after night in the uncomfortable corners of your automobile because no motel will accept you;

when you are humiliated day in and day out by nagging signs reading "white"
20 men and "colored";

when your first name becomes "nigger" and your middle name becomes "boy" (however old you are) and your last name becomes "John," and when your wife and mother are never given the respected title of "Mrs.";

when you are harried by day and haunted by night by the fact that you are a
25 Negro, living constantly at tip-toe stance, never quite knowing what to expect next, and plagued with inner fears and outer resentments;

when you are forever fighting a degenerating sense of "nobodiness"—

then you will understand why we find it difficult to wait.

Figurative Language

King uses figurative language throughout his letter, including metaphor, antithesis, alliteration, and anaphora.

Metaphor

Metaphor can best be described as a comparison between unlike things. Referring again to King's periodic sentence in "Letter from Birmingham Jail," we find the protesters characterized as dwelling in an "airtight cage of poverty," (line 6). Clearly, they are not in literal cages, but the imagery of the cage carries enormous visual power. It equates poverty with imprisonment.

Another metaphor from this passage is "ominous clouds of inferiority" that appear "in her little mental sky" (lines 11-12) when a six-year-old child cries upon being told that she cannot attend an amusement park because she is black. The tears and feelings of inferiority are equated with ominous clouds.

Antithesis

Antithesis--the juxtaposition of opposites, often in parallel structure—is a powerful device. Note the antithesis in the phrase "harried by day and haunted by night" (line 24) that King uses to describe living as a black person in American society at that time. Note also the antithesis in the phrase "inner fears and outer resentments" (line 26) that King uses to contrast the internal feelings and the external reality of a black person facing racism in America.

Alliteration

King makes extensive use of *alliteration*, which is the repetition of initial identical sounds in successive words. Here are two examples of King's alliteration in this passage:

- "... curse, kick, ... and even kill your black brothers ..." (lines 3-4)
- "... tongue twisted and your speech stammering ..." (line 7)

The first example shows alliteration of the *k* and *b* sounds, and the second example shows alliteration of the *t* and *s* sounds.

Anaphora

Anaphora is the use of repeated words at the beginnings of phrases, clauses, and sentences. King uses the phrase "*when you*" nine times to introduce clauses in his periodic sentence. In another pathos-laden passage, King again uses anaphora to highlight his point:

I **doubt that** you would have so warmly commended the police force
if you had seen its dogs sinking their teeth into unarmed, nonviolent Negroes.
I **doubt that** you would so quickly commend the policemen
if you were to observe their ugly and inhumane treatment of Negroes here in the city jail;
if you were to watch them push and curse old Negro women and young Negro girls;
if you were to see them slap and kick old Negro men and young boys;
if you were to observe them, as they did on two occasions, refuse to give us food because we wanted to sing our grace together.

King's stylistic use of the periodic sentence and figurative language enhance the rhetorical impact of his argument that nonviolent protest is the correct course of action in Birmingham. The devices also reveal him as a creative thinker, an excellent writer, and one of the most persuasive figures of the twentieth century.

While we have presented these ancient rhetorical tools as a way of analyzing a modern text, they can also be used for composing a modern argument as you make your way through the course in English Language and Composition. Practicing the use of these tools will eventually help you when you take the Advanced Placement English Language and Composition exam.

In the next chapter, we will look at modern approaches to making and synthesizing arguments.

Chapter 1 Review Questions

1. What is invention in rhetoric?
2. What is ethos?
3. What is logos?
4. What is pathos?
5. How do ethos, logos, and pathos work together to persuade an audience?
6. What is a syllogism?
7. What is an enthymeme?
8. How do you derive an enthymeme from a syllogism?
9. Why is an enthymeme more useful than a syllogism in analyzing and constructing an argument?
10. What is arrangement, and why is it important in analyzing and constructing arguments?
11. What is style?
12. What effect does style have in communicating an argument to an audience?

Chapter 2

Modern Approaches to Argument

In Chapter 1, you examined ancient rhetorical tools and applied them to a modern text. In this chapter, you will encounter a variety of modern approaches to argument. The rhetorical techniques and strategies presented in both chapters will provide you with the theoretical background for constructing your own arguments, synthesizing an array of sources to support a position, and analyzing the arguments that others construct.

The Rhetorical Triangle

The modern **rhetorical triangle** consists of five elements:

- writer
- audience
- message
- purpose
- rhetorical context

Traditionally, the rhetorical triangle contains the first three components: writer, audience, and message. Although the communication process is more complicated than can be captured by a graphic illustration, Figure 2-1 shows the process reduced to a simple triangle. The three points of the triangle are writer, audience, and message, and the rhetorical triangle is often connected to the three Aristotelian proofs, or appeals, of ethos (writer), logos (message), and pathos (audience) that you read about in Chapter 1.

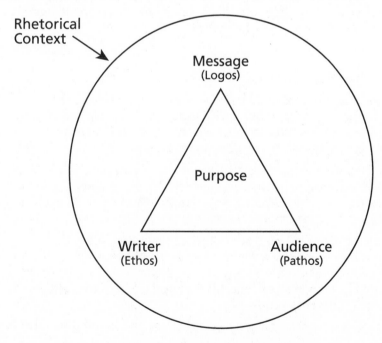

Fig. 2-1 The Rhetorical Triangle

Writer

The writer must ask the question "What can I do to build my credibility and make the audience trust my message?" In "Letter from Birmingham Jail," which we shall continue to analyze in Chapter 2, Dr. Martin Luther King, Jr., spends considerable time establishing his ethos. You recall that he does so by giving a warm greeting, finding common ground with his "fellow clergymen," and giving his opponents credit as "men of genuine good will." He also establishes that he is not an "outsider" because of his organizational ties to Birmingham and his calling to fight injustice wherever it exists.

Writing Effectively

You can build your ethos through the choices you make in terms of tone, style, and dealing with counter-arguments.

Audience

To have a message accepted by an audience, the writer should try to appeal to their emotions, which is why the audience is often linked with pathos in the rhetorical triangle.

Because he was also a clergyman, King understood his primary audience well. He knew what would appeal to their humanity and their consciences. In "Letter from Birmingham Jail," rather than sprinkle pathos throughout the letter, King chooses instead to concentrate the emotional appeal in one long periodic sentence. He makes the audience feel the pain of segregation, as he writes about "vicious lynch mobs," "hate-filled policemen," human beings "smothering in an airtight cage of poverty," the impossibility of explaining segregation to a child, and a list of "inner fears and outer resentments" that culminates in the cry, "then you will understand why we find it difficult to wait."

Writing Effectively

The writer must ask, "What values and beliefs do I appeal to in the audience? How can I engage both the audience's heart and mind?" The more you know about your audience, the better able you will be to find what will appeal to their emotions.

Message

In the rhetorical triangle, message is often linked with logos, the content of the communication. People sometimes confuse logos with logic. The logical argument is certainly an important component of logos; however, logos involves the entire content of the message, which goes well beyond the limits of logic.

For example, in "Letter from Birmingham Jail" King not only builds his own argument; he also refutes the major and minor premises of the clergymen's arguments, which are sometimes unstated. He points out their inconsistencies and provides evidence to counter their assertions. He writes,

> "You deplore the demonstrations taking place in Birmingham. But your statement, I am sorry to say, fails to express a similar concern for the conditions that brought about the demonstrations. I am sure that none of you would want to rest content with the superficial kind of social analysis that deals merely with effects and does not grapple with underlying causes."

Writing Effectively

As you construct and analyze arguments, ask, "What assumptions support the reasoning? What is the evidence?"

Balancing writer, audience, and message

In Figure 2-1, writer, audience, and message are the three points of an equilateral triangle. The triangle emphasizes the importance of the three elements working equally together, in balance. For example,

- If you put too much emphasis on message, you risk forgetting about the audience or establishing yourself insufficiently.

- If your emphasis is too much on the emotional appeal to the audience, then the content of your message might suffer, or the audience might not trust you.

- If you focus too much on yourself as the writer, then you might be dismissed as an egotist or a blowhard.

Writing Effectively

Seek to balance the three major elements of writer, audience, and message. These must work together to achieve the goal of your communication: your purpose.

Purpose

The purpose of your communication is your rhetorical goal. What are you trying to achieve with your message? In "Letter from Birmingham Jail," King was seeking to persuade the local clergymen of the rightness of his action, and help unite the African-American community. He also wanted the letter to reach out to the white political moderate, who he says "is more devoted to 'order' than to justice; who prefers a negative peace which is the absence of tension to a positive peace which is the presence of justice." King knew his audience would be resistant to his cause, so his purpose had to be clear and strong. The open letter format—which allowed his letter to be read by everyone—shows his purpose to be much larger than he initially suggested: he wanted not just to refute the claims of the clergymen, but also to persuade the community at large that his cause was right.

Writing Effectively

To identify the purpose of your communication, ask "What is my goal? What do I hope to achieve?" It is important that the goals be clear and specific. Unclear goals lead to unclear communication.

Rhetorical Context

The background or situation to which a persuasive message is addressed is considered **rhetorical context**. As the rhetorical situation changes, so should the response. Aristotle refers to the rhetorical context as those proofs that are *inartistic* or *extrinsic* because they are not under the control of the writer and do not emerge from the writer's creative efforts.

In "Letter from Birmingham Jail," the rhetorical context is the incarceration of King and his followers for breaking the law against public demonstrations. He was arrested on Good Friday, the day commemorating the crucifixion of Jesus Christ. King uses this rhetorical context to his advantage, allowing him to compare himself to Christ as well as to other religious and historical figures who had broken the law or who were considered extremists. Had King not been arrested on that day, he would not have had such a strong rhetorical context for his letter. King wrote:

> But though I was initially disappointed at being categorized as an extremist, as I continued to think about the matter I gradually gained a measure of satisfaction from the label. Was not Jesus an extremist for love: "Love your enemies, bless them that curse you, do good to them that hate you, and pray for them which
> 5 despitefully use you, and persecute you." Was not Amos an extremist for justice: "Let justice roll down like waters and righteousness like an ever-flowing stream." Was not Paul an extremist for the Christian gospel: "I bear in my body the marks of the Lord Jesus." Was not Martin Luther an extremist: "Here I stand; I cannot do otherwise, so help me God." And John Bunyan: "I will stay in jail to the end of my
> 10 days before I make a butchery of my conscience." And Abraham Lincoln: "This nation cannot survive half slave and half free." And Thomas Jefferson: "We hold these truths to be self-evident, that all men are created equal ..."

Writing Effectively

As a writer, consider how you can best tailor a response to the specific demands of a given situation. How should your response change as the rhetorical context changes?

Informal Logic: The Toulmin Scheme

Formal logic is an abstract discipline that deals with absolutes. Everyday life, however, does not operate in the realm of absolutes—it is messier, more complicated. Events in life are often random, so people must make decisions based on probability rather than absolute certainty. To bridge the gap between the absolute and the practical, philosopher Stephen Toulmin developed a model of informal logic commonly known as the **Toulmin scheme**.

Informal Logic

In 1958, Stephen Toulmin published a book titled *The Uses of Argument*, which has greatly influenced the study of both analyzing and making arguments. Toulmin's scheme was developed for use in the courtroom as a practical tool for persuading judges and juries. The model does not attempt to prove, but it gives good reasons and persuasive arguments. In the Toulmin scheme, there are reasonable arguments on either side. The model consists of the following:

- claim
- reasons
- warrant
- grounds
- backing
- conditions of rebuttal
- qualifier

In the Toulmin scheme, an enthymeme provides the claim, the reasons, and the warrant. As you recall from the analysis of the "Letter from Birmingham Jail" in Chapter 1, one of the local clergymen's objections to King's involvement was restated in the following enthymeme:

> *King should not be leading local protests because he is an outsider.*

To decide whether the claim in this enthymeme is sound, you need to examine the reasons and the underlying assumptions and decide whether the audience will accept and grant them.

Claim

In the Toulmin scheme, a **claim** is a statement of a position, a stand, or what you may have come to know as a thesis statement. A claim is an arguable statement. It is not a statement of the obvious; it presents an issue about which reasonable people might disagree. The claim in the enthymeme above is this:

King should not be leading local protests...

Reasons

Reasons support claims. An individual claim may have many supporting reasons for an argument. In the previous enthymeme, the stated reason is the following:

...because he is an outsider

Warrant

The **warrant** is the unstated assumption that makes the enthymeme work. The audience must accept the warrant in order to find an argument persuasive. The warrant is often the most vulnerable part of an argument because it appeals to the values and beliefs of an audience, which can be difficult to determine. Underlying the enthymeme is the local clergymen's warrant or unstated belief:

Outsiders should not be leading local protests.

Grounds

Claims, reasons, and warrants represent an argument in broad outline, stated in phrases or sentences. Of course, arguments involve much more than this. The **grounds** provide the actual evidence in support of the reasons. Grounds include facts, citations from authorities, examples, and statistics. Well-stated grounds make reasons more concrete for an audience.

In the statement that prompted Dr. King to write "Letter from Birmingham Jail," the local clergymen provide an example of grounds for their argument when they note that "we are now confronted by a series of demonstrations by some of our negro citizens, directed and led in part by outsiders."

Backing

Backing supports the warrant. If an audience already accepts the unstated assumption or warrant, then backing is unnecessary. However, if the person making the argument is unclear about the warrant or unfamiliar with the values and beliefs of the audience, then the writer must provide backing to support the warrant. Without it, the argument will not be persuasive to the audience.

In their statement of April 12, the Alabama clergymen give backing to support the warrant "Outsiders should not be leading local protests" by asserting that resolving these local problems requires people with "knowledge and experience of the local situation." It is to these statements that King reacts in his response.

Conditions of Rebuttal

No argument is complete without anticipating the counter-arguments, and the **conditions of rebuttal** bring up and address those counter-arguments. Rebuttal attacks the reasons and grounds and/or the warrant and backing.

In "Letter from Birmingham Jail," King refutes both the local clergymen's reasons (that he is an outsider) and their grounds (that local leaders are already handling the situation in a peaceful and lawful manner). King asserts that he is not an outsider because he has local ties to Birmingham, was invited there by local leaders, and has been called to fight injustice wherever it occurs—"Injustice anywhere is a threat to justice everywhere." In this way he rebuts the clergymen's warrant (outsiders should not be leading local protests) and their backing (outsiders lack sufficient knowledge of local issues). King adds that we are all interrelated, so it no longer makes sense to see the world in terms of insiders and outsiders.

Qualifier

A **qualifier** limits a claim. In the real world there are few absolutes or certainties, and this applies to analyzing and making arguments, too. Terms like *always* and *never* are problematic because opponents can often find exceptions to such broad statements. To remedy this situation, Toulmin introduced the qualifier, which limits the scope of the claim.

In "Letter from Birmingham Jail," one problem with the clergymen's argument is that they present their claims as absolute: they admit no justification for King to lead protests in Birmingham. Because the local clergymen do not limit their claim with a qualifier, King is able to provide numerous reasons why their claims are faulty.

Writing Effectively

Although both the six-part classical oration format and the Toulmin scheme are effective tools for making arguments, analyzing arguments, and synthesizing sources into arguments, the Toulmin scheme has an added advantage for you as a writer. Since it is based on probability, not formal logic, the Toulmin scheme allows for the possibility of dialogue between opposing views and deeper exploration of issues.

A Modern Alternative to Traditional Argument

The goal of traditional argument, from Aristotle to the modern day, is to defeat the opponent. This model centers on absolute victory and makes use of military terminology such as "attacking" one's opponent and developing rhetorical "strategy." In the 1960s, psychologist Carl Rogers developed an approach to counseling that in recent years has also influenced methods of argument.

The Rogerian Approach to Argument

The goals of **Rogerian argument** differ from those of the traditional approach in substantive ways. Although traditional argument seeks all-out victory over the opponent, Rogerian argument tries to find mutually acceptable solutions to problems using the following techniques:

- seeking common ground
- building trust
- reducing threat

In the traditional model, when people perceive that they are being attacked, they stop listening and become defensive and hostile. In Rogerian argument, the writer makes every effort to avoid confrontation. The writer does this by giving as much credit as possible to the opponents' counter-arguments, rather than simply dismissing these counter-arguments outright. In this framework, if opponents believe that their arguments are being understood and taken seriously, they will be more open to listening to the writer's position.

From the very start of the "Letter from Birmingham Jail," King attempts to build trust, seek common ground, and reduce threat by addressing his "opponents" as "My Dear Fellow Clergymen." He credits the clergymen with being "men of genuine good will," whose arguments "are sincerely set forth." He does not attack their character but instead emphasizes that they all share a common profession and a common goal of ending segregation.

Throughout the letter King makes references to biblical and historical figures and philosophers who would be familiar to the clergymen. He accepts some of the points in the clergymen's argument, such as the fact that the demonstrations in Birmingham were unfortunate. Toward the end of the letter, he verbally draws himself closer to his audience by switching pronouns from *I* and *you* to *we* when expressing his hope for the day when they will all sit down together as fellow clergymen.

Although King's letter is not totally Rogerian, he makes use of certain elements of the Rogerian approach, and these techniques make his argument more palatable to his audience.

Writing Effectively

The advantage of the Rogerian approach to argument is its emphasis on building bridges rather than tearing them down. As a writer you might face a rhetorical situation in which it is important for you to maintain a cordial relationship with your adversary. When this is the case, giving as much credit as you can to your opponent's points of view might be the best path to follow.

The Text Says/The Text Does Analysis

"The text says/the text does" analysis is a technique for close reading and rhetorical analysis of a text. The method consists of two elements:

- summary of the content of the text (what the text says)
- description of the construction, organization, and form of the text (what the text does)

We will refer to this method as a *says/does analysis*. Here is the concluding paragraph from Martin Luther King's "Letter from Birmingham Jail." It is followed by a *says* statement, then a *does* statement.

> I hope this letter finds you strong in the faith. I also hope that circumstances will soon make it possible for me to meet each of you, not as an integrationist or a civil rights leader but as a fellow clergyman and a Christian brother. Let us all hope that the dark clouds of racial prejudice will soon pass away and the deep fog of misunderstanding will be lifted from our fear-drenched communities, and in some not too distant tomorrow the radiant stars of love and brotherhood will shine over our great nation with all their scintillating beauty.

What The Text Says

To synthesize an argument in a text is to state the content very briefly. This sentence summarizes the concluding paragraph of "Letter from Birmingham Jail":

> I hope that we can meet again someday as Christian brothers in a time of racial harmony.

The concluding paragraph ties together all of King's previous arguments and re-establishes the personal tone of the opening paragraph. King also uses the double metaphor of raising the "fog of misunderstanding" from "our fear-drenched communities" to make his conclusion more vivid and memorable.

Says/does analysis is useful for breaking a piece of writing down into a simpler, more understandable form. It enables readers to examine a text in terms of its content as well as its structure.

Visual Arguments

Visual rhetoric is the incorporation of visual elements into an argument and the rhetorical impact of those images on an audience. Visual rhetoric includes photographs, drawings, graphs, charts, maps, posters, advertisements, Web pages, and cartoons, to name a few.

The claim that "a picture is worth a thousand words" has become a cliché, but it is nonetheless true. A visual image can make or amplify a claim just as words can, but visual images can often have a greater impact than words. Because visual images are processed by a different area of the brain than language is, visual images can strengthen an argument, exercise the imagination, and stimulate the brain in ways that words do not. Thus, when visual images are combined with text, together they can have a broader and more profound effect on the audience than words alone can.

If a printed edition of Dr. Martin Luther King's "Letter from Birmingham Jail" had included images of intolerance and photographs of King leading demonstrations and being taken to jail, the impact of the document would be quite different, possibly even inflammatory, despite King's moderate tone.

Sensitivity to the impact of visual rhetoric is useful in both analyzing and making arguments. You will find examples of visual rhetoric in Chapters 3 through 10 of this book. For instance, Chapter 3, "Photography," integrates a number of photographs with textual information. Chapter 4, "War," illustrates how photographs and bar graphs can be used as writing prompts for constructing and strengthening arguments. Chapter 9, "Food," uses both a painting and a cartoon to highlight the complexities of contemporary issues. Chapter 8, "Genes," provides a purposeful graphic and prompts for making your own visuals to support arguments. These chapters can also guide you in incorporating elements of visual rhetoric into your writing.

Chapter 2 Review Questions

1. What is the rhetorical triangle?
2. What is informal logic?
3. How is informal logic used to make an argument?
4. In informal logic, what is a claim?
5. How does a reason support a claim in informal logic?
6. What role does a warrant play in informal logic?
7. What is the goal of Rogerian rhetoric, and how does it differ from the goal of traditional argumentation?
8. What are the features of says/does analysis?
9. What are the components of visual rhetoric?
10. How can visual rhetoric be used to make or enhance an argument?

Chapter 3
Photography

Background

Photographs mesh with words. Writers and speakers often use photographic images as a means to illustrate their arguments or add dimension to their words. Anytime we view photographs, we "read" them as we "see" them. Because a thoughtful reading goes beyond the borders of a photograph, you think about the image's rhetorical function: how does an image make an argument or support an idea? What happens when you consider the interaction between an image and the purposeful set of words it accompanies?

A solid understanding of contemporary rhetoric demands that you appreciate that important place where words and images intersect and interact. The texts of this study cluster all involve pictures interacting, in various ways, with ideas expressed through words.

Readings

Donald M. Murray
The Stranger in the Photo Is Me

Dave Eggers
Woman Waiting to Take a Photograph

Freeman Patterson
Barriers to Seeing

N. Scott Momaday
Shadow Catcher

LIFE Magazine
The Power of Pictures

Susan Sontag
On Photography

Andy Grundberg
Photojournalism: A Blend of Artifice and Actuality

Donald M. Murray
The Stranger in the Photo Is Me

This essay first appeared on August 27, 1991, in Murray's weekly "Over 60" column in *The Boston Globe*. The author, a Pulitzer Prize-winning journalist and Professor of English at the University of New Hampshire, died in December 2006.

The author in England, 1944.

I was never one to make a big deal over snapshots; I never spent long evenings with the family photograph album. Let's get on with the living. To heck with yesterday, what are we going to do to-
5 morrow? But with the accumulation of yesterdays and the possibility of shrinking tomorrows, I find myself returning, as I suspect many over 60s do, for a second glance and a third at family photos that snatch a moment from time.

10 In looking at mine, I become aware that it is so recent in the stretch of man's history that we have been able to stop time in this way and hold still for reflection. Vermeer is one of my favorite painters because of that sense of suspended time, with both clock and
15 calendar held so wonderfully, so terribly still.

The people in the snapshots are all strangers. My parents young, caught before I arrived or as they were when I saw them as towering grown-
ups. They seemed so old then and so young now.
20 And I am, to me, the strangest of all.

There is a photograph of me on a tricycle before the duplex on Grand View Avenue in Wollaston I hardly remember; in another I am dressed in a seersucker sailor suit when I was 5
25 and lived in a Cincinnati hotel. I cannot remember the suit but even now, studying the snapshot, I am drunk on the memory of its peculiar odor and time is erased.

In the snapshots I pass from chubby to skin-
30 ny and, unfortunately, ended up a chub. Looking at the grown-ups in the snapshots I should have known.

In other snapshots, I am cowboy, pilot, Indian chief; I loved to dress up to become what I was
35 not, and suspect I still am a wearer of masks and costumes.

It would be socially appropriate to report on this day that I contemplate all those who are gone, but the truth is that my eyes are drawn back to
40 pictures of my stranger self.

And the picture that haunts me the most is one not in costume but in the uniform I proudly earned in World War II. I believe it was taken in England from the design of the barracks behind me. I have
45 taken off the ugly steelframed GI glasses, a touch of dishonesty for the girl who waited at home.

My overseas cap with its airborne insignia is tugged down over my right eye, my right shoulder in the jump jacket is lower because I have my
50 left hand in my pocket in rakish disregard for the regulation that a soldier in that war could never, ever stick a hand in a pocket.

The pockets that are empty in the photograph will soon bulge with hand grenades, extra am-
55 munition, food, and many of the gross of condoms we were issued before a combat jump. This GI item was more a matter of industrial merchandising than soldierly dreaming—or frontline reality.

60 The soldier smiles as if he knew his innocence and is both eager for its loss and nostalgic for those few years of naiveté behind him.

I try once more to enter the photograph and become what I was that day when autumn sunlight
65 dappled the barracks wall and I was so eager to experience the combat my father wanted so much for me. He had never made it to the trenches over there in his war.

When that photograph was taken, my father
70 still had dreams of merchandising glory, of a store with an awning that read Murray & Son. I had not yet become the person who had to nod yes at MGH when my father asked if he had cancer, to make the decision against extraordinary means
75 after his last heart attack. When this photo was taken, he had not yet grown old, his collars large, his step hesitant, his shoes unshined.

Mother was still alive, and her mother who really raised me had not died as I was to learn in a
80 letter I received at the front. The girl who wrote every day and for whom the photo was taken had not yet become my wife, and we had not yet been the first in our families to divorce two years later.

I had not yet seen my first dead soldier, had not
85 yet felt the earth beneath me become a trampoline as the shells of a rolling barrage marched across our position.

I had no idea my life would become as wonderful or as terrible as it has been; that I would
90 remarry, have three daughters and outlive one. I could not have imagined that I actually would be able to become a writer and eat — even overeat. I simply cannot re-create my snapshot innocence.

I had not had an easy or happy childhood, I
95 had done well at work but not at school; I was not Mr. Pollyanna, but life has been worse and far better than I could have imagined.

Over 60 we are fascinated by the mystery of our life, why roads were taken and not taken,
100 and our children encourage this as they develop a sense of family history. A daughter discovers a letter from the soldier in the photograph in England and another written less than a year later, on V-E day. She is surprised at how much I have
105 aged. I am not.

I would not wish for a child or grandchild of mine to undergo the blood test of war my father so hoped I would face as he had not. In photos taken not so many years later I have a streak of
110 white hair. It is probably genetic but I imagine it is the shadow of a bullet that barely passed me by, and I find I cannot enter the snapshot of the smiling soldier who is still stranger to me, still innocent of the heroic harm man can deliver to man.

First Reading

1. What textual and contextual elements indicate this column's particular audience?
2. Identify what you believe to be Murray's central argument. Where does his argument become clear? How do the essay's details and their arrangement, diction, tone, and structure contribute to its argument?
3. What explicit statements does Murray make about photographs? How do these statements contribute to the essay's purpose, if at all?
4. What is the importance of Murray's use of antithesis in the essay? How do such juxtapositions jibe with his argument?
5. How does Murray's comment on our "ability to stop time in this way" mesh with the inclusion of the photograph? How does the comment deepen our understanding of his argument?

6. Examine the photograph on page 20. How does the presence of the photograph itself contribute to Murray's effort to communicate? How, if at all, would the absence of the photograph change the essay's argument?

7. Consider the placement of the photograph in relation to the words of this text. What is the impact of presenting the image immediately following the essay's title? How would placing the photograph immediately after the essay rather than just before its opening paragraph alter your experience of the whole text?

8. Speculate: how would the absence of a caption alter your reading of or response to the essay?

9. Respond: how would replacing the existing caption with each of the following captions affect your reading?

    "Paratrooper Donald M. Murray, 1944"

    "The Stranger in England, 1944"

    "A soldier in rakish disregard..."

10. How would using the photograph below, either as a substitute for or in addition to the one that appears on page 20, alter your experience of Murray's essay? How would the inclusion of a photograph of the author as a child in the costume of a "cowboy, pilot, or Indian chief" affect your reading?

Annotate the essay, carefully noting the impact of particular words, phrases, and details upon your understanding of the text. Then answer these reading comprehension questions. After each response, explain what the question asked you to do or know, and why you answered as you did.

1. The central thrust of the writer's remarks is to

   (A) reflect upon diverse family events and relationships.
   (B) remember and honor the service of fallen comrades.
   (C) question the integrity and utility of photographs.
   (D) consider the relationship between innocence and experience.
   (E) summarize compelling moments of his life.

2. In paragraph 2 (lines 10–15), the writer does each of the following EXCEPT

   (A) reflect on previous comments.
   (B) illustrate an observation through a historical reference.
   (C) describe uncommon objects.
   (D) present a paradox.
   (E) explain a personal preference.

3. Paragraph 3 (lines 16–20) begins with a(n)

   (A) metaphoric recollection.
   (B) elaborate paradox.
   (C) figurative moment.
   (D) emphatic qualification.
   (E) declarative statement.

4. The writer's purpose in paragraph 7 (lines 37–40) is primarily to

   (A) introduce the importance of past experiences.
   (B) contemplate memories of his youthful parents.
   (C) suggest the impossibility of moving back in time.
   (D) personalize a particularly haunting memory.
   (E) create an image of life's improbabilities.

5. All of the following statements contribute to the importance of the word "haunts" in paragraph 8 (lines 41–46) EXCEPT

   (A) "photos that snatch a moment in time" (lines 8–9).
   (B) "with both clock and calendar held so wonderfully, so terribly still" (lines 14–15).
   (C) "And I am, to me, the strangest of all" (line 20).
   (D) "I am drunk on the memory of its particular odor and time is erased" (lines 27–28).
   (E) "and I suspect I still am a wearer of masks and costumes" (lines 35–36).

6. The rhetorical thrust of paragraph 9 (lines 47–52) is primarily

   (A) narrative.
   (B) descriptive.
   (C) argumentative.
   (D) persuasive.
   (E) comparative.

7. Paragraph 15 (lines 84–87) contains all of the following EXCEPT

   (A) concrete diction.
   (B) parallel syntax.
   (C) metaphor.
   (D) hyperbole.
   (E) understatement.

8. Recurring references to "time" in the essay emphasize its

   (A) triumph.
   (B) erasure.
   (C) passage.
   (D) suspension.
   (E) denial.

9. By focusing on a prominent photograph, the writer

   (A) emphasizes awareness of his lost innocence.
   (B) reconnects with his family.
   (C) concedes that he still wears masks and costumes.
   (D) recollects experiences as a soldier.
   (E) establishes nostalgia for his childhood.

10. The writer's stance in the last two paragraphs is best characterized as

   (A) a senior citizen experiencing regret over youthful decisions.
   (B) a veteran recognizing proud memories of service.
   (C) an individual encountering his younger persona.
   (D) a father longing to communicate with his daughters.
   (E) a son mourning his relationship with his father.

Writing

1. **Analysis** — Complete the following on-demand writing task. Study "The Stranger in the Photo Is Me," by Donald Murray. Then analyze how Murray uses both language and image to purposefully represent and explore his past.

2. **Argument** — Select several family photographs. Then, using one picture as a point of departure, write an essay that draws upon personal recollections and experiences, yet reaches beyond them to make and develop its argument. As you write and revise your essay, consider an audience that would appreciate the argument that emerges as you meld a particular photograph with thoughtfully chosen words and ideas.

Dave Eggers
Woman Waiting to Take a Photograph

In Eggers' vignette, the writer presents a view of a particular person poised, at a particular point in time, to take photographs. The writer punctuates this view with an intriguing closing statement that reaches beyond the immediate scene. The text first appeared in a London newspaper, *The Guardian*, on May 22, 2004.

The woman is a young woman. She wants to make a living as a photographer, but at the moment she is temping at a company that publishes books about wetlands preservation. On her days off she takes pictures, and today she is sitting in her car, across the street from a small grocery store called "The Go-Getters Market." The store is located in
5 a very poor neighborhood: the windows are barred and at night a roll-down steel door covers the storefront. The woman thus finds the name "Go-Getters" an interesting one, because it is clear that the customers of the market are anything but. They are drunkards and prostitutes and transients, and the young photographer thinks that if she can get the right picture of some of these people entering the store, she will make a picture that
10 would be considered trenchant, or even poignant—either way the product of a sharp and observant eye. So she sits in her Toyota Camry, which her parents gave her because it was four years old and they wanted something new, and she waits for the right poor person to enter or leave the store. She has her window closed, but will open it when the right person appears, and then shoot that person under the sign that says Go-Getters.
15 This, for the viewer of her photograph when it is displayed—first in a gallery, then in the hallway of a collector, and later in a museum when she has her retrospective—will prove that she, the photographer, has a good eye for the inequities and injustices of life, for hypocrisy and the exploitation of the underclass.

First Reading

1. What are the temporal boundaries of this vignette?
2. What is the perspective of the writer?
3. What does this text argue about photography, and about photographers?
4. How does the selection of details concerning the woman and her activities contribute to the text's point or argument?

Second Reading

1. How does the writer's repetition of term "Go-Getters" function in the text? How is each appearance of the term distinct?
2. What words and phrases suggest the writer's attitude toward the woman?
3. How does the final sentence of the vignette build on observed details?
4. What new idea or surprise emerges in the final sentence?

1. **Exposition** — In "Barriers to Seeing," Canadian photographer Freeman Patterson writes, "Making pictures can be a substitute for seeing and participating. The person who sees is involved, the person who looks is not." Write a purposeful vignette based upon an observation of someone you do not know in a public place who is unaware of you. Taking a cue from Patterson, see—do not merely look. Include speculative commentary as well as descriptive details.

2. **Argument** — Write an essay that compares and contrasts the act of seeing with the act of composing and taking a photograph. Make your essay appropriately personal by drawing upon your own experiences with photography in order to illustrate your points.

Freeman Patterson
Barriers to Seeing

In the preface to his 1985 book *Photography and the Art of Seeing*, the source of this passage, award-winning photographer Freeman Patterson of New Brunswick, Canada, writes that the photographer "best expresses a scene by using good composition, or visual design, to support the inherent design of the subject matter." However, he also argues that photographers who "merely follow the rules of composition" limit their own ability to respond to what they see.

On those frosty mornings when I grab my camera and tripod, and head out into the meadow behind my house, I quickly forget about me. I stop thinking about what I'll do with the photographs,
5 or about self-fulfillment, and lose myself in the sheer magic of rainbows in the grass; in the multicolored prisms of back-lighted crystals. I am lost in a world of glittering lights and dancing colors. I experience myself in what I see, and the result is
10 a tremendous exuberance which helps me make the best to use of my camera, and which lasts long after the frost has melted.

Letting go of self is an essential precondition to real seeing. When you let go of yourself, you aban-
15 don any preconceptions about the subject matter that might cramp you into photographing things in a certain, predetermined way. As long as you are worried about whether or not you will be able to make good pictures, or are concerned about en-
20 joying yourself, you are unlikely either to make the best photographs you can or to experience the joy of photography to the fullest. But when you let go, new conceptions arise from your direct experience of the subject matter, and new ideas and
25 feelings will guide you as you make pictures.

Preoccupation with self is the greatest barrier to seeing, and hardest one to break. You may be worrying about your job, or the kids, or other responsibilities, or you may be uneasy about your ability to
30 handle a new lens or to calculate exposure. There always seems to be something standing in the way of real freedom. Frederick Franck in *The Zen of Seeing* calls this the "Me cramp"; too much self-concern blocks direct experience of things outside
35 yourself. Sometimes the only way to overcome the cramp is through practice. You cannot relax your mind and body separately—they are too much a part of each other. In order to get the tightness and tenseness out of your body, you have to empty
40 your mind. It is like the connection between wind and water. The waves will not subside as long as the wind is blowing. Relaxing is the act of stopping the mental winds, so your body will be still.

Another barrier to seeing is the mass of stimuli
45 surrounding us. We are so bombarded with visual and other stimuli that we must block out most of them in order to cope. Instead of seeing everything, we select a few stimuli and organize these. Then, once we have achieved order in our lives,
50 we stick with the realities we have established. We seldom try to rediscover the possible value of ignored stimuli, and are reluctant to do so as long as the old ones still seem to be working. We develop a tunnel vision, which gives us a clear view of the
55 rut ahead of us, but prevents us from seeing the world around us.

A third major sight barrier is the labeling that results from familiarity. It was Monet, the painter, who said that in order to see we must forget the
60 name of the thing we are looking at. When we are children we think primarily in pictures, not in words. But this approach is played down when we go to school. The basic analytical skills (reading, writing, and arithmetic) are impressed upon
65 us as being more important than the appreciation of direct sensory experience, so we come to depend less and less on the part of the brain that encourages visual thinking. By grades three or four, many of us no longer regard painting or draw-
70 ing as being very important; we stop visualizing things freely, and put word labels on them instead. This pattern becomes so firmly established that, by adolescence, we hasten to catalogue everything we see. We rule out visual exploration,
75 and seldom discover the myriad facets of each object. As Frederick Franck so aptly expresses it, "By these labels we recognize everything, and no longer see anything. We know the labels on the bottles, but never taste the wine."

80 If you look at a fern and merely say, "Yes, that's a fern," you may not be seeing past the old, familiar label of its name. But if you really *see* a fern, you will notice its triangularity, individual leaf fibers, various shades of green, its sway and dance
85 before the wind. If you put your eyes close to the fern, so close that you cannot focus on the plant

at all, but only on objects beyond it, the fern will become a nebulous green haze which drifts across the background scene. You will have found dimensions and hidden beauty not included in the usual definition of a fern, while learning for yourself the difference between looking and seeing.

In viewing a photographer's work, do not let labels like "She's a portrait photographer" blind you to a beautiful landscape that she has made. Always try to understand the symbolic content of the photograph, or the meaning that the subject matter may have for the photographer.

Have you ever noticed, on returning from a holiday, your increased sensitivity to the details of your home? You glance around when you step in the door, and some things in the house may actually seem unfamiliar for a few minutes. You note that the living-room walls are more cream than ivory, that the English ivy looks spectacular in the west window. You even notice the evening light spilling across the little rug at the foot of the stairs, something you can't recall noticing before. But these moments pass quickly, familiarity is restored, everything is in its place; and you stop seeing once more.

How unfortunate it is that we don't respond with wonder every day to the magnificence of the English ivy. How sad that we don't see the light spilling across the little rug every evening. These sights are dismissed from mind and eye because they are so familiar, and their value as things-in-themselves goes unappreciated.

Where I live, people seldom notice the dandelions in the spring because there are so many of them. But, in southern Africa, a woman I know struggles to grow a little patch of dandelions in her garden. For her, dandelions are not familiar. On the other hand, she treats the colorful species of daisies which grows rampant in her area as too common, too familiar to be treasured.

A photographer who wants to see, a photographer who wants to make fine images, must recognize the value of the familiar. Your ability to see is not increased by the distance you put between yourself and your home. If you do not see what is all around you every day, what will you see when you go to Tangiers? The subject matter may be different, but unless you can get to the essence of the subject matter through keen observation, and express it through your photographs, it doesn't matter how exotic your locale.

Even the camera itself can be a barrier to seeing, in at least two ways. Susan Sontag, in *On Photography*, describes the first one: "A way of certifying experience, taking photographs is also a way of refusing it—by limiting experience to a search for the photogenic, by converting experiences into an image, a souvenir." Making pictures can be a substitute for seeing and participating. The person who sees is involved, the person who looks is not.

The camera is also a sight barrier because it does not see as the human eye does. We see a scene or situation in terms of both our senses and our experience. When we look at a landscape, we observe and remember only a few dominant features—enough to give us an impression of the landscape, which is often all that we need. But since a camera has no experience, it cannot select, so it records everything in its field of view. Its memory is perfect. For our purposes, then, the main difference between a person and a camera is that a person abstracts, but a camera does not.

People are constantly abstracting. They do it without thinking. So when they use a camera, they are often surprised to find that the scene the camera saw is not what they saw or, more precisely, not what they thought they saw. A major challenge in using a camera is learning to control it (and other tools and techniques) in order to produce a picture that shows what you perceived.

Except for the optical differences between the camera and human eye, all barriers to seeing are related to the first one—preoccupation with self. A good deal of our self-concern is a natural part of responsibilities of feeding our families, looking after our health, and paying our bills. But all these things can be done without closing our eyes to the remarkable world around us.

Seeing, in the finest and broadest sense, means using your senses, your intellect, and your emotions. It means encountering your subject matter with your whole being. Good seeing doesn't ensure good photographs, but good photographic expression is impossible without it.

First Reading

1. Relate the title of the essay to the content of the excerpted passage.

2. What shift distinguishes the first and second paragraphs? How does the shift relate to Patterson's audience?

3. Summarize the major barriers to seeing as enumerated by Patterson. Why does he present them in this particular order?

4. What is Patterson's most surprising comment? Why do you think so?

Second Reading

1. How does Patterson define "real freedom" (line 32) in paragraph 3? How does his definition relate to "real seeing" (line 14)?

2. In paragraph 5 (lines 57–79), Patterson asserts that, during childhood, the development of direct sensory experience involving visual thinking is minimized as basic analytical skills are emphasized. How does he further develop this assertion in the paragraph? How does the assertion lead to the development of additional points?

3. Identify the unfolding ideas in paragraphs 8 through 11. In paragraph 11, how does Patterson build support for his assertion concerning the "value of the familiar" (line 129)?

4. Explain how and why Patterson draws a distinction between a person and a camera in paragraph 13 (lines 148–160).

Writing

Argument — In paragraph 12 (lines 138–147), Patterson cites comments by Susan Sontag on the distinction between photography and experience. Write an essay in which you first summarize and then support, refute, or qualify Sontag's position. Support your response with appropriate evidence drawn from your own observation and experience.

N. Scott Momaday
Shadow Catcher

In this foreword to *Sacred Legacy: Edward S. Curtis and the North American Indian*, N. Scott Momaday introduces readers and viewers to a 2001 volume of photographs by and essays about Edward S. Curtis, who spent thirty years chronicling the Native inhabitants of North America.

Photography, at its best, is authentic art, an expression of the creative imagination informed by an original perception of the world. It is said that the camera, by virtue of its very presence, alters 5 reality. Too often a photograph is simply the static record of an image—an object, a figure, a place—in bare definition. A photograph commonly records a facade, the surface of a moment, a nick of geologic time. And as such it is necessarily a dis- 10 tortion, a kind of visible plane beyond which we cannot see. But in the hands of an extraordinary artist the camera can penetrate to a deeper level. For Edward Sheriff Curtis the camera was truly a magic box, a precision instrument that enabled 15 him to draw with light, to transcend the limits of ordinary vision, to see into the shadows of the soul. It is not by accident that he was called by his American Indian subjects "Shadow Catcher."

Some years ago I purchased a Curtis photograph 20 of Plains Indians on horseback, moving with travois[1] across an immense landscape of grasses. I had recently written *The Way to Rainy Mountain*, a story from oral tradition of the migration my Kiowa ancestors made from the Yellowstone to the South- 25 ern Plains, the last migration of the last culture to evolve in North America. I had not seen the photograph before. It struck me with such force that tears came to my eyes. I felt that I was looking into a memory in my blood. Here was a moment lost 30 in time, a moment I had known only in my imagination, suddenly verified, an image immediately translated from the mind's eye to the picture plane. More even than that, it was the evocation of a timeless and universal journey and of the spirit of a 35 people moving inexorably toward a destiny. There is a quality to the image, the composition, the invisible plane beyond the surface of the scene that is ineffable. It is a quality that informs the greatest art, and it is the standard in the Curtis photographs.

40 Taken as a whole, the work of Edward Curtis is a singular achievement. Never before have we seen the Indians of North America so close to the origins of their humanity, their sense of themselves in the world, their innate dignity and self-posses-

45 sion. These photographs comprehend more than an aboriginal culture, more than a prehistoric past—more, even, than a venture into a world of incomparable beauty and nobility. Curtis's photographs comprehend indispensable images of every human 50 being at every time in every place. In the focus upon the landscape of the continent and its indigenous people, a Curtis photograph becomes universal.

Edward Curtis preserved for us the unmistakable evidence of our involvement in the universe. 55 Curtis was acutely alive to evanescence; indeed, in a real sense it is his subject. The portraits here are of people whose way of life is coming rapidly to an end. We see the full awareness of this in their eyes. And yet these visages are not to be defined in terms 60 of despair. Rather, there is a general information of fortitude, patience, and something like assent, and above all composure and valor. In the face of such a man as Slow Bull, for example, there seem etched the very principles of the warrior ideal: bravery, 65 steadfastness, generosity, and virtue. We do not doubt that he is real in his mind and heart, in his word and in his vision. The same can be said of the portraits of Red Cloud, Chief Joseph, and Bear's Belly—in his bear robe—there is an amalgam of 70 man and wilderness, an equation that is a definition of the American Indian in relation to nature. And yet, in all of these photographs there is a privacy so profound as to be inviolable. A Navajo weaver sits at her loom before a canyon wall. She 75 is a silhouette; her loom is a geometry that seems essential to her being, organic, the extension of her hands into the earth itself. A young girl in her finery stands before her play tipi; she is every young girl who has ever lived upon the earth.

80 Edward Curtis wrote of himself, "While primarily a photographer, I do not see or think photographically; hence the story of Indian life will not be told in microscopic detail, but rather will be presented as a broad and luminous picture." 85 We must be grateful for this insight and for this intention: the world of these photographs is one in which breadth and luminosity are indispensable dimensions of spirit and reality.

---

1 travois: a wooden sled-like device used to drag equipment and supplies over difficult terrain

First Reading

1. Write a says/does statement for each of the essay's five paragraphs.
2. Before discussing your initial thoughts with peers, consider the impact of reading these five paragraphs without the benefit of any accompanying photographs by Edward S. Curtis.

Second Reading

1. In his first paragraph, Momaday makes an important claim. Identify the claim.
2. Create a public dialogue between Donald Murray, Freeman Patterson, and Scott Momaday concerning the relationship between writing and photography. Following their discussion, enter the discussion. What questions would you ask Murray? What would you ask Patterson? What would you ask Momaday? How do you think each person would respond?
3. Following are two photographs. On the left, from the National Archives, is a picture of the distinguished World War II and Korean War general, Douglas MacArthur. On the right is a portrait of Slow Bull, taken by Edward Sheriff Curtis. What, if anything, do you want or need to know about these images that you do not know upon viewing? How are these photographs related to each other? Does each photograph make a statement or argument of some kind or does each merely "appear" before the viewer?

Writing

Argument — Carefully reread the following passage from N. Scott Momaday's foreword and consider its broader implications. Then write a carefully reasoned essay that examines the validity of Momaday's comments. Support your argument by appropriately drawing upon your reading, observation, and personal experience.

Photography, at its best, is authentic art, an expression of the creative imagination informed by an original perception of the world. It is said that the camera, by virtue of its very presence, alters reality. Too often a photograph is simply the static record of an image—an object, a figure, a place—in bare definition. A photograph commonly records a facade, the surface of a moment, a nick of geologic time. And as such it is necessarily a distortion, a kind of visible plane beyond which we cannot see. But in the hands of an extraordinary artist the camera can penetrate to a deeper level.

This brief essay appeared without a named author in an introductory spread to a 1988 special issue of *LIFE*, a large-format weekly magazine that served as a photographic record for the mid-twentieth century. *LIFE* is no longer published.

Recall a moment from your childhood.

Recall a moment of joy.

Recall a moment from yesterday.

What you see are single frames in the album of memory. We have always had photo-
5　graphs, but for millennia these pictures remained invisible to all but their maker. Then we invented the camera, and suddenly it became possible to see inside another's mind. Among the several astonishing uses of photography, the first is that it is the instrument through which we share memory. There are others.

Photographs create collisions of time. We can shuffle decades with them—place an
10　Indy 500 racing machine next to a speedster of the 1920s, or a cavalry charge next to a carrier fleet. We can reach back 150 years and bring forth an instant of history.

They collapse space—put us in Moscow or Madagascar or on the moon. They allow us to become citizens of the world and, increasingly, of the universe.

They reveal what the eye cannot see. They take us inside a human cell or to the black-
15　est chamber of a deep cave. They can stretch the angle of vision and show us a landscape as only a hawk could see it.

They capture emotion. A grin, a grimace, a tear, a frown, a hug.

They record the past, its wars, its games, its glories, its injustices.

They celebrate life.

First Reading

1. Given the contextual detail that *LIFE* was designed for mass-market distribution, explain how the rhetor involves the audience in this text. Pay particular attention to the diction, the pronouns, and the character of details.

2. Identify the tone of the text, citing words and phrases that convey it.

3. Identify the central claim of this text.

Second Reading

1. Although brief, the text is rich in rhetorical figures. Identify and discuss how they contribute to the idea that photographs reveal what the eye cannot see.

2. Select three photographs that might be used to accompany this text, offering a rhetorical rationale for including each one. The picture or pictures you choose may be public or personal.

3. This text spanned two pages. A photograph of Labrador and Greenland, taken in 1984 from 227 miles above the Earth by an astronaut on the space shuttle *Challenger*, accompanied it. How would such a photograph impact the text for readers in the fall of 1988? How does this information affect your own regard for the text? Specifically, does the inclusion of such a photo from such a source suggest a particular understanding of the text?

4. Following is an image from the National Aeronautic and Space Administration (NASA) composed of photographs taken in 1992 from the spacecraft Galileo as the unmanned spacecraft sped from the Earth and Moon toward Jupiter. It may be viewed in color on the Web at http://grin.hq.nasa.gov/IMAGES/SMALL/GPN-2000-001437.jpg. How does the knowledge that the image was not taken by a person and that separate (although related) photographs were combined to form this view affect your regard for it?

Susan Sontag's influential commentaries concerning photographs were intriguing and controversial. She continued to consider and write about the impact of images on human culture until her death in 2005. The following passage is excerpted from her award-winning *On Photography*, published in 1977.

To photograph is to appropriate the thing photographed. It means putting oneself into a certain relation to the world that feels like knowledge—and, therefore, like power…. [P]rint seems a less treacherous form of leaching out the world, of turning it into a mental object, than photographic images, which now provide most of the knowledge people
5　have about the look of the past and the reach of the present. What is written about a person or an event is frankly an interpretation, as are handmade visual statements, like paintings or drawings. Photographed images do not seem to be statements about the world so much as pieces of it, miniatures of reality that anyone can make or acquire.

Photographs, which fiddle with the scale of the world, themselves get reduced, blown
10　up, cropped, retouched, doctored, tricked out. They age, plagued by the usual ills of paper objects; they disappear; they become valuable, and get bought and sold; they are reproduced. Photographs, which package the world, seem to invite packaging. They are stuck in albums, framed and set on tables, tacked on walls, projected as slides. Newspapers and magazines feature them; cops alphabetize them; museums exhibit them;
15　publishers compile them.

First Reading

1. Summarize the comparison Sontag expresses in the first paragraph.
2. Explain the force of the details Sontag includes in the second paragraph.

Second Reading

1. Identify several claims Sontag makes in the passage. Select what you believe to be her most remarkable claim and, drawing upon your own knowledge and experience, elaborate upon it.
2. Taken together, Sontag's claims suggest a particular stance. Compare how her stance relates to the positions taken in the Momaday and *LIFE Magazine* passages.

Writing

Argument with Visual Text Synthesis

In her 2003 book *Regarding the Pain of Others*, Susan Sontag writes that, unlike photographs, an individual's memory is "unreproducible—it dies with each person. What is called collective memory is not a remembering but a stipulating: that *this* is important, and this is the story about how it happened, with the pictures that lock the story in our minds." Sontag's position is that well-known photographs provide a shared but, unfortunately, artificial, selective, and therefore misleading record about what society deems as important about its history and character.

In a prepared essay of three to five pages, develop a position on the value that commonly known photographs can bring to a society. Research and refer to at least three well-known photographs that serve your argument.

Andy Grundberg
Photojournalism: A Blend of Artifice and Actuality

Andy Grundberg regularly wrote about photography for the *New York Times* in his column "Photography View." This particular column, prompted by a special issue of *LIFE*, appeared on January 10, 1988.

The current issue of *LIFE Magazine*, devoted to "The Year in Pictures" for 1987, features a remarkable portrait of Lt. Col. Oliver L. North. Taken by the photojournalist Harry Benson, it shows the star
5 of the summer's Iran-contra hearings in full-dress uniform, standing at attention next to an American flag. The camera's position, roughly waist-high, causes him to loom larger than life. A polished marble background adds to the heroic, even myth-
10 ic effect of the pose. One could say that Colonel North appears to be impersonating Charlton Heston impersonating Moses on the mountain.

This carefully lit and calculated image seems aimed at encapsulating the popular impression of
15 Colonel North as a kind of folk hero, and in this respect it succeeds quite well. But it is not by any stretch of the imagination a report on what went on during the Congressional inquiry. For that we have to turn the page, where we can find a less rhetorical,
20 and less interesting, news picture of Colonel North being sworn in before a full house of Congressmen, aides and—needless to say—press photographers.

The portrait and the news picture raise an important question: What kind of history do photographs
25 make? Is the aggregate visual record they produce a fairly faithful, albeit condensed, reflection of the events and spirit of our times for the future? Or is it something more ambiguous, selective and slippery, the still equivalent of a television docudrama?
30 One would assume that photographs are more reliable representations of historical events than, say, cave drawings or hieroglyphics. Those alive 150 years ago certainly thought so, since the invention of photography ended the practice of history painting
35 virtually overnight. Surely our image of the Napoleonic era would be more precise and accurate if we were to see it through the lens of a camera rather than through the eye of the painter Jacques Louis David.

But the camera's status as a mechanical record-
40 ing instrument does not mean that its images are necessarily any more innocent of bias than David's pigments. This is especially obvious today, when everyone from politicians to post-modernists is aware of how media images can be fabricated to
45 serve specific ends. In our century, the camera's ability to refashion the world is a given.

Still, it is significant that *LIFE*, which has long been considered the spiritual home of American photojournalism, should choose to use a plainly ar-
50 tificial, posed portrait of Colonel North rather than one of the thousands of "head shots" taken in the course of his testimony. It suggests that a symbolic photograph can supercede in importance a picture that purports to represent an event as it happens.
55 It suggests that photojournalism is as much artifice as actuality. It even suggests that in terms of representing history, photography is better at reproducing preconceptions than at revealing truths.

But there is a more profound lesson to be
60 gleaned from *LIFE's* "Pictures of the Year" issue, which is that photography lends credence to the belief that history is a matter of individuals and their actions. Those who believe otherwise—that economic, environmental, social and other factors
65 are the motivating forces of history—will look in vain for photographs to serve as evidence. Photography deals in appearances.

What picture might illustrate the impact of the nuclear-arms reduction pact, which to many minds was
70 the most significant event of the past year? An image of missile silos, or of warheads? The editors of *LIFE* have opted for a photograph of a smiling Gorbachev and a laughing Reagan, culled from their recent summit. This is a symbolic solution to a real dilemma.
75 But photography's affinity for individuals is not necessarily bad. Consider Alon Reininger's harrowing photographs of AIDS patients in the same issue of *LIFE*: What better way to bring home the devastating toll of the disease than to particularize its victims?
80 There is a flip side to this, however. Events without human faces tend to be left out of the pictorial record. In reporting on the October stock-market plunge, for example, *LIFE* resorts to drawings. At other times, faces take the place of the real
85 problem. The tendency of pictures to reduce history to personality frequently leads to the equation of celebrity with significance. In *LIFE's* case, eight pages of the "Pictures of the Year" issue are devoted to publicity portraits of Hollywood stars,
90 including Bette Midler, Cher and the male leads of "L.A. Law." These are not especially interesting photographs, much less "pictures of the year."

The reverse can happen just as easily. *LIFE*'s issue closes with three curious, glamorized portraits
95 of Fawn Hall, Jessica Hahn and Donna Rice—in the editors' words, "the girls of summer." The three women have nothing in common except roles in the careers of prominent men, but on Life's pages they are transformed from historical footnotes to
100 full-fledged celebrities. In makeup and designer clothes, they literally become models of notoriety.

This is not to take anything away from the photographers involved, who have done their best to give *LIFE* and its readers memorable images. Fran-
105 cesco Scavullo's picture of Miss Hall, in particular, is a convincing simulacrum of a *Cosmopolitan*-style fashion photograph, and I doubt that Miss Hall has ever looked more dashing. But if we compare this image with an earlier, thumbnail-size portrait
110 that shows her testifying before Congress, the gulf between image and reality seems to widen beneath our feet. One wonders: Is this the same *LIFE* magazine that gave us Robert Capa's D-Day photographs and countless other classics of photojour-
115 nalism? In a way, it isn't; the *LIFE* that nurtured the genre was a weekly, not the monthly we have now. But in another way it is, for if one looks back at the old weekly *LIFE* one will find it as full of calculated portraits and celebrity fluff as the current incarna-
120 tion. Even Gene Smith, whose credo was "Let truth be the prejudice," took liberties with what was in front of his camera. Photojournalism has never subscribed to the notion of "Just the facts, ma'am," even though that is what we somehow still expect.

First Reading

1. Annotate the text.
2. Working collaboratively, complete a says/does analysis.

Second Reading

1. Deepen your understanding of Grundberg's argument through research. Work either in teams or individually, eventually comparing notes with your classmates. Identify events, persons, television programs, products, and so on, that lend substance to Grundberg's argument. Using the Internet and other resources, locate images that might have accompanied this essay.
2. Report orally on your findings to your classmates, taking care to identify Grundberg's thesis. As part of your report, explain whether Grundberg's argument holds up today, years after he made it. Support your claim with specific references.

Writing

Synthesis

Suggested Preparation and Writing Time   one week following final reading assignment

Directions   The following task is based on the texts of this chapter, the photographs associated with these texts, and your additional research.

The task requires you to write a thoughtful essay of your own that integrates at least three of the sources used in this chapter and at least two additional sources. Refer to the sources in support of your own argument. Do not merely summarize the sources; *your own* argument is vital. Combine the sources in support of *your* argument.

Make certain that you attribute both direct and indirect citations, using the Modern Language Association (MLA) format. Conduct research appropriately and include a correct works cited page.

Introduction   Although photography has existed for less than 175 years, photographs are now certainly ubiquitous. Like words, "captured" images are seamlessly integrated into our lives. But do we sufficiently consider the complex nature of photography when we view photographs? How well developed is our awareness of both the opportunities and problems that accompany photographs?

Assignment   Write an essay in which you develop a position on the impact photographs have on our experience and representation of the world. Prepare a draft for a teacher/peer conference, then revise, and submit a final version.

Chapter 4

War

Background

Humans make war on one another. Historically, the purposes of war vary from aggression in order to acquire territory, to avenging or defending acts of aggression. Societies may engage in armed conflict to gain power, prestige, glory, honor, or goods. Although some societies are considered warrior nations and others peaceful, and while some societies achieve a given purpose for engaging in warfare, few escape the travails that result from armed conflict. Citizens of nations differ in attitudes regarding war, but ultimately the goal for most is a peaceful existence. There are those who say, "We must, we will go to war," and those who say, "We cannot, we will not go to war," and also those who say, "We should not go to war." Each society and each individual in a society, especially at this time, must choose.

Included in this chapter are essays, speeches, a photograph, a letter, a graph, and other texts that present different views of war, its intentions, and its results. Analyze the approaches taken by each writer, reading each text at least twice. Complete the accompanying activities, and consider your own position after evaluating all texts presented.

Readings

Marcus Tullius Cicero
On Duties

General Dwight D. Eisenhower
Message to Invasion Troops

Franklin D. Roosevelt Library
Untitled Photograph

Catiline
To His Army Before His Defeat in Battle

James Boswell
On War

President Dwight D. Eisenhower
Farewell Address

General Douglas MacArthur
Commencement Address: Michigan State University

Stockholm International Peace Research Institute
Patterns of Major Armed Conflicts, 1990–2005

Margaret Mead
Warfare: An Invention—Not a Biological Necessity

Mary Ewald
Letter to President Saddam Hussein

Marcus Tullius Cicero
On Duties

Cicero was, among other things, an orator, lawyer, politician, and philosopher. His life coincided with the decline and fall of the republic of Rome, and he was an important actor in many of the significant political events of his time. This is an excerpt from *On Duties*, which was written around 44 B.C.E.

[T]here are certain duties that we owe even to those who have wronged us. For there is a limit to retribution and to punishment; or rather, I am inclined to think, it is sufficient that the aggressor should be brought to repent of his wrong-doing, in order that he may not repeat the offence and that others may be deterred from doing wrong.
5 Then, too, in the case of a state in its external relations, the rights of war must be strictly observed. For since there are two ways of settling a dispute: first, by discussion; second; by physical force; and since the former is characteristic of man, the latter of the brute, we must resort to force only in case we may not avail ourselves of discussion. The only excuse, therefore, for going to war is that we may live in peace unharmed; and
10 when the victory is won, we should spare those who have not been blood-thirsty and barbarous in their warfare.

First Reading

1. Note key elements of the paragraph.
2. Write a one-sentence summary.
3. Write a brief statement of the claim.

Second Reading

1. Begin a working list of the topics of the arguments presented in the texts in this chapter; for example: Cicero—duties
2. As you work through these texts, add to your list notes about the most significant aspects of each speaker's argument.

General Dwight D. Eisenhower
Message to Invasion Troops

General Eisenhower delivered this message to the Allied Expeditionary Force prior to the 1944 Normandy Invasion. He also prepared a letter to President Franklin D. Roosevelt in the event of an Allied defeat. During World War II, General Eisenhower was the Supreme Commander of all Allied Expeditionary Forces in Europe, and with him lay the entire responsibility for the success or failure of the invasion. Allied Forces invaded Normandy, France, on June 6, 1944. Victory in Europe was declared on May 8, 1945.

Supreme Headquarters, Allied Expeditionary Force

Soldiers, Sailors and Airmen of the Allied Expeditionary Force!

You are about to embark upon the Great Crusade, toward which we have striven these many months. The eyes of the world are upon you. The hopes and prayers of lib-
5 erty-loving people everywhere march with you. In company with our brave Allies and brothers-in-arms on other Fronts, you will bring about the destruction of the German war machine, the elimination of Nazi tyranny over the oppressed peoples of Europe, and security to yourselves in a free world.

Your task will not be an easy one. Your enemy is well trained, well equipped and
10 battle-hardened. He will fight savagely.

But this is the year 1944! Much has happened since the Nazi triumphs of 1940–41. The United Nations have inflicted upon the Germans great defeats, in open battle, man-to-man. Our air offensive has seriously reduced their strength in the air and their capacity to wage war on the ground. Our Home Fronts have given us an overwhelming
15 superiority in weapons and munitions of war, and placed at our disposal great reserves of trained fighting men. The tide has turned! The free men of the world are marching together to Victory!

I have full confidence in your courage, devotion to duty, and skill in battle. We will accept nothing less than full Victory!
20 Good Luck! And let us all beseech the blessing of Almighty God upon this great and noble undertaking.

First Reading

1. Describe your initial response to General Eisenhower's letter. Be specific. How did it make you feel? What does it make you think about? How would you have felt had you been a member of the landing forces?
2. What kinds of dangers might you anticipate confronting on the day of the invasion? Describe what you expect would be your responsibility.

Second Reading

1. Note each of General Eisenhower's exclamations and explain what each suggests to the intended audience.
2. Note the allusions and explain how each contributes to Eisenhower's purpose in the letter.
3. Note repetitions and explain your ideas about how each repetition reinforces Eisenhower's purpose in the letter.

4. Consider Eisenhower's diction, and explain how words with positive and negative connotations contribute to his purpose.

5. Examine each of Eisenhower's emotional appeals. Then consider how the emotional appeals combine with logic to render a specific effect.

Writing

Argument — Rewrite General Eisenhower's letter as though you were a contemporary leader. Exhort your troops to desire victory and to be confident that it will come.

The following photograph shows members of the Allied forces wading ashore at Normandy on June 6, 1944.

In this photograph, the image represents a real event, and the photographer is inside the scene. Every photograph—in fact, every text regardless of the genre—exists within a context. This photograph exists within a context from the past. How does it mesh with its context? Consider the following questions.

First Reading

1. Upon what do you first focus in the photograph? What directed your focus to that element?
2. Describe your idea about the purpose of this photograph.
3. Consider several titles for the photo and choose one you find most suitable. Does your title change the way a viewer might consider the image? Explain why or why not.
4. How does the photograph tell a story?
5. Write a one-page story that explains the photograph.

Second Reading

1. When was the photograph generated and to what does it respond?
2. Explain your ideas about the intended audience? Be specific in your description. To answer "Allies of WWII" would be limited.
3. How do you expect viewers responded to the photograph in 1944, right after the invasion, and in 1946, after the war had ended? Would there be differences in the viewers' responses?
4. What elements unify the text? Write a list of everything you see before you decide.
5. Decide how the whole can be divided into parts.
6. How did this photographer manipulate the point of view to shape the composition?
7. Contrasts can shape complex and dramatic scenes. Explain how contrasts create drama in the photograph.
8. What seems most important in the photograph? Why? Consider the elements that are included and those elements that may have been left out.

Writing

1. **Analysis** — Write a one-page (250–500 words) analysis of the details that generated your response to the photograph. Consider such elements as contrasts of dark and light, point of view, and details. Introduce your analysis, present your thesis, and conclude by defending it.
2. **Argument** — Write from the point of view of a war correspondent and report General Eisenhower's response to this photograph, followed by the response of the mother of one member of the forces that landed at Normandy on D-Day.

Catiline
To His Army Before His Defeat in Battle

A conspirator against Rome, Catiline made this speech to his troops who were on their way into Gaul and trapped by the armies of Rome and Gaul at Pistoria, two hundred miles north of Rome. Catiline's forces were not as successful as General Eisenhower's, and he was killed in the battle that followed this speech delivered in 62 B.C.E.

I am well aware, soldiers, that words cannot inspire courage and that a spiritless army cannot be rendered active, or a timid army valiant, by the speech of its commander. Whatever courage is in
5 the heart of a man, whether from nature or from habit, so much will be shown by him in the field; and on him whom neither glory nor danger can move, exhortation is bestowed in vain, for the terror in his breast stops his ears.
10 I have called you together, however, to give you a few instructions, and to explain to you, at the same time, my reasons for the course which I have adopted. You all know, soldiers, how severe a penalty the inactivity and cowardice of Lentu-
15 lus has brought upon himself and us; and how, while waiting for reinforcement from the city, I was unable to march into Gaul. In what situation our affairs now are, you all understand as well as myself. Two armies of the enemy, one on the side
20 of Rome, and the other on that of Gaul, oppose our progress; while the want of corn and of other necessaries, prevents us from remaining, however strongly we may desire to remain, in our present position. Whithersoever we would go, we must
25 open a passage with our swords.
I conjure you, therefore, to maintain a brave and resolute spirit and to remember, when you advance to battle, that on your own right hands depend riches, honor, and glory, with the enjoyment
30 of your liberty and of your country. If we conquer, all will be safe; we shall have provisions in abundance, and the colonies and corporate towns will open their gates to us. But if we lose the victory through want of courage, those same places will

35 turn against us, for neither place nor friend will protect him whom his arms have not protected. Besides, soldiers, the same exigency does not press upon our adversaries as presses upon us; we fight for our country, for our liberty, for our life;
40 they contend for what but little concerns them, the power of a small party. Attack them, therefore, with so much the greater confidence, and call to mind your achievements of old.
We might, with the utmost ignominy, have
45 passed the rest of our days in exile. Some of you, after losing your property, might have waited at Rome for assistance from others. But because such a life, to men of spirit, was disgusting and unendurable, you resolved upon your present course. If you
50 wish to quit it, you must exert all your resolution, for none but conquerors have exchanged war for peace. To hope for safety in flight, when you have turned away from the enemy the arms by which the body is defended, is indeed madness. In battle,
55 those who are most afraid are always in most danger; but courage is equivalent to a rampart.
When I contemplate you, soldiers, and when I consider your past exploits, a strong hope of victory animates me. Your spirit, your age, your
60 valor, give me confidence—to say nothing of necessity, which makes even cowards brave. To prevent the numbers of the enemy from surrounding us, our confined situation is sufficient. But should fortune be unjust to your valor, take care not to
65 lose your lives unavenged; take care not to be taken and butchered like cattle, rather than fighting like men, to leave your enemies a bloody and mournful victory.

First Reading

1. Does the first paragraph appeal to ethics, logic, or emotion? Explain how you know.
2. The second paragraph (lines 10–25) presents Catiline's purpose. Find his declaration of purpose.
3. The third paragraph (lines 26–43) is a cause-and-effect explanation that constitutes a logical appeal. Trace Catiline's if/then reasoning.
4. The fourth paragraph (lines 44–56) points out what Catiline and his army "might" have done had they not been resolved to their course. What purpose does this paragraph serve?
5. The fifth paragraph (lines 57–68) constitutes Catiline's emotional appeal. Explain its persuasive qualities.

Second Reading

1. Note each element of metaphoric language and explain how that element contributes to Catiline's purpose.
2. Notice that Catiline begins the speech with first person singular point of view and shifts to first person plural at the end of paragraph two. Explain his purpose in this shift and why he maintains that point of view for the remainder of the speech.

Writing

Analysis and Argument — In a two-page essay, compare Catiline's speech to General Eisenhower's message on page 39. Refer to specific elements of each speech, and determine which speech you consider more persuasive. Explain your reasoning.

James Boswell
On War

James Boswell was a lawyer and writer from Scotland. He wrote this essay in 1777 after a European tour. Boswell begins by expressing his amazement at the preparations men make for war and ends by suggesting that his amazement continues, but in the body of the essay he presents sound evidence to support his claim that war is "irrational."

While viewing, as travelers usually do, the remarkable objects of curiosity at Venice, I was conducted through the different departments of the Arsenal; and as I contemplated the great
5 storehouse of mortal engines, in which there is not only a large deposit of arms, but men are continually employed in making more, my thoughts *rebounded*, if I may use the expression, from what I beheld; and the effect was, that I was first as it were
10 stunned into a state of amazement, and when I recovered from that, my mind expanded itself in reflections upon the horrid irrationality of war.

What those reflections were I do not precisely recollect. But the general impression dwells upon
15 my memory; and however strange it may seem, my opinion of the irrationality of war is still associated with the Arsenal of Venice.

One particular however I well remember. When I saw workingmen engaged with grave assiduity
20 in fashioning weapons of death, I was struck with wonder at the shortsightedness, the *caecae mentes*[1] of human beings, who were thus soberly preparing the instruments of destruction of their own species. I have since found upon a closer study
25 of man, that my wonder might have been spared; because there are very few men whose minds are sufficiently enlarged to comprehend universal or even extensive good. The views of most individuals are limited to their own happiness; and
30 the workmen whom I beheld so busy in the Arsenal of Venice saw nothing but what was good in the labour for which they received such wages as procured them the comforts of life. That their immediate satisfaction was not hindered by a
35 view of the remote consequential and contingent evils for which alone their labours could be at all useful, would not surprise one who has had a tolerable share of experience in life. We must have the telescope of philosophy to make us perceive
40 distant ills; nay, we know that there are individuals of our species to whom the immediate misery of others is nothing in comparison with their own advantage – for we know that in every age there

have been found men very willing to perform the
45 office of executioner ever for a moderate hire.

To prepare instruments for the destruction of our species at large, is what I now see may very well be done by ordinary men, without starting, when they themselves are to run no risk. But I
50 shall never forget, nor cease to wonder at a most extraordinary instance of thoughtless intrepidity which I had related to me by a cousin of mine, now a lieutenant-colonel in the British army, who was upon guard when it happened. A soldier
55 of one of the regiments in garrison at Minorca, having been found guilty of a capital crime, was brought out to be hanged. They had neglected to have a rope in readiness, and the shocking business was at a stand. The fellow, with a spirit and
60 alertness which in general would, upon a difficult and trying emergency, have been very great presence of mind and conduct, striped the lace off his hat, said this will do, and actually made it serve as the fatal chord.

65 The irrationality of war is, I suppose, admitted by almost all men: I almost say all; because I have met myself with men who attempted seriously to maintain that it is an agreeable occupation and one of the chief means of human happiness. I
70 must own that although I use the plural number here, I should have used the dual, had I been writing in Greek; for I never met with but two men who supported such a paradox; and one of them was a tragick poet, and one a Scotch Highlander.
75 The first had his imagination so in a blaze with heroic sentiments, with the 'pride, pomp, and circumstance of glorious war,' that he did not avert to its miseries, as one dazzled with the pageantry of a magnificent funeral thinks not of the pangs
80 of dissolution and the dismal corpse. The second had his attention so eagerly fixed on the advantage which accrued to his *clan* from the 'trade of war,' that he could think only of it as a good.

We are told by some writers, who assume the
85 character of philosophers, that war is necessary to take off the superfluity of the human species, or at

---

1 *Caecae mentes:* "blind minds"

least to rid the world of numbers of idle and profligate men who are a burden upon every community, and would grow an insupportable burden, were they to live as long as men do in the usual course of nature. But there is unquestioningly no reason to fear a superfluity of mankind, when we know that although perhaps the time 'when every rood of land maintain'd its man' is a poetical exaggeration, yet vigorous and well directed industry can raise sustenance for such a proportion of people in a certain space of territory, as is astonishing to us who are accustomed to see only moderate effects of labour; and when we also know what immense regions of the terrestrial globe in very good climates are uninhabited. In these there is room for millions to enjoy existence. In cultivating these, the idle and profligate, expelled from their original societies, might be employed and gradually reformed, which would be better surely, than continuing the practice of periodical destruction, which is also indiscriminate, and involves the best equally with the worst of men.

I have often thought that if war should cease over all the face of the earth, for a thousand years, its reality would not be believed at such a distance of time, notwithstanding the faith of authentick records in every nation. Were mankind totally free from every tincture of prejudice in favour of those gallant exertions which could not exist were there not the evil of violence to combat; had they never seen in their own days, or been told by father or grandfathers, of battles, and were there no traces of the *art of war*, I have no doubt that they would treat as fabulous or allegorical, the accounts in history, of prodigious armies being formed, of men who engaged themselves for an unlimited time, under the penalty of immediate death, to obey implicitly the orders of commanders to whom they were not attached either by affection or by interest; that these armies were sometimes led with toilsome expedition over vast tracts of land, sometimes crouded into ships, and obliged to endure tedious, unhealthy, and perilous voyages; and that the purpose of all this toil and danger was not to obtain any comfort or pleasure, but to be in a situation to encounter other armies; and that those opposite multitudes the individuals of which had no cause to quarrel, no ill-will to each other, continued for hours engaged with patient and obstinate perseverance, while thousands were slain, and thousands crushed and mangled by the diversity of wounds.

We who have from our earliest years had our minds filled with scenes of war of which we have read in the books that we most revere and most admire, who have remarked it in every revolving century, and in every country that has been discovered by navigators, even in the gentle and benign regions of the southern oceans; we who have seen all the intelligence, power and ingenuity of our nation employed in war, who have been accustomed to peruse Gazettes, and have had our friends and relations killed or sent home to us wretchedly maimed; we cannot without a steady effort of reflection be sensible of the improbability that rational creatures should act so irrationally as to unite in deliberate plans, which must certainly produce the direful effects which war is known to do. But I have no doubt that if the project for a perpetual peace which the Abbé de St Pierre sketched, and Rousseau[2] improved, were to take place, the incredulity of war would after the lapse of some ages be universal.

Were there any good produced by war which could in any degree compensate its direful effects; were better men to spring up from the ruins of those who fall in battle, as more beautiful material forms sometimes arise from the ashes of others; or were those who escape from its destruction to have an increase of happiness; in short, were there any great beneficial effect to follow it, the notion of its irrationality would be only the notion of narrow comprehension. But we find that war is followed by no general good whatever. The power, the glory, or the wealth of a very few may be enlarged. But the people in general, upon both sides, after all the sufferings are passed, pursue their ordinary occupations, with no difference from their former state. The evils therefore of war, upon a general view of humanity are as the French say, *à pure perte*[3], a mere loss without any advantage, unless indeed furnishing subjects for history, poetry, and painting. And although it should be allowed that mankind have gained enjoyment in these respects, I suppose it will not be seriously said, that the misery is overbalanced. At any rate, there is already such a store of subjects, that an addition to them would be dearly purchased by more wars.

I am none of those who would set up their notions against the opinion of the world; on the contrary, I have such a respect for that authority, as to doubt my own judgement when it opposes that of numbers probably as wise as I am. But when I maintain the irrationality of war, I am not contradicting the opinion, but the practice of the

---

2 **Rousseau:** Jean Jacques Rousseau (1717–1778) was a French philosopher and social reformer.

3 *À pure perte:* "uselessly," "to no purpose"

world. For, as I have already observed, its irrationality is generally admitted. Horace calls Hannibal, *demens*[4], a madman; and Pope gives the same appellation to Alexander the Great and Charles XII: From Macedonia's madman to the Swede.

How long war will continue to be practised, we have no means of conjecturing. Civilization, which it might have been expected would have abolished it, has only refined its savage rudeness. The irrationality remains, though we have learnt *insanire certa ratione modoque*[5], to have a method in our madness.

That amiable religion which 'proclaims peace on earth,' hath not as yet made war to cease. The furious passions of men, modified as they are by moral instruction, still operate with much force; and by a perpetual fallacy, even the conscientious in each contending nation think they may join in war, because they each believe they are repelling an aggressor. Were the mild and humane doctrine of those Christians, who are called Quakers[6], which Mr Jenyns has lately embellished with his elegant pen, to prevail, human felicity would gain more than we can well conceive. But perhaps it is necessary that mankind in this state of existence, the purpose of which is so mysterious, should ever suffer the woes of war.

To relieve my readers from reflections which they may think too abstract, I shall conclude this paper with a few observations upon actual war.

In ancient times when a battle was fought man to man, or as somebody has very well expressed it, was a group of duels, there was an opportunity for individuals to distinguish themselves by vigour and bravery. One who was a '*robustus acri militia*[7], hardy from keen warfare,' could gratify his ambition for fame, by the exercise of his own personal qualities. It was therefore more reasonable then, for individuals to enlist, than it is in modern times; for, a battle now is truly nothing else than a huge conflict of opposite engines worked by men, who are themselves as machines directed by a few; and the event is not so frequently decided by what is actually done, as by accidents happening in the dreadful confusion. It is as if two towns in opposite territories should be set on fire at the same time, and victory should be declared to the inhabitants of that in which the flames were least destructive. We hear much of the conduct of generals; and Addison himself has represented the Duke of Marlborough[8] directing an army in battle, as an 'angel riding in a whirlwind and directing the storm.' Nevertheless I much doubt if upon many occasions the immediate schemes of a commander have had certain effect; and I believe Sir Callaghan O'Bralachan in Mr Macklin's *Love A la mode* gives a very just account of modern battle: 'There is so much doing every where that we cannot tell what is doing any where.'

First Reading

1. Briefly describe your first impression of Boswell's essay.
2. What information can you derive from the date and the title? State Boswell's claim. Consider the essay in light of your own experience, and consider how that experience contributes to your response to Boswell's claim.
3. Jot down questions you would like to ask Boswell and speculate about his answers.

Second Reading

1. How does the structure of the essay order the ideas? Trace the focus of each paragraph to determine the movement of ideas. Generally, you can describe the focus with a word or two. For example, you could label the focus of the first paragraph as "amazement." The focus is often, but not always, stated directly.
2. Explain how each footnote contributes to your understanding of Boswell's essay.

---

4 *Demens*: "out of one's mind"

5 *Insanire certa ratione modoque*: From the Latin poet Horace, "to have a method in one's madness"

6 Quakers believe in a philosophy that promotes personal nonviolence.

7 *Robustus acri militia*: From the Latin poet Horace, "(made) strong by intense military exercise"

8 **Addison… Marlborough:** Joseph Addison (1672–1719) was a famous essayist of the period. John Churchill (1650–1722), first Duke of Marlborough, was one of England's greatest generals. He won many important battles against the French.

3. Note each example Boswell includes and explain how that example contributes to his claim.

4. Note sections or paragraphs as appeals to logic, emotion, or ethics.

5. What would General Eisenhower say to James Boswell?

Complete the following reading comprehension questions. After each one, explain what the question asked you to do or know and why you answered as you did.

1. Which of the following best describes the rhetorical function of the first two paragraphs?

   (A) the initiation of emotional appeals
   (B) the presentation of the writer's thesis
   (C) the introduction of the writer's amazement at the work he saw
   (D) the beginning of a series of associations
   (E) the introduction of his reflections

2. In context, the expression "the telescope of philosophy" in paragraph 3 (lines 18–45) is best interpreted to have which of the following meanings?

   (A) a method of viewing information
   (B) a reference to unforeseen consequences
   (C) a way to study the future
   (D) an instrument of vision
   (E) an insight based on wisdom

3. The writer's observation about "The irrationality of war" in paragraph 5 (lines 65–83) is best described as an example of which of the following?

   (A) dismissively objective
   (B) sincerely apologetic
   (C) ridiculously pejorative
   (D) mockingly dismissive
   (E) admittedly humorous

4. The writers referred to in paragraph 6 (lines 84–108) view warfare as

   (A) essential to humanity.
   (B) burdensome on a society.
   (C) insupportable by sound thinkers.
   (D) indiscriminately waged.
   (E) exaggerated argument.

5. Which of the following rhetorical devices is most in evidence in the second sentence of paragraph 7 (lines 109–139), which begins "Were mankind totally free from every tincture of prejudice…"

   (A) abstract propositions
   (B) objective description
   (C) paradoxical imagery
   (D) historical generalizations
   (E) extended metaphor

6. The writer's purpose in paragraph 8 (lines 140–160) is best described as

   (A) anticipating future objections to refute.
   (B) providing a contrast to paragraph 6.
   (C) presenting an illustration of paragraph 7.
   (D) reinforcing the allusions in paragraph 7.
   (E) introducing a generalization supported in paragraph 9.

7. All of the following are referred to by the implied abstraction "rationality" in the essay EXCEPT

   (A) moderation.
   (B) plausibility.
   (C) perspicacity.
   (D) reflection.
   (E) responsibility.

8. The structure of paragraph 13 (lines 220–252) is best described as

   (A) a concession followed by a series of examples.
   (B) a movement from the serious to the absurd.
   (C) a claim followed by supporting details.
   (D) a historical example followed by allusions.
   (E) a reflection followed by details.

9. The writer's tone in the essay as a whole is best described as

   (A) superficial and capricious.
   (B) formal and analytical.
   (C) strident and ludicrous.
   (D) altruistic and excessive.
   (E) vexatious and provocative.

Writing

Analysis — Write an explanation of how one rhetorical strategy illustrates and furthers Boswell's claim.

President Dwight D. Eisenhower
Farewell Address

Bringing to the Presidency his prestige as commanding general of the victorious forces in Europe during World War II, President Eisenhower worked incessantly during his two terms to ease the tensions of the Cold War. He pursued moderate policies concentrated on maintaining world peace. In his farewell address, delivered on January 17, 1961, after two terms in office, the president urges continued concentration on policies to maintain peace.

My fellow Americans:

Three days from now, after half a century in the service of our country, I shall lay down the responsibilities of office as, in traditional and solemn cer-
5 emony, the authority of the Presidency is vested in my successor. This evening I come to you with a message of leave-taking and farewell, and to share a few final thoughts with you, my countrymen. Like every other citizen, I wish the new President,
10 and all who will labor with him, Godspeed. I pray that the coming years will be blessed with peace and prosperity for all. Our people expect their President and the Congress to find essential agreement on issues of great moment, the wise resolution of
15 which will better shape the future of the Nation.

My own relations with the Congress, which began on a remote and tenuous basis when, long ago, a member of the Senate appointed me to West Point, have since ranged to the intimate during the
20 war and immediate post-war period, and, finally, to the mutually interdependent during these past eight years. In this final relationship, the Congress and the Administration have, on most vital issues, cooperated well, to serve the national good rather
25 than mere partisanship, and so have assured that the business of the Nation should go forward. So, my official relationship with the Congress ends in a feeling, on my part, of gratitude that we have been able to do so much together.

30 We now stand ten years past the midpoint of a century that has witnessed four major wars among great nations. Three of these involved our own country. Despite these holocausts America is today the strongest, the most influential and most pro-
35 ductive nation in the world. Understandably proud of this pre-eminence, we yet realize that America's leadership and prestige depend, not merely upon our unmatched material progress, riches and military strength, but on how we use our power in the
40 interests of world peace and human betterment. Throughout America's adventure in free government, our basic purposes have been to keep the

peace; to foster progress in human achievement, and to enhance liberty, dignity and integrity among
45 people and among nations. To strive for less would be unworthy of a free and religious people. Any failure traceable to arrogance, or our lack of comprehension or readiness to sacrifice would inflict upon us grievous hurt both at home and abroad.
50 Progress toward these noble goals is persistently threatened by the conflict now engulfing the world. It commands our whole attention, absorbs our very beings. We face a hostile ideology—global in scope, atheistic in character, ruthless in purpose,
55 and insidious in method. Unhappily the danger it poses promises to be of indefinite duration. To meet it successfully, there is called for, not so much the emotional and transitory sacrifices of crisis, but rather those which enable us to carry forward
60 steadily, surely, and without complaint the burdens of a prolonged and complex struggle—with liberty at stake. Only thus shall we remain, despite every provocation, on our charted course toward permanent peace and human betterment.

65 Crises there will continue to be. In meeting them, whether foreign or domestic, great or small, there is a recurring temptation to feel that some spectacular and costly action could become the miraculous solution to all current difficulties. A huge
70 increase in newer elements of our defense; development of unrealistic programs to cure every ill in agriculture; a dramatic expansion in basic and applied research—these and many other possibilities, each possibly promising in itself, may be suggested
75 as the only way to the road we wish to travel.

But each proposal must be weighed in the light of a broader consideration: the need to maintain balance in and among national programs—balance between the private and the public econo-
80 my, balance between cost and hoped for advantage—balance between the clearly necessary and the comfortably desirable; balance between our essential requirements as a nation and the duties imposed by the nation upon the individual; bal-
85 ance between action of the moment and the na-

tional welfare of the future. Good judgment seeks balance and progress; lack of it eventually finds imbalance and frustration. The record of many decades stands as proof that our people and their government have, in the main, understood these truths and have responded to them well, in the face of stress and threat. But threats, new in kind or degree, constantly arise. I mention two only.

A vital element in keeping the peace is our military establishment. Our arms must be mighty, ready for instant action, so that no potential aggressor may be tempted to risk his own destruction. Our military organization today bears little relation to that known by any of my predecessors in peace time, or indeed by the fighting men of World War II or Korea. Until the latest of our world conflicts, the United States had no armaments industry. American makers of plowshares could, with time and as required, make swords as well. But now we can no longer risk emergency improvisation of national defense; we have been compelled to create a permanent armaments industry of vast proportions. Added to this, three and a half million men and women are directly engaged in the defense establishment. We annually spend on military security more than the net income of all United States corporations. This conjunction of an immense military establishment and a large arms industry is new in the American experience. The total influence—economic, political, even spiritual—is felt in every city, every state house, every office of the Federal government. We recognize the imperative need for this development. Yet we must not fail to comprehend its grave implications. Our toil, resources and livelihood are all involved; so is the very structure of our society. In the councils of government, we must guard against the acquisition of unwarranted influence, whether sought or unsought, by the military-industrial complex. The potential for the disastrous rise of misplaced power exists and will persist. We must never let the weight of this combination endanger our liberties or democratic processes. We should take nothing for granted. Only an alert and knowledgeable citizenry can compel the proper meshing of huge industrial and military machinery of defense with our peaceful methods and goals, so that security and liberty may prosper together.

Akin to, and largely responsible for the sweeping changes in our industrial-military posture, has been the technological revolution during recent decades. In this revolution, research has become central; it also becomes more formalized, complex, and costly. A steadily increasing share is conducted for, by, or at the direction of, the Federal government. Today, the solitary inventor, tinkering in his shop, has been over shadowed by task forces of scientists in laboratories and testing fields. In the same fashion, the free university, historically the fountainhead of free ideas and scientific discovery, has experienced a revolution in the conduct of research. Partly because of the huge costs involved, a government contract becomes virtually a substitute for intellectual curiosity. For every old blackboard there are now hundreds of new electronic computers. The prospect of domination of the nation's scholars by Federal employment, project allocations, and the power of money is ever present and is gravely to be regarded. Yet, in holding scientific research and discovery in respect, as we should, we must also be alert to the equal and opposite danger that public policy could itself become the captive of a scientific-technological elite. It is the task of statesmanship to mold, to balance, and to integrate these and other forces, new and old, within the principles of our democratic system—ever aiming toward the supreme goals of our free society. Another factor in maintaining balance involves the element of time. As we peer into society's future, we—you and I, and our government—must avoid the impulse to live only for today, plundering, for our own ease and convenience, the precious resources of tomorrow. We cannot mortgage the material assets of our grandchildren without risking the loss also of their political and spiritual heritage. We want democracy to survive for all generations to come, not to become the insolvent phantom of tomorrow.

Down the long lane of the history yet to be written America knows that this world of ours, ever growing smaller, must avoid becoming a community of dreadful fear and hate, and be, instead, a proud confederation of mutual trust and respect. Such a confederation must be one of equals. The weakest must come to the conference table with the same confidence as do we, protected as we are by our moral, economic, and military strength. That table, though scarred by many past frustrations, cannot be abandoned for the certain agony of the battlefield.

Disarmament, with mutual honor and confidence, is a continuing imperative. Together we must learn how to compose difference, not with arms, but with intellect and decent purpose. Because this need is so sharp and apparent I confess that I lay down my official responsibilities in this field with a definite sense of disappointment. As one who has witnessed the horror and the lingering sadness of war—as one who knows that another war could utterly destroy this civilization which has been so slowly and painfully built over thousands of years—I wish I could say tonight that a lasting peace is in sight. Happily, I can say that war has been avoided. Steady progress toward our ultimate goal has been made. But, so much remains to be done. As a private citizen, I shall never cease to do what little I can to help the world advance along that road.

So—in this my last good night to you as your President—I thank you for the many opportunities you have given me for public service in war and peace. I trust that in that service you find some things worthy; as for the rest of it, I know you will find ways to improve performance in the future. You and I—my fellow citizens—need to be strong in our faith that all nations, under God, will reach the goal of peace with justice. May we be ever unswerving in devotion to principle, confident but humble with power, diligent in pursuit of the Nation's great goals. To all the peoples of the world, I once more give expression to America's prayerful and continuing aspiration:

We pray that peoples of all faiths, all races, all nations, may have their great human needs satisfied; that those now denied opportunity shall come to enjoy it to the full; that all who yearn for freedom may experience its spiritual blessings; that those who have freedom will understand, also, its heavy responsibilities; that all who are insensitive to the needs of others will learn charity; that the scourges of poverty, disease and ignorance will be made to disappear from the earth, and that, in the goodness of time, all peoples will come to live together in a peace guaranteed by the binding force of mutual respect and love.

First Reading

1. What previous knowledge do you have about the period of President Eisenhower's two terms? Make a brief list of social, cultural, and political elements that you know about the world in the 1950s.

2. The president's address was delivered via radio and television to the nation, but his entire audience can be described by its diversity. Consider both the national and the global audience. How might different elements of his audience respond to the farewell address?

3. Write a brief description of your own response and explain why you respond as you do.

Second Reading

1. The president's first two paragraphs are personal expressions from a public figure, and through them he presents ethical appeals. Name the focus of each paragraph and explain how the appeals in each paragraph are developed.

2. Paragraphs 3 through 5 (lines 30–75) contain the president's comments about the standing of the nation at the end of his second term. Name the focus of each paragraph and explain how the president addresses the issues he describes. In addition to simple paraphrase, add your own thoughts about the president's choice of rhetorical devices.

3. Paragraphs 6, 7, and 8 (lines 76–172) address specific elements facing the United States at the time. These three paragraphs are primarily logical appeals, but they contain diction that might constitute elements of emotional appeal. Explain the president's reasoning in each paragraph. Again, in addition to simple paraphrase, add your own thoughts about the president's choice of rhetorical devices.

4. Paragraph 8 (lines 133–172) begins the president's conclusion. Using the strategies in questions 2 and 3, name the focus of each of the last four paragraphs and explain how the president achieves his purpose in each paragraph.

Writing

1. **Analysis** — Carefully read President Eisenhower's farewell address. Analyze the rhetorical strategies in the president's speech that reveal his attitude toward the United States' position in the global society at that time.

2. **Argument** — Read the president's speech carefully. Find what you believe is the most compelling imperative he presents about society's future. Then write an essay in which you consider the validity of that imperative today for Americans and for the global society.

General Douglas MacArthur
Commencement Address: Michigan State University

The following commencement address was delivered in 1961 by MacArthur, the retired but prominent and controversial United States Army General who commanded American forces in the Pacific during World War II and in the Korean War.

Overshadowing all other problems you will face, intruding upon every thought and action, encompassing all that you hold most dear, dictating not only the past but your very future, is the master problem of global war. How, you can well ask, did such an institution as war become so integrated with man's life and civilization? How has it grown to be the most vital factor in our existence?

It started in a modest enough way as a sort of gladiatorial method of settling disputes between conflicting tribes. One of the oldest and most classical examples is the Biblical story of David and Goliath. Each of the two contesting groups selected its champion. They fought, and based upon the outcome, an agreement resulted. Then, as time went on, small professional groups known as armies replaced the individual champions. And these groups fought in some obscure corner of the world, and victory or defeat was accepted as the basis of an ensuing peace. And from then on, down through the ages, the constant record is an increase in the character and strength of the forces with the rate of increase always accelerating. From a small percentage of the population it finally engulfed all. It is now the nation in arms. Within my own life I have witnessed much of the evolution. At the turn of the century, when I joined the Army, the target was one enemy casualty at the end of a rifle, a pistol, a bayonet, a sword. Then came the machine gun designed to kill by the dozens. After that the heavy artillery raining death upon the hundreds. Then the aerial bomb to strike by the thousands—followed by the atom explosion to reach the hundreds of thousands. Now electronics and other processes of science have raised the destructive potential to encompass millions. And with restless hands we work feverishly in dark laboratories to find the means to destroy all at one blow.

But this very triumph of scientific annihilation—this very success of invention—has destroyed the possibility of war being a medium for the practical settlement of international differences. The enormous destruction to both sides of closely matched opponents makes it impossible for even the winner to translate it into anything but his own disaster.

The late war, even with its now antiquated armaments, clearly demonstrated that the victor had to bear in large part the very injuries inflicted on his foe. We expended billions of dollars and untold energies to heal the wounds of Germany and Japan.

Global war has become a Frankenstein monster to destroy both sides. No longer can it be a successful weapon of international adventure. If you lose, you are annihilated. If you win, you stand only to lose. No longer does it possess even the chance of the winner of a duel—it contains now only the germs of double suicide.

Time was when victory in war represented a shortcut to power, a place in the sun, economic wealth, and accelerated prosperity. It was the final weapon of statecraft, the apotheosis of political diplomacy. Its application, however, was regulated, controlled, and limited by the basic principle that a great nation that entered upon war and did not see it through to victory would ultimately suffer all the consequences of defeat. This is what happened to us in Korea. With victory within our grasp and without the use of the atom bomb which we needed no more then than against Japan, we failed to see it through. Had we done so we would have destroyed Red China's capability of waging modern war for generations to come. Our failure to win that war was a major disaster to the free world. Its fatal consequences are now increasingly being felt in the military rise of Red China into a mighty colossus which threatens all of continental Asia and bids fair to emerge as the balance of military power in the world. This would jeopardize freedom on all continents.

The great question is, can global war now be outlawed from the world? If so, it would mark the greatest advance in civilization since the Sermon on the Mount. It would lift at one stroke the darkest shadow which has engulfed mankind from the beginning. It would not only remove fear and bring security; it would not only create new moral and spiritual values; it would produce an economic wave of prosperity that would raise the world's standard of living beyond anything ever dreamed of by man. The hundreds of billions of dollars now spent in mutual preparedness could conceivably abolish poverty from the face of the earth. It would accomplish even more than this; it would at one stroke reduce the international tensions that seem to be insurmountable now to matters of probable solution. This would not, of course, mean the abandonment of all armed forces, but it would reduce them to the simpler problems of internal order and international police. It would not mean Utopia at one fell stroke, but it would mean that the great roadblock now existing to the development of the human race would have been cleared.

You will say at once that although the abolition of war has been the dream of man for centuries every proposition to that end has been promptly discarded as impossible and fantastic. But that was before the science of the past decade made mass destruction a reality. The argument then was along spiritual and moral lines, and lost. But now the tremendous evolution of nuclear and other potentials of destruction has suddenly taken the problem away from its primary consideration as a moral and spiritual question and brought it abreast of scientific realism. It is no longer an ethical question to be pondered solely by learned philosophers and ecclesiastics but a hard core one for the decision of the masses whose survival is the issue. This is as true of the Soviet side of the world as of the free side—as true behind the Iron Curtain as in front of it. The ordinary people of the world, such as you and I, whether free or slave, are all in agreement on this solution; and this, perhaps, is the only thing in the world they do agree upon, but it is the most vital and decisive of all. We are told that we must go on indefinitely as at present—with what at the end none say—there is no definite objective. The search for a final solution is but passed along to those who follow and,

at the end, the problem will be exactly that which we face now.

It may take another cataclysm of destruction to prove the bald truth that the further evolution of civilization cannot take place until global war is abolished. This is the one issue upon which both sides can agree, for it is the one issue upon which both sides will profit equally. It is the one issue in which the interests of both are completely parallel. It is the one issue which, if settled, might settle all others.

The present tensions with their threat of national annihilation are fostered by two great illusions. The one is a complete belief on the part of the Soviet world that the capitalistic countries are preparing to eventually attack them and that sooner or later we intend to strike. And the other is a complete belief on the part of the capitalistic countries that the Soviets are preparing the attack on us and that sooner or later they intend to strike. Both are wrong. Each side, so far as the masses are concerned, is desirous of peace. Both dread war. But the constant acceleration of preparation may, without specific intent, ultimately precipitate a kind of spontaneous combustion.

Many will tell you, with mockery and ridicule, that the abolition of war can only be a dream, that it is but the vague imaginings of a visionary. But we must go on or we will go under. And criticism is that the world has no plan which will enable us to go on. We have suffered the blood and the sweat and the tears. Now we seek the way and the truth and the light. We are in a new era. The old methods and solutions for this vital problem no longer suffice. We must have new thoughts, new ideas, new concepts. We must break out of the strait-jacket of the past. We must have sufficient imagination and moral courage to translate this universal wish—which is rapidly becoming a universal necessity—into actuality. And until then we must be fully prepared, whatever the cost, lest we perish.

First Reading

1. What is the effect of MacArthur's description of "the master problem of global war" in paragraph 1?

2. In paragraph 2, MacArthur briefly traces the history of warfare. Paraphrase this paragraph. To what does "Frankenstein monster" (line 54) generally refer? What is the effect of the allusion?

3. In paragraph 6 (lines 61–82), MacArthur describes "Red China" as a "mighty colossus." To what effect?

4. In paragraph 7 (lines 83–106), what does MacArthur urge us to consider as desirable? What evidence does he present?

5. In paragraph 10 (lines 144–157), MacArthur says, "But the constant acceleration in preparation may, without specific intent, ultimately precipitate a kind of spontaneous combustion." Briefly explain why you would or would not agree with him.

Second Reading

1. What basic information does MacArthur seem to expect his audience to know about global war? How can you tell?

2. What possible reasons might MacArthur have for presenting a brief history of warfare in paragraph two? Explain why you think this paragraph is placed after the introduction.

3. Where does MacArthur present the basic claim in his speech? Where and how does he add dimensions to this claim?

4. MacArthur, himself a warrior general, uses strong language—"scientific annihilation" (line 40) and "fatal consequences" (line 77)—to argue for "the abolition of war." Find other examples of such language in the speech. Do you consider this language necessary, or could he have made his point with more neutral language? Explain.

5. Reread paragraph 7 (lines 83–106). How does MacArthur intertwine logical and emotional appeals? How does this combination further his argument?

6. MacArthur begins his conclusion by reminding his audience that some people will argue that "the abolition of war can only be a dream" (line 159). How effective is his conclusion? Explain.

Writing

1. **Analysis** — Write an essay in which you analyze the rhetorical strategies MacArthur uses to convey his beliefs about global war.

2. **Argument** — Following MacArthur's example, write a speech that argues a position about an aspect of our global society that requires urgent attention in your consideration.

3. **Synthesis** — Compare MacArthur's speech with President Eisenhower's Farewell Address and with Margaret Mead's essay on page 58. In an essay that synthesizes the three sources for support, develop a position in response to the following question: Is war an inevitable element of human existence? Refer to each source in your essay.

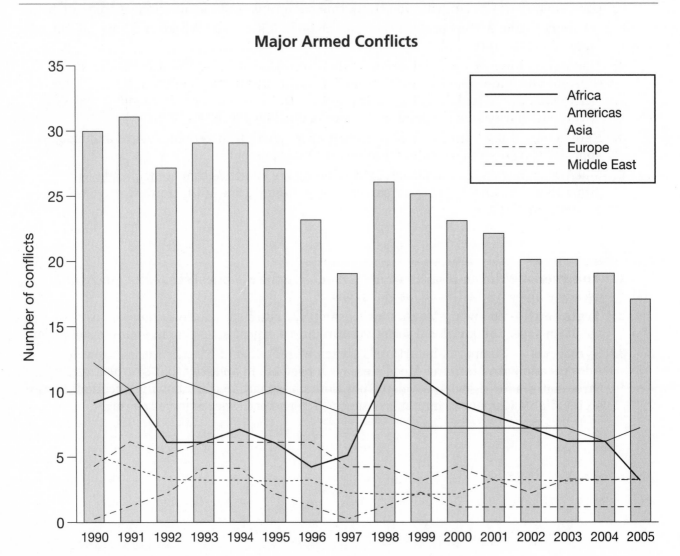

Stockholm International Peace Research Institute
Mikael Eriksson and Peter Wallensteen
Patterns of Major Armed Conflicts, 1990–2005

The task of the Institute is to conduct research on questions of conflict and cooperation, with the aim of contributing to an understanding of the conditions for peaceful solutions of international conflicts and for a stable peace. The following is from the 2005 SIPRI Yearbook.

Major Armed Conflicts

Legend:
- Africa
- Americas
- Asia
- Europe
- Middle East

y-axis: Number of conflicts

x-axis: 1990 1991 1992 1993 1994 1995 1996 1997 1998 1999 2000 2001 2002 2003 2004 2005

Regional distribution and total number of major armed conflicts, 1990–2005.

First Reading

1. What is your eye drawn to first? What is your overall impression?
2. What information can you glean from the title and the dates of the graph?
3. For what audience was the graph designed? Be specific.
4. What is the purpose of the words that are included with the graph?
5. What details, if any, would you consider have been omitted?

Second Reading

1. List three specific ideas presented by the graph and explain why you think they are important.
2. What issues of global importance does the graph suggest?
3. What questions would you ask Eriksson and Wallensteen? Speculate about their answers.
4. What argument do Eriksson and Wallensteen make with the graph?
5. How might viewers find this graph useful? Consider proponents and opponents of armed conflict.

Margaret Mead
Warfare: An Invention—Not a Biological Necessity

Mead was a cultural anthropologist who contributed greatly to our understanding of human behavior. She wrote on subjects ranging from mental and spiritual health to ethics and overpopulation. At the time of her death in 1978, she was the most famous anthropologist in the world. This essay was written in 1940.

Is war a biological necessity, a sociological inevitability, or just a bad invention? Those who argue for the first view endow man with such pugnacious instincts that some outlet in aggres-
5 sive behavior is necessary if man is to reach full human stature. It was this point of view which lay behind William James's famous essay, 'The Moral Equivalent of War', in which he tried to retain the warlike virtues and channel them in new direc-
10 tions. A similar point of view has lain behind the Soviet Union's attempt to make competition between groups rather than between individuals. A basic, competitive, aggressive, warring human nature is assumed, and those who wish to outlaw
15 war or outlaw competitiveness merely try to find new and less socially destructive ways in which these biologically given aspects of man's nature can find expression. Then there are those who take the second view: warfare is the inevitable
20 concomitant of the development of the state, the struggle for land and natural resources, of class societies springing not from the nature of man, but, from the nature of history. War is nevertheless inevitable unless we change our social system and
25 outlaw classes, the struggle for power, and possessions; and in the event of our success warfare would disappear, as a symptom vanishes when the disease is cured.

One may hold a sort of compromise position
30 between these two extremes; one may claim that all aggression springs from the frustration of man's biologically determined drives and that, since all forms of culture are frustrating, it is certain each new generation will be aggressive and
35 the aggression will find its natural and inevitable expression in race war, class war, nationalistic war, and so on. All three of these positions are very popular today among those who think seriously about the problems of war and its pos-
40 sible prevention, but I wish to urge another point of view, less defeatist, perhaps, than the first and third and more accurate than the second: that is, that warfare, by which I mean recognized conflict between two groups as groups, in which each

45 group puts an army (even if the army is only fifteen pygmies) into the field to fight and kill, if possible, some of the members of the army of the other group—that warfare of this sort is an invention like any other of the inventions in terms of
50 which we order our lives, such as writing, marriage, cooking our food instead of eating it raw, trial by jury, or burial of the dead, and so on. Some of this list anyone will grant are inventions: trial by jury is confined to very limited portions
55 of the globe; we know that there are tribes that do not bury their dead but instead expose or cremate them; and we know that only part of the human race has had the knowledge of writing as its cultural inheritance. But, whenever a way
60 of doing things is found universally, such as the use of fire or the practice of some form of marriage, we tend to think at once that it is not an invention at all but an attribute of humanity itself. And yet even such universals as marriage and the
65 use of fire are inventions like the rest, very basic ones, inventions which were, perhaps, necessary if human history was to take the turn that it has taken, but nevertheless inventions. At some point in his social development man was undoubtedly
70 without the institution of marriage or the knowledge of the use of fire.

The case for warfare is much clearer because there are peoples even today who have no warfare. Of these the Eskimos are perhaps the most
75 conspicuous examples, but the Lepchas of Sikkim described by Geoffrey Gorer in Himalayan Village are as good. Neither of these peoples understands war, not even defensive warfare. The idea of warfare is lacking, and this idea is as essential
80 to really carrying on war as an alphabet or a syllabary is to writing. But, whereas the Lepchas are a gentle, unquarrelsome people, and the advocates of other points of view might argue that they are not full human beings or that they had never been
85 frustrated and so had no aggression to expand in warfare, the Eskimo case gives no such possibility of interpretation. The Eskimos are not a mild and meek people; many of them are turbulent

and troublesome. Fights, theft of wives, murder, cannibalism, occur among them—all outbursts of passionate men goaded by desire or intolerable circumstance. Here are men faced with hunger, men faced with loss of their wives, men faced with the threat of extermination by other men, and here are orphan children, growing up miserably with no one to care for them, mocked and neglected by those about them. The personality necessary for war, the circumstances necessary to goad men to desperation are present, but there is no war. When a traveling Eskimo entered a settlement, he might have to fight the strongest man in the settlement to establish his position among them, but this was a test of strength and bravery, not war. The idea of warfare, of one group organizing against another group to maim and wound and kill them was absent. And, without that idea, passions might rage but there was no war.

But, it may be argued, is not this because the Eskimos have such a low and undeveloped form of social organization? They own no land, they move from place to place, camping, it is true, season after season on the same site, but this is not something to fight for as the modern nations of the world fight for land and raw materials. They have no permanent possessions that can be looted, no towns that can be burned. They have no social classes to produce stress and strains within the society which might force it to go to war outside. Does not the absence of war among the Eskimos, while disproving the biological necessity of war, just go to confirm the point that it is the state of development of the society which accounts for war and nothing else?

We find the answer among the pygmy peoples of the Andaman Islands in the Bay of Bengal. The Andamans also represent an exceedingly low level of society; they are a hunting and food-gathering people; they live in tiny hordes without any class stratification; their houses are simpler than the snow houses of the Eskimo. But they knew about warfare. The army might contain only fifteen determined pygmies marching in a straight line, but it was the real thing none the less. Tiny army met tiny army in open battle, blows were exchanged, casualties suffered, and the state of warfare could only be concluded by a peacemaking ceremony.

Similarly, among the Australian aborigines, who built no permanent dwellings but wandered from water hole to water hole over their almost desert country, warfare—and rules of "international law"—were highly developed. The student of social evolution will seek in vain for his obvious causes of war, struggle for lands, struggle for power of one group over another, expansion of popula-

tion, need to divert the minds of a populace restive under tyranny, or even the ambition of a successful leader to enhance his own prestige. All are absent, but warfare as a practice remained, and men engaged in it and killed one another in the course of a war because killing is what is done in wars.

From instances like these it becomes apparent that an inquiry into the causes of war misses the fundamental point as completely as does an insistence upon the biological necessity of war. If a people have an idea of going to war and the idea that war is the way in which certain situations, defined within their society, are to be handled, they will sometimes go to war. If they are a mild and unaggressive people, like the Pueblo Indians, they may limit themselves to defensive warfare, but they will be forced to think in terms of war because there are peoples near them who have warfare as a pattern, and offensive, raiding, pillaging warfare at that. When the pattern of warfare is known, people like the Pueblo Indians will defend themselves, taking advantage of their natural defenses, the mesa village site, and people like the Lepchas, having no natural defenses and no idea of warfare, will merely submit to the invader. But the essential point remains the same. There is a way of behaving which is known to a given people and labeled as an appropriate form of behavior; a bold and warlike people like the Sioux or the Maori may label warfare as desirable as well as possible, a mild people like the Pueblo Indians may label warfare as undesirable, but to the minds of both peoples the possibility of warfare is present. Their thoughts, their hopes, their plans are oriented about this idea—that warfare may be selected as the way to meet some situation.

So simple peoples and civilized peoples, mild peoples and violent, assertive peoples, will all go to war if they have the invention, just as those peoples who have the custom of dueling will have duels and peoples who have the pattern of vendetta will indulge in vendetta. And, conversely, peoples who do not know of dueling will not fight duels, even though their wives are seduced and their daughters ravished; they may on occasion commit murder but they will not fight duels. Cultures which lack the idea of the vendetta will not meet every quarrel in this way. A people can use only the forms it has. So the Balinese have their special way of dealing with a quarrel between two individuals: if the two feel that the causes of quarrel are heavy, they may go and register their quarrel in the temple before the gods, and, making offerings, they may swear never to have anything to do with each other again.... But in other societies, although individuals might feel as full of animosity and as unwilling to have any further contact as do the Balinese, they cannot register their quarrel with the gods and go on quietly about their business because registering quarrels with the gods is not an invention of which they know.

Yet, if it be granted that warfare is, after all, an invention, it may nevertheless be an invention that lends itself to certain types of personality, to the exigent needs of autocrats, to the expansionist desires of crowded peoples, to the desire for plunder and rape and loot which is engendered by a dull and frustrating life. What, then, can we say of this congruence between warfare and its uses? If it is a form which fits so well, is not this congruence the essential point? But even here the primitive material causes us to wonder, because there are tribes who go to war merely for glory, having no quarrel with the enemy, suffering from no tyrant within their boundaries, anxious neither for land nor loot nor women, but merely anxious to win prestige which within that tribe has been declared obtainable only by war and without which no young man can hope to win his sweetheart's smile of approval. But if, as was the case with the Bush Negroes of Dutch Guiana, it is artistic ability which is necessary to win a girl's approval, the same young man would have to be carving rather than going out on a war party.

In many parts of the world, war is a game in which the individual can win counters—counters which bring him prestige in the eyes of his own sex or of the opposite sex; he plays for these counters as he might, in our society, strive for a tennis championship. Warfare is a frame for such prestige-seeking merely because it calls for the display of certain skills and certain virtues; all of these skills—riding straight, shooting straight, dodging the missiles of the enemy and sending one's own straight to the mark—can be equally well exercised in some other framework and, equally, the virtues endurance, bravery, loyalty, steadfastness—can be displayed in other contexts. The tie-up between proving oneself a man and proving this by a success in organized killing is due to a definition which many societies have made of manliness. And often, even in those societies which counted success in warfare a proof of human worth, strange turns were given to the idea, as when the plains Indians gave their highest awards to the man who touched a live enemy rather than to the man who brought in a scalp—from a dead enemy—because the latter was less risky. Warfare is just an invention known to the majority of human societies by which they permit their young men either to accumulate prestige or avenge their honor or acquire loot or wives or slaves or sago lands or cattle or appease the blood lust of their gods or the restless souls of the recently dead. It is just an invention, older and more widespread than the jury system, but none the less an invention.

But, once we have said this, have we said anything at all? Despite a few stances, dear to the instances of controversialist, of the loss of the useful arts, once an invention is made which proves congruent with human needs or social forms, it tends to persist. Grant that war is an invention, that it is not a biological necessity nor the outcome of certain special types of social forms, still once the invention is made, what are we to do about it? The Indian who had been subsisting on the buffalo for generations because with his primitive weapons he could slaughter only a limited number of buffalo did not return to his primitive weapons when he saw that the white man's more efficient weapons were exterminating the buffalo. A desire for the white man's cloth may mortgage the South Sea Islander to the white man's plantation, but he does not return to making bark cloth, which would have left him free. Once an invention is known and accepted, men do not easily relinquish it. The skilled workers may smash the first steam looms which they feel are to be their undoing, but they accept them in the end, and no movement which has insisted upon the mere abandonment of usable inventions has ever had much success. Warfare is here, as part of our thought; the deeds of warriors are immortalized in the words of our poets, the toys of our children are modeled upon the weapons of the soldier, the frame of reference within which our statesmen and our diplomats work always contains war. If we know that it is not inevitable, that it is due to historical accident that warfare is one of the ways in which we think of behaving, are we given any hope by that? What hope is there of persuading nations to abandon war, nations so thoroughly imbued with the idea that resort to war is, if not actually desirable and noble, at least inevitable whenever certain defined circumstances arise?

In answer to this question I think we might turn to the history of other social inventions, and inventions which must once have seemed as finally entrenched as warfare. Take the methods of trial which preceded the jury system: ordeal and trial by combat. Unfair, capricious, alien as they are to our feeling today, they were once the only methods open to individuals accused of some offense. The invention of trial by jury gradually replaced these methods until only witches, and finally not even witches, had to resort to the ordeal. And for a long time the jury system seemed the best and finest method of settling legal disputes,

but today new inventions, trial before judges only or before commissions, are replacing the jury sys-
315 tem. In each case the old method was replaced by a new social invention. The ordeal did not go out because people thought it unjust or wrong; it went out because a method more congruent with the institutions and feelings of the period was in-
320 vented. And, if we despair over the way in which war seems such an ingrained habit of most of the human race, we can take comfort from the fact that a poor invention will usually give place to a better invention.
325 For this, two conditions, at least, are necessary. The people must recognize the defects of the old

invention, and someone must make a new one. Propaganda against warfare, documentation of its terrible cost in human suffering and social waste,
330 these prepare the ground by teaching people to feel that warfare is a defective social institution. There is further needed a belief that social invention is possible and the invention of new methods which will render warfare as out of date as the
335 tractor is making the plough, or the motor car the horse and buggy. A form of behavior becomes out of date only when something else takes its place, and, in order to invent forms of behavior which will make war obsolete, it is a first requirement to
340 believe that an invention is possible.

First Reading

1. Name the focus of each paragraph and briefly describe the movement of ideas in Mead's argument.
2. What viewpoints does Mead present to explain how some peoples view war?
3. What limitations does she see in the first two viewpoints?
4. What elements of human behavior does Mead examine? Explain her attitude toward these behaviors.
5. What assumptions does Mead reject in her explanations of human behavior?

Second Reading

1. Mead classifies humans as "simple peoples" and "civilized peoples." Then she examines different facets of behavior in various elements of each group. How does her examination of facets of human behavior further her argument?
2. Mead classifies war as an "invention." Do you consider her classification and explanation valid? Explain your reasoning.
3. Mead contends that, historically, some inventions deemed necessary have been replaced. What inventions in your personal experience would support Mead's argument? Can you think of any current inventions that seem utterly necessary, but that you can also imagine could be replaced in your lifetime? Examine both concrete inventions and those inventions of behavior that Mead discusses.
4. What complications could you anticipate if the global society accepted Mead's view of warfare as a defective invention and decided to make a new one?

Writing

1. **Analysis** — Read carefully the essay by Margaret Mead. Then, in a well-written essay, analyze how the rhetorical strategies Mead uses persuade the global society to consider abandoning war as a bad invention that needs replacing.
2. **Argument** — As you study Margaret Mead's essay, carefully consider her assertion that "people must recognize the defects of the old invention, and someone must make a new one." Then using your own critical understanding of contemporary society as evidence, write a carefully argued essay that agrees or disagrees with Mead's assertion.

Mary Ewald
Letter to President Saddam Hussein

Iraq invaded Kuwait on August 2, 1990, and was condemned by a UN Security Council resolution that called on Iraq to withdraw immediately. Four days later, another UN resolution imposed economic sanctions on Iraq with the stated purpose of compelling Iraq's military forces to leave Kuwait. After receiving this letter from Mary Ewald, mother of civilian captive Thomas Ewald, Iraqi leader Saddam Hussein ordered the young man released.

September 4, 1990

President Saddam Hussein
c/o Ambassador al-Machat

Dear Mr. President:

5   I am writing to you to send my student son, Thomas Hart Benton Ewald, home to his family. He was taken, I think, from the SAS Hotel in Kuwait City.

I feel I have the obligation to appeal to you for two reasons. First, my family has been a staunch friend to the Arabs. My husband, Tom's father, was on the White House Staff when President Eisenhower caused the French, British, and Israelis to pull out of Suez.
10 One of the first non-Arab meetings at the Washington Mosque was the one which I, as president of the Radcliffe (Harvard) Club of Washington, arranged to explain Muslim culture. I am also a poet who has written about Arabia. I have sent my youngest, well-loved son to work in an Arab country, hoping he would help bring peace between our cultures. Instead, after two days, he was caught up in war. It seems unjust that I, who
15 have given to you so generously, should have my son taken away from me in return. You have the power to right this wrong.

Second, my son is asthmatic, so severely crippled as a child that we thought we could never raise him. He needs medication and a doctor's care. I beg you, in the name of Allah, let my son go.

20   Yours truly,

Mary Ewald

First Reading

1. Describe your initial response to Ewald's letter.
2. Underline and label the concrete and abstract nouns.

Second Reading

1. Label Ewald's appeals as ethical, logical, or emotional.
2. Make brief notes about the effect of each of the appeals.

Writing

Analysis — Carefully read the letter from Mary Ewald to Iraqi president Saddam Hussein. Then, write an essay in which you analyze the techniques Ewald uses in her attempt to secure her son's release.

Chapter 5

Beauty

Background

Over time and across cultures, the mystery of beauty has vexed as well as captivated many people. Beauty has been the subject of persistent and varied attempts to define it, to capture it, to market it, to replicate it, to ignore it, to use it, to enhance it, and to celebrate it. The clichés about beauty are many, but they are difficult to dismiss. Everyone seems to accept that beauty is viably present and often sought. However, its importance and its role in our lives remain the subject of vigorous discussion and wonder. Why is beauty the object of both admiration and envy? Why does the pursuit of beauty bring us pain as well as pleasure? This chapter focuses upon texts that offer views and viewpoints on human beauty, specifically human female beauty.

Readings

Matthew Zimmerman
Marilyn Monroe, New York, 1954

C.E. Gomes
Swahili Woman

Jean Godfrey-June
Why I Wear Purple Lipstick

Nancy Etcoff
What Is Beauty and How Do We Know It?

Kathy Peiss
Hope—and History—in a Jar

Alex Kuczynski
What is Beautiful?

Christine Rosen
The Democratization of Beauty

Virginia Postrel
The Truth About Beauty

> (Left) **Matthew Zimmerman**
> Marilyn Monroe, New York, 1954
> (Right) **C. E. Gomes**
> Swahili Woman, *circa* 1900

Each of the photographs below captures and conveys the image of a woman whom different observers in different cultural contexts refer to as beautiful. Study the photographs then answer the questions that follow.

First Reading

1. What is your personal response to the Zimmerman photo of Marilyn Monroe?
2. What is your personal response to the Gomes photo of an unnamed Swahili woman?
3. How do the images address different audience expectations? What is the likely audience for the Zimmerman photograph? What is the likely audience of the Gomes photograph?
4. How is the subject matter of the images similar? Identify specific features.
5. How is the subject matter of the images distinct? Again, identify specific features.

Second Reading

1. Are these images contrived or do they convey truth? Explain your response.
2. The continuing audience for the Zimmerman photo is consistent with the continuing interest in its subject. How do you account for the interest? How does the presence of such interest impact a reading of this image?
3. Unlike the Zimmerman photograph, the Gomes portrait is largely unknown. Does such unfamiliarity make the Gomes photo more difficult to read? Explain.
4. Does the Zimmerman photograph carry meaning beyond its subject? How, for example, does it remind its current viewers of an ideal?
5. Is beauty evident in both images?
6. What arguments do the respective photographs make about human beauty? About perfection? About culture?

Writing

1. **Analysis** — These photographs are public in character. That is, they were taken with a broad audience in mind. View them carefully and then write an essay of no more than one page that considers the distinction between public and private beauty.
2. **Argument** — Write an essay in which you propose competing definitions of human beauty as represented by three photographs: these two and a third photograph of your own choosing that is preferably of an adult. Write specifically about each image in your response.

"Why I Wear Purple Lipstick" is the final essay in a 1997 book by Dorothy Schefer that attempts, through its many collected comments, images, and essays, to answer the question posed by the book's title: *What Is Beauty? New Definitions from the Fashion Vanguard.*

Beauty trends arise for exactly the same reasons that a boot-cut pant, a maxi coat, or an unexpectedly chunky heel induces in many of us that pre-verbal, hunter/gatherer, foaming at the mouth, let-me-at-it lust for the new, the different. We're bored, we long to reinvent ourselves, to shake things up. It's that little bit of Madonna in everyone that
5 says to the world, "Thought you had me all figured out? HA!"… and moves on.

Many—but certainly not all—beauty trends emerge backstage at fashion shows, as makeup artists and hairstylists interpret what a given designer has done with the clothes that season; as the models travel from one show to the next (often with ten minutes in between), their faces transmit the last show's news to the team working on the next one.
10 If it's modern, if some aspect of it applies to the show at hand, it's taken up, adapted, and further cemented as "The Look of the Season," be it darker lips, slicked-back hair, or baby-blue toenail polish.

Beauty trends are rarely about being beautiful. At ground zero, they're about shock, daring, imagination: Being first on the block to wear a green-gray nail polish called
15 "Mildew," or to try the new "skunk stripe" highlights before anyone else does requires serious cojones, or at the very least, a love of the spotlight.

Being second or third on the block involves the opposite impulse. Like a secret hand-shake between a clique of nine-year-old girls, a gloss of pink-frosted lipstick, or a bar-rette pinned just so signifies membership, belonging. With beauty products, this second
20 stage of a trend can take on an evangelical tone, as the first-wave "pioneers" convert their friends and associates.

How one wears one's hair and exactly what shade of lipstick one selects is, in the grand scheme of things, silly, useless information. Silly and useless in the same way that one prefers a certain vintage from a particular vineyard, or grills one's vegetables just
25 so. It's about pleasure, choices, and changes—the little ones that make us human.

First Reading

1. Explain how the title of the essay represents its subject.
2. Describe the essay's tone, identifying words and phrases that convey it.
3. Where in the essay does the author establish her credentials as someone sufficiently knowledgeable to comment on this subject?

Second Reading

1. Summarize the content of each paragraph of the essay by writing a statement for each one based on *the text says analysis*. Effectively represent each paragraph's information.
2. Identify the function of each paragraph of the essay by properly sequencing the following *the text does* statements.
   a. Provides additional focus on the identified phenomenon with specific examples of how it develops.

    b. Identifies the existence of a particular kind of phenomenon and relates it to specific developments that owe their existence to particular kind of human behavior. Elaborates by making a broad, inclusive assertion, and then elaborates with an illustrative reference to a widely recognized cultural figure.

    c. Characterizes human behaviors and preferences related to the subject using slightly demeaning language. Immediately elaborates by repeating the demeaning words from the previous sentence, placing them in a broader and more positive context. Closes with a strong assertion linking human behavior, human pursuits, and human identity.

    d. Makes a defining assertion about the phenomenon in the first sentence. Elaborates in the following sentence, offering a subsequent assertion, two vexing illustrations, and an explanation for human behavior related to the phenomenon.

    e. Cites contrasting human behavior, then clarifies with three illustrative similes. Two words in the final sentence strengthen a comparison with a different human enterprise, one seemingly unrelated to the phenomenon that is the essay's subject.

3. Locate a magazine advertisement that illustrates an important element of Godfrey-June's argument.

Writing

Argument — In her 1984 book *Women and Beauty*, actress Sophia Loren says that the large beauty business, faced with both the diversity of how people look and the pursuit of profits, trumpets the idea of "ideal" beauty. Loren writes:

> "It is largely for business reasons that fashions change so much from year to year, and the woman who is deemed 'beautiful' this year is outdated the next. But ideal beauty is a mirage. Altering your hairstyle to the 'perfect' style for your face or discovering an extraordinary new night cream or eye shadow or this season's popular new dress designer will certainly alter your appearance, but real beauty is not just a matter of looking up-to-date."

In an essay of up to three pages, explore the relationship between Loren's comments and Godfrey-June's argument. Be sure to illustrate your thinking with appropriate evidence drawn from your reading, observation, and experience.

Nancy Etcoff is a practicing psychologist and member of the faculty of Harvard Medical School. The text that follows, from the introductory chapter of her 1999 book, *Survival of the Prettiest: The Science of Beauty*, is Etcoff's initial response to two persistent and powerful questions about beauty.

We are always sizing up other people's looks: our beauty detectors never close up shop and call it a day. We notice the attractiveness of each face we see as automatically as we register whether or not they look familiar. Beauty detectors scan the environment like radar: we can see a face for a fraction of a second (150 msec. in one psychology experiment) and rate its beauty, even give it the same rating we would give it on longer inspection. Long after we forget many important details about a person, our initial response stays in our memory.

Beauty is a basic pleasure. Try to imagine that you have become immune to beauty. Chances are, you would consider yourself unwell—sunk in a physical, spiritual, or emotional malaise. The absence of a response to physical beauty is one sign of profound depression—so prevalent that the standard screening measures for depression include a question about changes in the perception of one's own physical attractiveness.

But what is beauty? As you will see, no definition can capture it entirely. I started by mining what those who peddle beauty as a business had to say, thinking that they might have concrete details about their criteria rather than airy abstractions to float. Aaron Spelling, creator of "Baywatch" and "Melrose Place," said, "I can't define it, but I know it when I walk into the room." I talked with a modeling agency that books top male models, and they were more descriptive: "It's when someone walks in the door and you almost can't breathe. It doesn't happen often. You can feel it rather than see it. I mean someone you literally can't walk past in the street." It is noteworthy that the experts describe the experience of seeing beauty, and not what beauty looks like. On that end, all I got was that they should be young and tall and have good skin. But it was a start.

The Oxford English Dictionary defines the word "beautiful" as "Excelling in the grace of form, charm of coloring, and other qualities, which delight the eye and call forth admiration: a. of the human face and figure: b. of other objects." As a secondary definition it states "In modern colloquial use the word is often applied to anything that a person likes very much." The dictionary that my computer network provides says that beauty "give[s] pleasure to the senses or pleasurably exalts the mind or spirit."

The dictionaries define beauty as something intrinsic to the object (its color, form, and other qualities) or simply as the pleasure an object evokes in the beholder (The philosopher Santayana called beauty "pleasure objectified.") If we follow a time line of ideas on beauty, the pendulum clearly swings from one direction to the other. For the ancient Greeks, beauty was like a sixth sense. In the twentieth century, when Marcel Duchamp could make a toilet the subject of high art, and Andy Warhol could do the same for a soup can, beauty came to reside not in objects themselves but in the eye that viewed those objects and conferred beauty on them.

Although the *object* of beauty is debated, the experience of beauty is not. Beauty can stir up a snarl of emotions but pleasure must always be one (tortured longings and envy are not incompatible with pleasure). Our body responds to it viscerally and our names for beauty are synonymous with physical cataclysms and bodily obliteration—breathtaking, femme fatale, knockout, drop-dead gorgeous, bombshell, stunner, and ravishing. We experience beauty not as rational contemplation but as a response to physical urgency.

In 1688, Jean de La Bruyere expressed these transgender wishes, "to be a girl and a beautiful girl from the age of thirteen to the age of twenty-two and then after that to be a man." There is tremendous power in a young woman's beauty. In 1957, Brigitte Bardot was twenty-three years old and she had starred in the film *And God Created Woman*. That year, the magazine *Cinemonde* even reported that a million lines had been devoted to her in French dailies, and two million in the weeklies, and that this torrent or words was accompanied by 29,345 images of her. *Cinemonde* even reported that she was the subject of forty-seven percent of French conversation! In 1994, the model Claudia Schiffer spent four minutes modeling a black velvet dress on Rome's Spanish Steps. According to British journalists covering the "event" for the *Daily Telegraph*, four and a half million people watched and the city came to "a standstill."

95 Perhaps these are media-driven frenzies, no more real than the canned laughter chortling from our television screens. But small epiphanies are common in daily life. The most lyrical description of an encounter with beauty—solitary, spontaneous, with an unknown other—comes in James 100 Joyce's *Portrait of the Artist as a Young Man* when Stephen Dedalus sees a young woman standing by the shore with "long, slender, bare legs," and a face "touched with the wonder of mortal beauty." Her beauty is transformative and gives form 105 to his sensual and spiritual longings. "Her image had passed into his soul for ever and no word had broken from the holy silence of his ecstasy.... A wild angel had appeared to him, the angel of mortal youth and beauty, an envoy from the fair courts 110 of life, to throw open before him in an instant of ecstasy the gates of all the ways of error and glory. On and on and on and on!"

Ezra Pound had a moment of recognition that inspired him to write a two-line poem "In a sta-
115 tion at the Metro," which comprised these brief sentences: "The apparition of these faces in the crowd: Petals, on a wet, black bough." Later, Pound described how he came to write it. "Three years ago in Paris I got out of a Metro train at
120 La Concorde, and saw suddenly a beautiful face, and then another beautiful woman, and I tried all day to find words for what this had meant to me, and I could not find any words that seemed to me worthy or as lovely as that sudden emo-
125 tion.... In a poem of this sort one is trying to record the precise instant when a thing outward and objective transforms itself or darts into a thing inward and subjective."

It is difficult to put into words why a particu-
130 lar set of eyes or a certain mouth move us while others do not. Even for the poets, it is often beyond language. Looking to the object of beauty, we confront centuries of struggle to capture beauty's essence.

First Reading

1. Discuss the importance of the use of the pronoun *we* in the first paragraph.
2. How does the absence of the pronoun *we* in paragraph 2 (lines 12–20) indicate an important shift? Point to similar shifts in the passage.
3. What is Etcoff's most compelling assertion?
4. How does structure play a role in this section? Discuss the selection and arrangement of details.

Second Reading

1. Etcoff makes frequent references to other sources. Why?
2. Starting on line 28, Etcoff cites a conversation with a modeling agency. How does it serve her purpose to report a portion of that particular discussion?
3. Paragraph 6 (lines 64–74) is pivotal. In it, Etcoff draws a distinction between the object of beauty, which she says is debated, and the experience of beauty, which she claims is not debated. Do you agree with her claims?
4. What is behind this tactic? How does she prepare her reader for this move? Is her tactic effective?
5. Why is "event" in line 91 in quotation marks?
6. Relate Zimmerman's photograph of Marilyn Monroe to the content of paragraphs 7 and 8 (lines 75–112).
7. In paragraph 8, Etcoff shifts focus from media frenzies to "small epiphanies [that] are common in daily life" (lines 96–97). She offers a quotation-and-explication of a passage from James Joyce, a remarkably uncommon writer. What is the impact of this juxtaposition?
8. How does the ninth paragraph (lines 113–128) build upon the main idea of the previous paragraph?

9. Etcoff writes "It is difficult to put into words why a particular set of eyes or a certain mouth move us while others do not" (lines 129–131). How would you dispute this view?

Writing

Argument — In the opening three paragraphs of this passage, Nancy Etcoff argues that although all of us are alert to beauty and need the pleasure of its experience, we have difficulty defining it. To articulate her own definition of beauty, Etcoff suggests several realms of human endeavor, knowledge, and experience, such as art, commerce, language, history, and literature, in which portions of such a definition might be found.

In an argumentative essay, pursue Etcoff's suggestion and present a viable definition of beauty after researching, identifying, and considering several different sources that inform your own thinking on the subject.

Kathy Peiss
Hope—and History—in a Jar

In her 1998 book *Hope in a Jar*, professor Kathy Peiss provides a compelling social history as she examines beauty culture and its implications for commerce and community in the United States. In this excerpt, the book's introductory chapter, Peiss illuminates some of the complex context around "the act of beautifying."

In 1938 the cosmetics firm Volupté introduced two new lipsticks. *Mademoiselle* magazine explained that one was for "girls who lean toward pale-lacquered nails, quiet smart clothes and tiny
5 strands of pearls," the other "for the girl who loves exciting clothes, pins a strass [paste] pin big as a saucer to her dress, and likes to be just a leetle bit shocking." One had a "soft mat finish" while the other covered the lips "with a gleaming lus-
10 tre." The names of these lipsticks were Lady and Hussy. As *Mademoiselle* put it, "Each of these two categories being as much a matter of mood as a matter of fact, we leave you to decide which you prefer to be."[1]
15 The assumptions behind this promotion are arresting. For nineteenth century Americans, lady and hussy were polar opposites—the best and worst of womanhood—and the presence or absence of cosmetics marked the divide. Reddened
20 cheeks and darkened eyelids were signs of female vice, and the "painted woman" provoked disgust and censure from the virtuous. But by the 1930s, lady and hussy had become "types" and "moods." Female identities once fixed by parent-
25 age, class position, social etiquette, and sexual codes were now released from small swiveling cylinders. Where "paint" implied a concealing mask, the term "makeup," in common usage by the 1920s, connoted a medium of self-expression
30 in a consumer society where identity had become a purchasable style. Women could choose the look of gentlewoman or prostitute—and apparently Hussy outsold Lady five to one!

Lady and Hussy lipsticks mark a sea change, not
35 only in the meaning of cosmetics, but in conceptions of women's appearance and identity. How did this fundamental transformation take place?

How did a sign of disrepute become the daily routine of millions? And how did a "kitchen physic,"
40 as homemade cosmetics were once called, become a mass market industry?

Small objects sometimes possess great moral force, and the usual answers to these questions have been charged with disapproval and criticism.
45 Cosmetics have been condemned as symptomatic of all that is wrong in modern consumer society: Their producers create false needs, manipulate fears and desires, and elevate superficiality over substance, all to sell overpriced goods that do not
50 deliver on their promises. Today the most formidable judgments about cosmetics often come from feminists who, since the 1960s, have argued that powerful male-dominated consumer industries and mass media have been a leading cause of wom-
55 en's oppression. In this view, the beauty industry has added to, even to some extent supplanted, the legal and economic discriminations that have for so long subordinated women. Manufactured images of ideal beauty and supermodel glamour
60 have come to dominate women's consciousness. And the act of beautifying, though it seems enticing and freely chosen, is really compulsory work, so narcissistic, time-consuming, and absorbing as to limit women's achievements.[2]
65 To many critics, the story begins and ends there. But this view is partial and in many respects, wrong. For one thing, this business for women was largely built *by* women. In the early stages of the developing cosmetics industry, from
70 the 1890s to the 1920s, women formulated and organized "beauty culture" to a remarkable extent. The very notion of femininity, emphasizing women's innate taste for beauty, opened opportunities for women in this business, even as it restricted

---

1 *Mademoiselle* 7 (June 1938): 13. John J. Pollock, "Smart Merchandising and Fashion tie-Ups Multiply Volupté Sales," *Sales Management*, 20 April 1939, 17.

2 See, for instance, Naomi Wolf, *The Beauty Myth* (New York: Morrow, 1991); Sandra Lee Bartky, *Femininity and Domination* (New York: Routledge, 1990); Dean MacCannell and Juliet Flower MacCannell, "The Beauty System," in Nancy Armstrong and Leonard Tennenhouse, eds., *The Ideology of Conduct* (New York: Methuen, 1987), 206-238. For a more complex view, see Susan Bordo, *Unbearable Weight: Feminism, Western Culture and the Body* (Berkeley: Univ. of California Press, 1993).

them elsewhere. And women seized their chances, becoming entrepreneurs, inventors, manufacturers, distributors, and promoters. Handicapped in pursuing standard business practices, they resourcefully founded salons, beauty schools, correspondence courses, and mail-order companies; they pioneered in the development of modern franchising and direct-sales marketing strategies. The beauty trade they developed did not depend upon advertising as its impetus. Rather, it capitalized on patterns of women's social life—their old customs of visiting, conversation, and religious observance, as well as their new presence in shops, clubs, and theaters.

Strikingly, many of the most successful entrepreneurs were immigrant, working-class, or black women. Coming from poor, socially marginal backgrounds, they played a surprisingly central role in redefining mainstream ideals of beauty and femininity in the twentieth century. Focusing new attention on the face and figure, they made the pursuit of beauty visible and respectable. In many ways, they set the stage for Madison Avenue, whose narrowly drawn images of flawless beauty bombard us today. But before the rise of the mass market, these early businesswomen served up a variety of visions of womanly beauty. Elizabeth Arden was a Canadian immigrant and "working girl" who remade herself into a symbol of haute femininity; she carved a "class market" for cosmetics by catering to the social prestige and power of wealthy and upwardly mobile white women. They consciously created job opportunities for women, addressed the politics of appearance, and committed their profits to their community. Indeed, the history of these businesswomen flatly contradicts the view that the beauty industry worked only *against* women's interests.

What about the women who bought and used beauty products? Cosmetics have often figured in the old stereotype of women as vain and foolish, a stereotype contemporary critics too often reinforce. How could a rational being eat arsenic to improve her complexion, spread hormones on her face, believe promises of a wrinkle-free future, and pay exorbitant prices for an ounce of prevention?

Answering these questions requires us to listen more closely to women's own voices and to consider how they understood beautifying in their own lives. Remarkably, women from across the country, from different social classes and racial-ethnic groups, enthusiastically embraced cosmetics—especially makeup—in the early twentieth century. This acceptance was no mere fad or fashion, but a larger change in the way women perceived their identities and displayed them on the face and body. For some, cosmetic use quickly became a self-diminishing habit: Women reported as early as the 1930s that advertising and social pressures to be attractive lowered their self-esteem. Others, however, boldly applied their lipsticks in public and asserted their right to self-creation through the "makeover" of self-image.

Today the possibility of transformation through cosmetics is often belittled as delusion, "hope in a jar" that only masks the fact of women's oppression. In truth, women knew then—as they do now—precisely what they were buying. Again and again they reported their delight in beautifying—in the sensuous creams and tiny compacts, the riot of colors, the mastery of makeup skills, the touch of hands, the sharing knowledge and advice. Indeed, the pleasures of fantasy and desire were an integral part of the product—and these included not only dreams of romance and marriage, but also the modern yearning to take part in public life.

Beauty culture, then, should be understood not only as a type of commerce but as a system of meaning that helped women navigate the changing conditions of modern social experience. "Modernity" is, to be sure, a slippery concept. It describes the paradoxical effects of an urban, capitalist order—its rationalized work, bureaucracy, and efficiency, on the one hand, its fleeting encounters, self-consciousness, and continuous novelty, on the other. Women's rendezvous with modernity brought them into a public realm that was not always welcoming.[3] Their changing status as workers, consumers, and pleasure seekers was acknowledged cosmetically: During the nineteenth century, the "public woman" was a painted prostitute; by its end, women from all walks of life were "going public": Women crowded onto trolleys, promenaded the streets, frequented the theaters, and shopped in the new

---

3 For insights into women, modernity, and consumption, see Anne Friedberg, *Window Shopping: Cinema and the Postmodern* (Berkeley: Univ. of California Press, 1993); Gilles Lipovetsky, *The Empire of Fashion: Dressing Modern Democracy* (Princeton: Princeton University Press, 1994); Victoria de Grazia with Ellen Furlough, ed., *The Sex of Things: Gender and Consumption in Historical Perspective* (Berkeley: Univ. of California Press, 1966); Hilary Radner, *Shopping Around: Feminine Culture and the Pursuit of Pleasure* (New York: Routledge, 1995); Janet Wolff, *Feminine Sentences: Essays on Women and Culture* (Berkeley: Univ. of California Press, 1990). See also Judith L. Goldstein, "The Female Aesthetic Community," in George E. Marcus and Fred R. Myers, eds., *The Traffic in Culture* (Berkeley: Univ. of California Press, 1995), 310-329.

palaces of consumption. They found jobs not only in the traditional work of domestic service, sewing, and farming, but also in offices, stores, and other urban occupations that required new kinds of face-to-face interactions. A new "marriage market" substituted dating for courtship, and the dance hall for the front porch; a new sense of sexual freedom emerged.

For women experiencing these social changes, the act of beautifying often became a lightning rod for larger conflicts over female autonomy and social roles. Among white women, for example, popular concern centered on the morality of visible makeup—rouge, lipstick, mascara, and eye shadow. In the black community, beauty culture was explicitly a political issue, long before the contemporary feminist movement made it so. Skin whiteners and hair straighteners were the tokens in a heated debate: Against charges of white emulation and self-loathing, many black women invoked their rights to social participation and cultural legitimacy precisely through their use of beauty aids.

Still, for all the efforts to fix the meaning of cosmetics in relation to beauty standards, ideals of femininity, profit-making, and politics, the significance of these substances remains elusive. What do women declare when they "put on a face"? Is making up an act of deception, a confirmation of natural female identity, a self-conscious "put on"? By the light of today's TV shopping channels, as celebrities hawk their cosmetic lines, it may seem that the promise of beauty is nothing but a commercial myth that binds women to its costly pursuit. Critics are not wrong to address the power of corporations, advertisers, and mass media to foster and profit from this myth. But they have overlooked the web of intimate rituals, social relationships, and female institutions that gave form to American beauty culture. Over the decades, mothers and daughters have taught each other about cosmetics, cliques have been formed around looks, women have shared their beauty secrets and, in the process, created intimacy. Not only tolls of deception and illusion, then, these little jars tell a rich history of women's ambition, pleasure, and community.

First Reading

1. Annotate the passage with care.
2. Identify instances where Peiss asserts and elaborates upon her own views.
3. Note instances where Peiss presents conflicting viewpoints.
4. Note the selection and use of detail.
5. What common tactic does Peiss employ in paragraphs 3 (lines 34–41), 7 (lines 113–120), and 12 (lines 194–216)?

Second Reading

1. Identify the function of each paragraph, then group paragraphs that serve to support a particular point.
2. Identify structural features of the passage, particularly shifts in focus and transitions.
3. Describe the content of footnote 1.
4. What subject does Peiss address in footnote 2?
5. Compare the function of footnote 3 with that of footnote 1.
6. Peiss refers to numerous other texts in footnotes 2 and 3. Explain how these references serve her purpose.

Writing

Analysis — Reread with care Kathy Peiss's introduction to the book *Hope—and History—in a Jar*. Then, write an essay in which you analyze how Peiss uses the resources of language to represent distinct viewpoints on beauty culture in the United States and to present her own argument.

Alex Kuczynski is a columnist for the *New York Times*. In her 2006 book *Beauty Junkies*, she explores numerous topics concerning the pursuit of beauty, including cosmetic surgery and its place in contemporary commerce and culture. In this excerpt, she explains and illustrates where our ideas about beauty come from.

The survival of the cosmetic surgery industry is based on the notion that a relatively specific ideal of beauty exists and that it is something that can be achieved through purchase. It has long
5 been a commonplace in anthropology that every culture has its own standards defining beauty. But in American culture, where standards are set by a vast array of media, from reality television to airbrushed magazine covers, the param-
10 eters have been rapidly narrowing. Full lips, large breasts, a nipped-in waist, lean thighs: we're fast approaching an ideal in womanhood in which an adult female looks like a woman on top, with full breasts and large pink lips, and a twelve-year-old
15 boy (minus external genitalia) on the bottom, with slim hips and a tiny bottom.

So, just what is beauty these days? What is considered beautiful?

There is a cartoon version of beauty such as
20 one sees on the reality programs that take pudgy, snaggle-toothed Americans and put them through a brutal round of cosmetic surgery. At the climax of each program the participants emerge, transformed, to the oohs and ahs of family, friends, and
25 surgeons. But as the patients make their appearances week after week, viewers begin to notice an eerie similarity. "They all get a chin implant, all get a brow lift, all get their lips done," said Dr. Z. Paul Lornec, a New York plastic surgeon.
30 The cheeks of the patients are all planed upward, the lips uniformly swollen to rubber-doll proportions, the breast so ample it looks as if the women who bear them might topple over from the weight. And they all get hair extensions: scalp
35 hair in humans grows longer than it does in other primates, and we use it to signal good health, status and youth. Hair extensions are an überadvertisement of health and fecundity, a perfect example of the folly of attempting to outdo nature.
40 (Folly, because eventually the extensions become stringy and lose their bonds, and the bearer leaves trails of hair wherever she goes.) The men all receive superhero chins. Mouths are crammed with huge white Chiclets.

45 The look is cookie-cutter beauty, Dr. Peter B. Fodor, the president of the American Society for Aesthetic Plastic Surgery, told me. "There is a sameness to them all that is chilling," he said.

Critics of American popular culture have long
50 looked down their noses at the quest for bland conformity. We are a nation, they say, of follow-me consumerism. We all wear the same clothes, eat at the same restaurants, and drive the same SUVs. But these television shows signal something far deeper:
55 the herd mentality has reached alarming new levels. Are we now going to have the same face—one that looks like whoever is on the cover of *Us* magazine?

Of course, the assembly-line look ultimately damages the notion of personal identity. When
60 faces and bodies are remade in the image of the Platonic pop-star ideal, all ties to personal identity—even to one's own family—are lost. The husband of one of the contestants on *The Swan* e-mailed me confidentially after his wife's appear-
65 ance on the program, complaining that she, while certainly looking more attractive, cried herself to sleep at night because she no longer looked like her mother or her sister. She was unmoored, physically, from her own past.

70 "She feels lost," he wrote.

Of seventeen candidates on the first season of *The Swan*, all receive[d] tooth veneers, sixteen had liposuction, fifteen had forehead lifts, thirteen had nose jobs, thirteen had lip augmentations,
75 and eleven had breast augmentations. Dr. Randal Haworth, one of two surgeons on *The Swan*, said the "graduates" all bore a certain resemblance to one another partly for technical reasons. "There is a finite number of procedures you can do," he told
80 me, "And when humans think of beauty, they go to those hot points—nose brows, lips—and that's what we work hard to define."

But there may have been other reasons, Surgeons on such a program may not only listen to
85 the patient's requests; they may also think of the show as an infomercial for their services. In other words, they are going to think of what is most broadly appealing to the mass market.

In some social sets, it is a simple fact of life that one will have some major procedure every year. In 2004, for example, when Lionel Richie's thirty-seven-year-old wife, Diane, filed for divorce in Los Angeles, her list of financial demands included $20,000 a year for plastic surgery. She also stated in her lawsuit that by her own conservative estimate she spent at least $3,000 a month on dermatology, $600 a month on hair care, $1,000 a month on laser hair removal, $10,000 to $15,000 a month on clothing, and $500 to $600 on vitamins.[1] (Later the same year, she was charged with aiding and abetting Daniel Tomas Fuente Serrano, who was using her home to host "pumping parties" and give non-FDA-approved injections to women such as Shawn King, wife of Larry King.)[2]

And who most women want to look like is no surprise.

"Our religion is celebrity, and our gods are celebrities," Haworth said. "When we conform to the dictates of taste, that's who we look to."

No better example of the celebrity notion of beauty exists than MTV's *I Want a Famous Face*, in which teenagers and people in their twenties describe to a surgeon who they want to look like. A twenty-three-year-old transsexual named Jessica wanted to look like Jennifer Lopez. So she got breast implants, cheek implants, and an eyebrow lift and had her hairline lowered. Mike and Matt, twenty-year-old twin brothers from Arizona, wanted to look like Brad Pitt. They both got rhinoplasty, chin implants, and porcelain veneers, One woman, Kacey Long, inspired by the movie *Erin Brockovich*, decided to have breast implants so she could look more like Julia Roberts (even though Roberts's ample bosoms in that movie were created with the help of push-up bras and rubber "chicken-cutlet" bra inserts). *I Want a Famous Face* later broadcast the surgery Long had to remove the implants, which had created serious medical complications.

Notions of beauty are often fixed to class. Dr. Terry Dubrow, the other *Swan* surgeon, said the women on the show turned out looking alike because they are all relatively young and come from a similar socioeconomic background, so they share—and want to look like—a similar beauty prototype. "The younger girls think that beauty is raised cheeks, a higher brow, bigger breasts, and fuller lips," Dubrow said. "You know, Pam Anderson."

Of course, women have long tried to look like cultural icons, whether it's Twiggy or Angie Dickinson. But there is something much more chilling in the way that patients today see Pamela Anderson, an obvious and proud consumer of cosmetic surgery, as a paradigm of beauty. It is as if we have elevated artifice above humanity and the look of the fake over the natural contours of the authentic.

First Reading

1. What do you believe to be the author's most important observations and claims?
2. Where and how does Kuczynski establish the assertive tone of the passage?
3. How does Kuczynski claim authority over her subject?
4. Describe the variations in the pace of the passage and their effect.
5. By the end of the passage, has Kuczynski answered the questions posed in paragraph 2 (lines 17–18)?
6. Where in the passage do you most actively question the author? Explain.

Second Reading

1. Why does Kuczynski precede the two questions that comprise the second paragraph with an emphatic first paragraph?
2. Explain the relationship between paragraph 2 and the two paragraphs that follow (lines 19–44).
3. Why is paragraph 5 (lines 45–48) remarkably brief?
4. Where does Kuczynski use extensive description to support her argument?

1 Diane Ritchie divorce petition against Lionel Ritchie,
  http://www.thesmokinggun.com/archive/ritchiediv7.html.
2 "Lionel Ritchie's Estranged Wife Charged," *Associated Press Online*, November 17, 2004.

5. Identify portions of the passage where Kuczynski appeals to emotion.

6. Identify portions of the passage where Kuczynski appeals to logic.

Writing

1. **Analysis** — After rereading Kuczynski's text with care, write an essay in which you analyze the strategies she uses to develop her perspective on cosmetic surgery.

2. **Argument** — Carefully consider the comments by Alex Kuczynski on the American pursuit of beauty and its implications. Then write an essay in which you support, refute, or qualify Kuczynski's claim that popular beauty ideals compel contemporary Americans to "elevate artifice above humanity and the look of the fake over the natural contours of the authentic."

Christine Rosen
The Democratization of Beauty

Senior editor of *The New Atlantis* and resident fellow at the Ethics and Public Policy Center, the author regularly observes and comments on issues involving ethics, technology, and policy. In this excerpt from a 2004 essay, Rosen considers the implications of the growth of the popularity of cosmetic surgery on American culture.

The contemporary cosmetic surgery industry is a lavish smorgasbord of options for the American consumer. A partial list of the procedures available include: Cheek implants, mentoplasty (chin aug-
5 mentation), collagen and fat injections, otoplasty (pinning back the ears), blepharoplasty (eyelid tightening), rhytidectomy (facelift), forehead lifts, hair transplantation (using scalp reduction, strip grafts, and plugs), rhinoplasty (nose job), brachio-
10 plasty (arm lift), breast augmentation, mastopexy (breast tightening), breast reduction, buttock lift, thigh lift, calf implants, pectoral implants, ab-dominoplasty (tummy tuck), penile enlargements and implants, and the ever-popular Botox (where
15 diluted doses of the botulinum toxin are injected into wrinkles) and liposuction (the removal of de-posits of fat using a suction cannula).

According to the American Academy of Cos-metic Surgery, approximately 860,000 cosmetic
20 surgery procedures were performed in 2002, most-ly on women, although men accounted for 150,000 procedures. One-third of cosmetic surgery patients are between the ages of 35 and 50; another 22 per-cent are between the ages of 26 and 34. And 18 per-
25 cent of people getting cosmetic surgery are under the age of 25. Instead of the smoke and mirrors of the old freak show, we now have, online, hundreds of "before and after" pictures of cosmetic surgery patients—all of them encouraging a belief in the
30 surgeon's power of total transformation.

Aging is not the only problem cosmetic sur-gery seeks to solve—it also offers a solution to the American obsession with our waistlines. In his book *Battleground of Desire: The Struggle for
35 Self-Control in Modern America*, Peter Stearns notes how, as early as 1916, popular magazines were equating control of one's weight with the health of one's character. The first diet cookbook, published in 1900, stated matter-of-factly in its preface, "An
40 excess of flesh is looked upon as one of the most objectionable forms of disease." Liposuction, a technique for removing deposits of fat using a tool called a suction cannula, was developed by French surgeon Yves-Gerard Illouz in the 1970s,

45 and it is the most popular invasive cosmetic sur-gery procedure: 74,000 people had liposuction in 2002 alone.

The language of artistic achievement suffuses the industry: surgeons describe their work as
50 "body sculpting" or "body contouring," and lipo-suction is known as "blind subcutaneous sculptur-ing." But the anodyne terms mask physically bru-tal procedures. The trauma of this kind of surgery can be considerable. As Ryan Murphy, the creator
55 of the FX network's plastic surgery drama *Nip/Tuck* told the *New York Times* jocularly, "one plas-tic surgeon told me that getting your face done is basically the equivalent of going through a car window at 70 miles an hour and surviving." His
60 show is one that revels in gory details. "I think the public thinks that this is delicate surgery, and these surgeons treat the face as if it were porcelain," he said. "And in fact they treat it like it was sirloin."

The faces and bodies of many celebrities tes-
65 tify to the unhealthy lure of excessive physical transformation: Michael Jackson's many surgeries have left him nearly unrecognizable, and Jocelyn Wildenstein, a terrifying spectacle of a socialite, has had multiple surgeries, including an enormous
70 chin implant, lip implants, facelifts, and eyelifts so that her face would have the features of a large cat. Respectable surgeons do try to vet candidates for surgery to avoid encouraging the activities of these "scalpel slaves." "I wish we had a question-
75 naire that could warn us," [plastic surgeon] Dr. [George] Weston said. "We sit down with patients in consultation, but we're both interviewing each other." Weston concedes that if he refuses to op-erate on someone who is obviously mentally un-
80 stable or who has unreasonable expectations for surgery, "they'll eventually find someone else to operate on them."

More mundane dangers exist for people who undergo cosmetic surgery. One study, conducted
85 by a plastic surgeon in 2000 and described by Da-vid and Sheila Rothman, found that "the rounded mortality rate for liposuction surgery in the late 1990s hovers near 20 per 100,000." Compare that

to the 3 per 100,000 rate for hernia operations. In the space of only a few months this year, several widely publicized cosmetic surgery deaths—notably that of 54-year-old novelist Olivia Goldsmith, who had checked into an Upper East Side hospital for a chin tuck—have prompted halfhearted handwringing in the media, but no discernible slackening of interest among consumers. "We educate our patients about the risks," says Dr. Weston, "and you're safer in my operating room than you are driving on the Capitol Beltway." But it is still surgery. Complications can arise from inappropriate use of anesthesia, heart attacks, and post-surgical blood clots.

As with any lucrative enterprise, cosmetic surgery also has its share of fringe practitioners—men and women who lack board certification (or, in some cases, even medical training) who advertise their services, often targeting lower-income groups with lower prices than legitimate surgeons. Earlier this spring, Dean Faiello, who in 2002 had pled guilty to practicing medicine without a license, was arrested in Costa Rica and charged with murder after the body of investment banker Maria Cruz was found, encased in concrete, at Faiello's former Newark, New Jersey home. Ms. Cruz had gone to Faiello's makeshift clinic in Manhattan for a cosmetic laser procedure to remove a growth from her tongue and died, likely as a result of the anesthesia Faiello administered.

Despite the risks, demand grows—and continues to trickle down the social scale. Cosmetic surgery, once the province of celebrities, has in the last several decades begun to appeal to other public figures, including politicians. Former Senate Majority Leader Bob Dole's post-retirement facelift led to lucrative advertising work for Pepsi and Viagra, and his new, tensile look is not the only one inside the Beltway. House Minority Leader Nancy Pelosi's official website unwittingly features two images that represent commendable examples of human achievement in architecture: the Golden Gate Bridge in her home state of California, and Ms. Pelosi's own stretched, lifted, and resculpted visage. Beltway observers have also remarked on Senator Joseph Biden's flourishing hairplugs. Commenting on the American scene recently, a reporter for an Australian newspaper noted, "It's hardly surprising that while Bill Clinton's presidential campaign of the 1990s was haunted by whispers of infidelity, the first rumor to dog the campaign of ... Senator John Kerry was that he had had Botox injections in his patrician forehead." Today, after setting aside his plough, Cincinnatus would have to get a quick mini-lift and chemical peel before returning to rule Rome.

Our vices are also reflected in new cosmetic treatments. Surgery to cure bunions and other foot ailments is increasing, and women are even having their toes shortened (at a cost of $2,500 per toe) and feet injected with collagen so that they can wear the high-heeled, pointy-toed shoes now in fashion—despite the real risks such surgeries carry, including permanent nerve damage.

The latest trend is "Age Dropping," with increasingly younger men and women its target market. Like the fable of the grasshopper and the ant, women in particular are being warned that, like the industrious ant, they should shore up their supply of youth and beauty by having an increasing number of carefully calibrated nips, tucks, and peels performed in their thirties so that they don't end up, like the hapless grasshopper, without an adequate supply in their winter years. Writing recently in the *New York Times Magazine*, beauty editor Mary Tannen confessed to pangs of doubt about her own decision to resist plastic surgery. "Perhaps I am deluded in thinking that my jowls are an advertisement for courage, proclaiming that I'm not afraid of growing old," she writes. "Maybe they are shrieking that I am a clueless loser who doesn't have the wherewithal to have my chin taken care of." In certain social milieus such as hers, she notes, "the lifted face has started to seem normal, leaving the unlifted one looking, well, strange."

When I asked Dr. Weston what he would recommend as a preventative, "age-dropping" measure for a thirty-year-old female of average height and weight (which I happen to be), he hesitated, noting, "everybody's face is different," but quickly told me not to smoke and to stay out of the sun. He added that there were a lot of procedures that could be performed in one's thirties to forestall the worst effects of aging. Another surgeon, Dr. Gerald Imber, is more forthright in his support of preventive measures—so much so that he wrote an entire book, *The Youth Corridor*, outlining the best methods of age dropping. "My philosophy," Imber writes in the introduction, "advocates preventing wrinkles, rather than curing them, and smaller procedures and earlier surgery for generally younger patients, in order to maintain one's appearance throughout the adult years in what I call the Youth Corridor." The book includes dramatic pencil sketches of a woman's face becoming progressively more haggard, like Dorian Gray's portrait, because she failed to follow Dr. Imber's multi-point strategy for wrinkle-free golden years.

What "age dropping" and other trends suggest is a diminishing tolerance for imperfection and aging. Writing in *The New Yorker* in 2001, Malcolm

Gladwell noted that "we have come to prefer a world where the distractible take Ritalin, the depressed take Prozac, and the unattractive get cosmetic surgery to a world ruled, arbitrarily, by those fortunate few who were born focused, happy, and beautiful. Cosmetic surgery is not 'earned' beauty, but then natural beauty isn't earned, either. One of the principal contributions of the late twentieth century was the moral deregulation of social competition—the insistence that advantages derived from artificial and extraordinary intervention are no less legitimate than the advantages of nature." The inevitable result is a sense that, in certain settings such as the corporate boardroom or Capitol Hill, cosmetic surgery is beginning to be considered a career necessity.

Meanwhile, democratization sends this message ever further down the income scale. The average cosmetic surgery patient is not rich. As historian Haiken notes, "only 23 percent of patients come from families earning more than $50,000 per year. Families with incomes under $25,000 account for 30 percent of patients, while those earning between $25,000 and $50,000 account for another 35 percent." "The worst perception of cosmetic surgery is that it's for the rich, vain, and foolish," Dr. Weston told me. "The reality is that most people are middle class and most people save their money for it. You can have almost anything done for the price of a used car. It's considered a tremendous value."

The future of cosmetic surgery is a story of continual expansion and increased consumer demand. In the years to come, "there will be more cosmetic surgery done than all surgical procedures combined," predicts Dr. Weston. Techniques are improving, and the surgeon's work is becoming more difficult to spot. "If cosmetic surgery looks like cosmetic surgery, it's not good cosmetic surgery," he says. "You don't want someone to say 'nice facelift.'... You want to hear, 'Gosh, you look good, did you lose weight?' or ideally, 'My God, are you in love?' Then you know it's really good cosmetic surgery."

Non-surgical treatments are expected to continue to increase in popularity as well. New injectable gel-like substances with names such as CosmoDerm, Hylaform, and Juvederm are hitting the market as wrinkle fillers. The *New York Times* reported last year that "it's not unusual for women in New York to spend $2,000 every few months on fillers, which run about $500 a treatment and last around six months." New treatments for hair loss are also coming down the cosmetic pipeline, such as "follicular unit transplantation," a procedure that purports to be a vast improvement over the crop-rotation-like aesthetic of first-generation hair plugs. Overall, industry projections are rosy: as *Medical Devices & Surgical Technology Week* recently reported, "demand for materials and equipment used in cosmetic surgery procedures will advance over 11 percent annually to $1.8 billion in 2007."

Cosmetic surgery is even going global. The *Washington Post* recently reported on the increasing acceptance of such practices in China, particularly a procedure to create creases in women's eyelids to give the eyes a rounder, more Westernized look. Breast implants are also popular, "a status symbol, an indication of an ability to afford the accouterments of a wealthy life." Hardly the great leap forward Chairman Mao had in mind, but further evidence of the cross-cultural lure of physical perfection.

The democratizing trend in cosmetic surgery is nowhere more evident than with liposuction and breast implants, which speak to two American obsessions: weight and sex. Liposuction is the most popular invasive cosmetic procedure, but it is not a permanent weight-loss solution. People who regain weight after liposuction look as if they never had the procedure to begin with; indeed, some patients report looking worse, because the new fat deposits itself in strangely misshapen ways on their previously vacuumed hips and thighs. Still, websites like liposite.com offer galleries of anonymous before and after liposuction pictures, and it is not unusual to find images of 19-year-old women who are by no means overweight but seem intent on resculpting their bodies to suit the reigning slim-hipped, thin-thighed ideal.

With breast implants, the democratic message has flowed down to meet a demand that originally traveled from the bottom of the respectable social scale up: once the province of strippers and porn actresses, breast implants eventually became popular among Hollywood celebrities. Today, it is middle class American women who scrimp and save to achieve the figures they've always wanted. According to a recent industry newsletter, "breast implants are the most significant single product type in the cosmetic-surgery market, alone accounting for 20 percent of demand, and will continue to be among the highest profile products." In 2002 alone, nearly 34,000 women had breast implants. Although liposuction is the most popular invasive cosmetic procedure, accounting for 74 percent of all such procedures performed in 2003, the demand for breast augmentation has increased at a faster pace. It is also the procedure (after rhinoplasty and otoplasty) with the youngest average age for patients—33 years old.

Breast implants are a good example of some of the ironies of our pragmatic, democratic approach to cosmetic surgery. Women who get them to feel more sexually attractive are making a strange bargain. In the process of *looking* more sexually appealing, they rob themselves of several uniquely female experiences. Women with breast implants frequently report a loss of sensation in their breasts, eliminating a site of natural sexual pleasure. They cannot breastfeed their children, eliminating both the bonding and health benefits of this practice. They must, on average, have their implants replaced or adjusted every ten years, and rippling, hardening, and significant movement of the implant and surrounding tissue are common. And popular culture, always a fickle beast, suggests that a quiet backlash against implants is building, with purveyors of pornography increasingly touting their "all natural" performers.

It is not clear if this shift from artificial to natural (like the trend in popular "natural foods" sales) will make a permanent mark. Beauty standards change as often as the seasons. But lately, popular culture has offered more insight into our collective embrace of cosmetic surgery. Alongside our paeans to the transformative power of plastic surgery rests a fascinated disgust with its extremes. There is a lurid subculture devoted to documenting the cosmetic surgery of celebrities, for example, who often deny having altered their appearance. Websites such as www.awfulplasticsurgery.com adopt a "gotcha!" tone and feature galleries of pictures documenting starlets' shrinking noses and ballooning bustlines—a *concours d'elegance* of the human body.

Televised burlesques satisfy a similar impulse, one not far removed from the freak shows of carnivals past. Programs such as *Extreme Makeover*, which deploys radical plastic surgery to transform unattractive women into glamorous sirens, and *Nip/Tuck*, a plastic surgery drama told through the somewhat jaundiced eyes of two Miami plastic surgeons, have proven wildly popular. The latest show in the plastic surgery oeuvre is Fox's *The Swan*, which "takes women described as ugly ducklings and puts them under the cosmetic surgery knife, fixes their teeth, lets them see a shrink, makes them work out, styles their hair, does their makeup" and turns them into "swans," according to the *San Francisco Chronicle*. There is a twist, of course. The women are not allowed to look in a mirror for three months, after which time they see themselves briefly before being shuttled off to a beauty contest where they face savage competition from other former ducklings. The show so pushes the limits of taste that it drove the cheeky but reli-

able television critic for Salon.com nearly apoplectic: "*The Swan* is bad for you. It's bad for me," she wrote, after watching the premier episode. "Openly reject those who discuss this show. Go ahead. Ostracize them. Limit their freedom of speech. Let the FCC roll its cannons onto this battlefield."

Employing a more documentary style, MTV's *I Want a Famous Face* tracks men and women (and even a pre-op transsexual) who are so enamored of modern celebrities that they endure major plastic surgery to look more like them. A recent episode chronicled the misadventures of Sha, a 19-year-old woman from Texas whose ambition in life is to become a *Playboy* centerfold. To further her aim, she receives enormous breast implants, lip implants, and chin liposuction in an effort to ape the appearance of former Playmate Pamela Anderson. The show shows only brief snippets of the actual surgery—zooming in on Sha's anesthetized face as her surgeon crams the huge lip implants into place with a large, metal, chopstick-like tool. As he sews up her newly enhanced chest, the surgeon quips, "This ought to satisfy *Playboy*!" The camera then lingers over Sha one day later, mummified in bandages and weeping in agony.

Unlike *Extreme Makeover*, MTV gives a nod to surgeries gone bad; they interview another former aspiring Playmate who endured a similarly challenging transformation, but who, several years later and with enormous breast implants beginning to ripple and relocate on her chest, has had little luck finding work. This cautionary tale fails to dissuade Sha; even the recommendation of a *Playboy* scout, who gently tells her that the magazine is opting for a more "natural" look these days, fails to prompt second thoughts. By the end of that week's episode, Sha, recovered from surgery, is proudly posing for a special issue of *Playboy* called "Voluptuous Vixens" and is by her own account very happy with her surgery. "I want to be somebody," she says, tossing a marabou boa over her shoulder as she preens for the camera. "I want to be famous." It is not difficult to imagine, a few decades hence, a "where are they now?" show that tracks down these carved up exhibitionists to see how they are holding up.

All of these shows are far more extreme expressions of older cultural tropes. In 1924, the *New York Daily Mirror* sponsored a "Homely Girl contest," with an advertisement that read: "Who is the homeliest girl in New York? *Daily Mirror* wants to find her—for a great opportunity awaits her." The paper promised the winner the full surgical services of Dr. W. A. Pratt and an opera audition; the winner was a sweatshop worker named Rosa Travers, according to historian Haiken. Less than twenty years later, *Good Housekeeping* featured the fairy-tale transformation of a "dowdy" and "rather untidy" girl with a big nose who, thanks to "a brief five days in the hospital" and the "skilled surgical hands" of an unnamed doctor, now had a nose of "pleasant proportions" which she accessorized with "a brand-new pompadour" and "a touching new-born vanity."

Popular culture has produced a few critiques of plastic surgery, too. The *Twilight Zone* tackled the topic on a few episodes in the 1960s, and in 1996, John Carpenter produced a critically panned movie called *Escape from L.A.*, which touched on the West Coast's obsessive commitment to appearance and cosmetic surgery. In this futuristic action flick, the city of Los Angeles has become a depraved penal colony, with Beverly Hills a neighborhood inhabited by polysurgical addicts who capture newcomers and harvest their body parts, all under the watchful rule of the Surgeon General of Beverly Hills, whose hands are made of scalpels. The social message of the film is somewhat undermined by inadvertent moments of high camp, such as a scene where a doctor, examining the breasts of a recently-captured woman, exclaims in horror, "My God, they're real!"

Popular culture currently rewards (with fifteen minutes of fame and free surgeries) a clatch of Americans who are clearly eager to have their worth judged by the fickle democratic masses. The viewing audience might observe this circus from an ironic distance, but it is clear that the impulse to measure success by outward appearance has more adherents than merely the contestants on reality television shows. Cosmetic surgery—better, cheaper, more widespread—encourages this kind of measurement. What it doesn't offer is a solution to an intransigent fact: no matter how much surgery a person has, there will always be someone younger, more naturally beautiful and outwardly appealing. And democratic culture, which tends to cater to the well-being of the body more than the well-being of the soul, will continue to seek out and reward those younger, more beautiful people. The ultimate futility of cosmetic surgery is perhaps the least remarked upon of its features.

In the end, cosmetic surgery is in some sense self-defeating, since it cannot permanently stop the process of aging. And yet, many of us know formerly dewlapped matrons and love-handled forty-something rogues who are objectively much happier after their surgeries; indeed, some people experience more satisfaction from a "marriage abdominoplasty" (combination lipo and tummy tuck) than they do in their own marriages. In a free society, why should anyone stand in the way

of another person's transformation from tatterdemalion to goddess? Isn't this simply the laudable and democratic pursuit of happiness?

If opponents of cosmetic surgery are too quick to dismiss those who claim great psychological benefits, boosters are far too willing to dismiss those who raise concerns. Cosmetic surgery might make individual people happier, but in the aggregate it makes life worse for everyone. By defining beauty up—fifty is *literally* the new forty if a critical mass of people are getting face-lifted and Botoxed—the pressure to conform to these elevated standards increases. So, too, does the amount of time and money we spend on what is ultimately a futile goal: cheating time. Even for men and women who have objectively achieved success—the award-winning novelist, the high-flying CEO—the refusal to meet these beauty standards will brand you as uncompetitive, evidence to the contrary notwithstanding.

The risk is not a society of beautiful but homogeneous mannequins. "Most of my patients want to look more like themselves than they've looked in a long time," Dr. Weston told me. "They don't want to look like someone else." The danger is a growing intolerance for what we would naturally look like without constant nipping, tucking, peeling, and liposuctioning. In the process, it contributes to that "philosophy of fatigue" and "disappointment with achievements" that Paul Nystrom, an early and astute critic of modern marketing techniques, argued led to society's embrace of "more superficial things in which fashion reigns."

In part, the discomfort some people have with cosmetic surgery is a discomfort about the particular form of denial it represents: a denial of bodily limits. The language of cosmetic surgery does everything to obscure this. Something "cosmetic" is not supposed to be a permanent alteration, as plastic surgery is. And humans are not "plastic," but beings embodied in tissue, flesh, and bone that will, at a certain point, resist our efforts to remold it. But the freedom to do what we will with ourselves, which is the model for cosmetic surgery, presents a real challenge when we start thinking about permanent alterations to the human body. As a case study for how we might act in the genetic future, cosmetic surgery—which is individualistic, consumer-oriented, largely unregulated, and invokes the therapeutic language so popular today—is hardly a reassuring model.

In the 1990s, a French performance artist named Orlan embarked on a multi-stage cosmetic surgery art installment that involved having surgery performed that would give her the chin of the Venus de Milo, Mona Lisa's forehead, and Psyche's nose, among other things. Pictures of one of her "performances" show a partially anesthetized Orlan reclining on an operating room table, draped in a surreal, mirrored gown and speaking into a cordless microphone. Buzzing about are surgeons and nurses decked out in scrubs designed by Issey Miyake and Paco Rabanne. But Orlan has other enthusiasms. As the *New York Times* noted, she "grandly proclaims her work to be 'a fight against nature and the idea of God' and also a way to prepare the world for widespread genetic engineering." Orlan offers us a disturbing peek into our future.

In the end, the questions raised by cosmetic surgery pose a special challenge for conservatives. Conservatives advocate free markets and individual autonomy (albeit linked to personal responsibility), but profess horror at the logical excesses of this view. We cringe when commercial culture throws up a Michael Jackson or an *Extreme Makeover*, but on what grounds do we argue for their end? Like our new reproductive technologies, cosmetic surgery collides with intimate, personal choices about the kind of lives we want to lead. And it becomes difficult to argue against the exercise of choice either legally or politically.

Perhaps this is the point at which culture becomes more important than policy, and the direct engagement with our cultural extremes a way of helping us find a more rational center. In the end, democratic culture seeks authenticity, but it doesn't always find it in the old forms where conservatives tend to feel more comfortable. And so we need to ask less threatening but no less fundamental questions—questions about the excesses of individualism and the extremes of democracy, questions about what are and what are not genuine social goods, and questions about how we measure success and failure.

We are not yet a nation of Narcissi, content to stare happily into the pool, our surgically enhanced self-esteem intact but our character irrevocably compromised. But we would do well to be more engaged in the culture that is encouraging us to move in that direction. "There are no grades of vanity, there are only grades of ability in concealing it," Mark Twain purportedly wrote. Concealing our desire for physical perfection behind a mask of democratic or therapeutic rhetoric will ultimately do us no good. We should, instead, bring cosmetic surgery out into the open, not merely to please our taste for voyeurism, but to understand how we might handle new and increasingly sophisticated techniques for empowering our vanity—techniques which stand to make that vanity much harder to conceal and to control.

First Reading

1. Identify Rosen's most compelling statement. Explain and defend your choice.
2. Specify portions of the text that indicate her assumptions about who is reading it. What knowledge and background does she assume her audience has?
3. Define Rosen's attitude toward her audience. What words and phrases convey that attitude?

Second Reading

1. Explain the relationship between the essay's title and the content of this excerpt. Indicate particular details that best illuminate the relationship.
2. Describe the tone of the excerpt, pointing to language and ideas that support your description.
3. Note where Rosen cites various credentialed authorities and recognized figures and explain why she does so.
4. Rosen makes several historical references to publications and television programs from decades ago. Identify how she uses two of these references to develop her argument.
5. Evaluate the conclusion of Rosen's essay. Explain how she leads up to her closing comment and explain its importance.
6. Distinguish Rosen's views on cosmetic surgery from those of Kuczynski.

Analysis and Argument — In lines 200–212, Christine Rosen cites Malcolm Gladwell, who wrote that "we have come to prefer a world where the distractible take Ritalin, the depressed take Prozac, and the unattractive get cosmetic surgery to a world ruled, arbitrarily, by those fortunate few who were born focused, happy, and beautiful." In a prepared essay, explain how Rosen uses Gladwell's comment to enhance her own argument, and then develop a position of your own in response to his claim.

Virginia Postrel
The Truth About Beauty

A contributing editor of *The Atlantic Monthly*, Virginia Postrel observed a multinational corporation's "campaign for real beauty" for months. In 2007, she wrote the following based upon her observations.

Cosmetics makers have always sold "hope in a jar"—creams and potions that promise youth, beauty, sex appeal, and even love for the women who use them. Over the last few years, the market
5 ers at Dove have added some new-and-improved enticements. They're now promising self-esteem and cultural transformation. Dove's "Campaign for Real Beauty," declares a press release, is "a global effort that is intended to serve as a starting
10 point for societal change and act as a catalyst for widening the definition and discussion of beauty." Along with its thigh-firming creams, self-tanners, and hair conditioners, Dove is peddling the crowd-pleasing notions that beauty is a media cre
15 ation, that recognizing plural forms of beauty is the same as declaring every woman beautiful, and that self-esteem means ignoring imperfections.

Dove won widespread acclaim in June 2005 when it rolled out its thigh-firming cream with
20 billboards of attractive but variously sized "real women" frolicking in their underwear. It advertised its hair-care products by showing hundreds of women in identical platinum-blonde wigs— described as "the kind of hair found in maga
25 zines"—tossing off those artificial manes and celebrating their real (perfectly styled, colored, and conditioned) hair. It ran print ads that featured atypical models, including a plump brunette and a ninety-five-year-old, and invited readers to
30 choose between pejorative and complimentary adjectives: "Wrinkled or wonderful?" "Oversized or outstanding?" The public and press got the point, and Dove got attention. Oprah covered the story, and so did the *Today* show. Dove's cam
35 paign, wrote *Advertising Age*, "undermines the basic proposition of decades of beauty-care advertising by telling women—and young girls—they're beautiful just the way they are."

Last fall, Dove extended its image building
40 with a successful bit of viral marketing: a seventy-five-second online video called *Evolution*. Created by Ogilvy & Mather, the video is a close-up of a seemingly ordinary woman, shot in harsh lighting that calls attention to her uneven skin tone,
45 slightly lopsided eyes, and dull, flat hair. In twen-

ty seconds of time-lapse video, makeup artists and hair stylists turn her into a wide-eyed, big-haired beauty with sculpted cheeks and perfect skin. It's *Extreme Makeover* without the surgical gore.
50 But that's only the beginning. Next comes the digital transformation, as a designer points-and-clicks on the model's photo, giving her a longer, slimmer neck, a slightly narrower upper face, fuller lips, bigger eyes, and more space between her
55 eyebrows and eyes. The perfected image rises to fill a billboard advertising a fictitious line of makeup. Fade to black, with the message "No wonder our perception of beauty is distorted." The video has attracted more than 3 million YouTube views.
60 It also appears on Dove's campaignforrealbeauty.com Web site, where it concludes, "Every girl deserves to feel beautiful just the way she is."

Every girl certainly wants to, which explains the popularity of Dove's campaign. There's only
65 one problem: Beauty exists, and it's unevenly distributed. Our eyes and brains pretty consistently like some human forms better than others. Shown photos of strangers, even babies look longer at the faces adults rank the best-looking. Whether you
70 prefer Nicole Kidman to Angelina Jolie, Jennifer Lopez to Halle Berry, or Queen Latifah to Kate Moss may be a matter of taste, but rare is the beholder who would declare Holly Hunter or Whoopi Goldberg—neither of whom is homely—more
75 beautiful than any of these women.

For similar reasons, we still thrill to the centuries-old bust of Nefertiti, the Venus de Milo, and the exquisite faces painted by Leonardo and Botticelli. Greta Garbo's acting style seems stilted to
80 day, but her face transcends time. We know beauty when we see it, and our reactions are remarkably consistent. Beauty is not just a social construct, and not every girl is beautiful just the way she is.

Take Dove's *Evolution* video. The digital trans
85 formation is fascinating because it magically makes a beautiful woman more striking. Her face's new geometry triggers an immediate, visceral response—and the video's storytelling impact is dependent on that predictable reaction. The video
90 makes its point about artifice only because most

people find the manipulated face more beautiful than the natural one.

In *Survival of the Prettiest: The Science of Beauty*, Nancy Etcoff, a psychologist at Harvard Medical School, reported on experiments that let people rate faces and digitally "breed" ever-more- attractive composite generations. The results for female faces look a lot like the finished product in the Dove video: "thinner jaws, larger eyes relative to the size of their faces, and shorter distances between their mouths and chins" in one case, and "fuller lips, a less robust jaw, a smaller nose and smaller chin than the population average" in another. These features, wrote Etcoff, "exaggerate the ways that adult female faces differ from adult male faces. They also exaggerate the youthfulness of the face." More than youth, the full lips and small jaws of beautiful women reflect relatively high levels of female hormones and low levels of male hormones—indicating greater fertility—according to psychologist Victor Johnston, who did some of these experiments.

More generally, evolutionary psychologists suggest that the features we see as beautiful—including indicators of good health like smooth skin and symmetry—have been rewarded through countless generations of competition for mates. The same evolutionary pressures, this research suggests, have biologically programmed human minds to perceive these features as beautiful. "Some scientists believe that our beauty detectors are really detectors for the combination of youth and femininity," wrote Etcoff. Whether the beauty we detect arises from nature or artifice doesn't change that visceral reflex.

Perhaps surprisingly, Etcoff herself advised Dove on several rounds of survey research and helped the company create workshops for girls. Dove touts her involvement (and her doctorate and Harvard affiliation) in its publicity materials. She sees the campaign as a useful corrective. Media images, Etcoff notes in an e-mail, are often so rarefied that "they change our ideas about what people look like and what normal looks like ... Our brains did not evolve with media, and many people see more media images of women than actual women. The contrast effect makes even the most beautiful non-model look less attractive; it produces a new 'normal.'"

Dove began its campaign by recognizing the diverse manifestations of universally beautiful patterns. The "real women" pictured in the thigh-cream billboards may not have looked like supermodels, but they were all young, with symmetrical faces, feminine features, great skin, white teeth, and hourglass shapes. Even the most zaftig

had relatively flat stomachs and clearly defined waists. These pretty women were not a random sample of the population. Dove diversified the portrait of beauty without abandoning the concept altogether.

But the campaign didn't stop there. Dove is defining itself as the brand that loves regular women—and regular women, by definition, are not extraordinarily beautiful. The company can't afford a precise definition of *real beauty* that might exclude half the population—not a good strategy for selling mass-market consumer products. So the campaign leaves *real beauty* ambiguous, enabling the viewers to fill in the concept with their own desires. Some take *real beauty* to mean "nature unretouched" and interpret the *Evolution* video as suggesting that uncannily beautiful faces are not merely rare but nonexistent. Others emphasize the importance of character and personality: Real beauty comes from the inside, not physical appearance. And *Advertising Age*'s interpretation is common: that Dove is reminding women that "they're beautiful just the way they are."

Another Dove ad, focusing on girls' insecurities about their looks, concludes, "Every girl deserves to feel good about herself and see how beautiful she really is." Here, Dove is encouraging the myth that physical beauty is a false concept, and, at the same time, falsely equating beauty with goodness and self-worth. If you don't see perfection in the mirror, it suggests, you've been duped by the media and suffer from low self-esteem.

But adult women have a more realistic view. "Only two percent of women describe themselves as beautiful" trumpets the headline of Dove's press release. Contrary to what the company wants readers to believe, however, that statistic doesn't necessarily represent a crisis of confidence; it may simply reflect the power of the word *beautiful*. Dove's surveys don't ask women if they think they're unattractive or ugly, so it's hard to differentiate between knowing you have flaws, believing you're acceptably but unimpressively plain, and feeling worthlessly hideous. In another Dove survey, 88 percent of the American women polled said they're at least somewhat satisfied with their face, while 76 percent said they're at least somewhat satisfied with their body. But dissatisfaction is not the same as unhappiness or insecurity.

Like the rest of the genetic lottery, beauty is unfair. Everyone falls short of perfection, but some are luckier than others. Real confidence requires self-knowledge, which includes recognizing one's shortcomings as well as one's strengths. At a recent conference on biological manipulations, I heard a philosopher declare during lunch that she'd never have plastic surgery or even dye her hair. But, she confessed, she'd pay just about anything for fifteen more IQ points. This woman is not insecure about her intelligence, which is far above average; she'd just like to be smarter. Asking women to say they're beautiful is like asking intellectuals to say they're geniuses. Most know they simply don't qualify.

First Reading

1. What does the title of the essay suggest about its content?
2. Identify the subject of the essay.
3. How does the "Campaign for Real Beauty" provide Postrel with the context for her argument?
4. Identify Postrel's main argument.

Second Reading

1. Where does Postrel's attitude toward the "Campaign for Real Beauty" first become evident? How does she develop that attitude at key points in the essay?
2. In paragraph 5, Postrel states, "Beauty exists, and it's unevenly distributed" (lines 65–66). Explain how she uses her summary account of the "Evolution" video (lines 41–62) to illustrate her stance.
3. The cliché that "we know beauty when we see it" appears in lines 80–81. Given the title of the essay, is Postrel's use of this line justified? Why or why not?
4. In lines 93–139, Postrel makes direct references to the observations of psychologist Nancy Etcoff (see pages 68–69). Why does she reveal Etcoff's role as an adviser to a beauty products company after citing her as an authority?
5. How does Postrel emphasize "real beauty" in paragraph 12, lines 152–169? Why does she offer distinct definitions of the term?
6. What central idea is illustrated by the details of the essay's last paragraph? Explain the impact of the final two sentences.

Writing

Synthesis

Suggested Preparation and Writing Time   one week following the final reading assignment.

If "the truth about beauty" isn't what the "Campaign for Real Beauty" says it is, then what is it? Write a scene that represents a thoughtful yet spirited conversation about beauty's truth involving June Godfrey-June, Nancy Etcoff, Kathy Peiss, Alex Kuczynski, Christine Rosen, and Virginia Postrel. Give the speakers authentic voices by effectively using the sources of this chapter. After you prepare a full early draft for a teacher or peer conference, write and submit a final version that adds your own perspective, presence, and voice to the discussion.

Chapter 6
Nature

Background

As humans, we watch the events occurring in our world. Sometimes, by chance or by choice, we watch from a distance, or watch from close at hand. As watchers, we always react in some way, very often with merely a passing thought to the images we see, and at other times we pause to consider the significance of the events or the landscapes we see. How often have you spent time looking closely at an ant, a moth or a worm? Consider the images you have seen of the effects of the 2004 tsunami or Hurricane Katrina in 2005, and consider your reaction to those images.

From the petroglyphs of prehistoric peoples to widely read publications of today, humans record interactions with the natural world. We scratch images on cave walls, and we photograph or capture nature through some other medium. At times we reflect, and at other times we applaud or recoil or mourn. Also, from earliest times some among us have clearly understood how dependent is our existence upon the natural world. Contemporary events indicate that our relationship with the natural elements has become interdependent, and the responsibility for the success of a continued relationship with nature belongs to the human animal. In the introduction to *The Norton Book of Nature Writing*, Robert Finch and John Elder argue that nature writing should offer "vivid and compelling chronicles of engagement with the perpetual mystery of human existence in a physical and biological universe." This is how we view the selections in this chapter. How human animals continue the relationship with the natural world remains to be seen.

Readings

Annie Dillard
Pilgrim at Tinker Creek

Henry David Thoreau
Walden

Gilbert White
The Natural History and Antiquities of Selborne

Lewis Thomas
The Lives of a Cell

Diane Ackerman
A Natural History of the Senses

NASA
Earth from Apollo 17

Chief Seattle, Suquamish
Respect

Tim Flannery
The Weather Makers

Vaclav Havel
The Quiver of a Shrub in California

Annie Dillard
Pilgrim at Tinker Creek

This excerpt from "The Fixed" in *Pilgrim at Tinker Creek*, written in 1974, focuses on a single aspect of human interaction with nature.

Once, when I was ten or eleven years old, my friend Judy brought in a Polyphemus moth cocoon. It was January; there were doily snowflakes taped to the schoolroom panes. The teacher kept the cocoon in her desk all morning and brought it out when we were getting restless before recess. In a book we found what the adult moth would look
5   like; it would be beautiful. With a wingspread of up to six inches, the Polyphemus is one of the few huge American silk moths, much larger than, say, a giant or tiger swallowtail butterfly. The moth's enormous wings are velveted in a rich, warm brown, and edged in bands of blue and pink delicate as a watercolor wash. A startling "eyespot," immense, and deep blue melding to an almost translucent yellow, luxuriates in the center of each
10 hind wing. The effect is one of a masculine splendor foreign to the butterflies, a fragility unfurled to strength. The Polyphemus moth in the picture looked like a mighty wraith, a beating essence of the hardwood forest, alien-skinned and brown, with spread, blind eyes. This was the giant moth packed in the faded cocoon. It was an oak leaf sewn into a plump oval bundle; Judy had found it loose in a pile of frozen leaves.
15 We passed the cocoon around; it was heavy. As we held it in our hands, the creature within warmed and squirmed. We were delighted, and wrapped it tighter in our fists. The pupa began to jerk violently, in heart stopping knocks. Who's there? I can still feel those thumps, urgent through a muffling of spun silk and leaf, urgent through the swaddling of many years, against the curve of my palm, We kept passing it around, When it
20 came to me again it was hot as a bun; it jumped half out of my hand. The teacher intervened. She put it, still heaving and banging, in the ubiquitous Mason jar.

It was coming. There was no stopping it now, January or not. One end of the cocoon dampened and gradually frayed in a furious battle. The whole cocoon twisted and slapped around in the bottom of the jar. The teacher fades, the classmates fade, I fade: I
25 don't remember anything but that thing's struggle to be a moth or die trying. It emerged at last, a sodden crumple. It was a male; his long antennae were thickly plumed, as wide as his fat abdomen. His body was very thick, over an inch long, and deeply furred. A gray furlike plush covered his head; a long tan furlike hair hung from his wide thorax over his brown-furred segmented abdomen. His multijointed legs, pale and powerful,
30 were shaggy as a bear's. He stood still, but he breathed.

He couldn't spread his wings. There was no room. The chemical that coated his wings like varnish, stiffening them permanently, dried, and hardened his wings as they were. He was a monster in a Mason jar. Those huge wings stuck on his back in a torture of random pleats and folds, wrinkled as a dirty tissue, rigid as leather. They made a single
35 nightmare clump still wracked with useless, frantic convulsions.

The next things I remember, it was recess. The school was in Shadyside, a busy residential part of Pittsburgh. Everyone was playing dodgeball in the fenced playground or racing around the concrete schoolyard by the swings. Next to the playground a long delivery drive sloped downhill to the sidewalk and street. Someone—it must have been the
40 teacher—had let the moth out. I was standing in the driveway, alone, stock-still, but shivering. Someone had given the Polyphemus moth his freedom, and he was walking away.

He heaved himself down the asphalt driveway by infinite degrees, unwavering. His hideous crumpled wings lay glued and rucked on his back, perfectly still now, like a collapsed tent. The bell rang twice; I had to go. The moth was receding down the drive-
45 way, dragging on. I went; I ran inside. The Polyphemus moth is still crawling down the driveway, crawling down the driveway hunched, crawling down the driveway on six furred feet, forever.

First Reading

1. Describe your initial response to the Dillard excerpt. Be specific. How did it make you feel? What does it make you think about? How would you have felt had you been watching the events from a distance?
2. Find the images that suggest beauty. Explain the incongruity in finding beauty in a moth.
3. Who was Polyphemus? Explain the allusion to Polyphemus in the moth's name.
4. Find the paradoxical elements in Dillard's description of the moth.
5. Explain how Dillard's comparison of the moth to a bear in paragraph 3 (lines 22–30) suggests that a thing huge and powerful exists.

Second Reading

1. Read carefully to find the sequence of causes and effects that lead to the irreconcilable change in the moth. Paraphrase the events.
2. Since Dillard tells about the activities of children and a teacher, what do such subjects suggest about unintended consequences?
3. Explain the significance of the building of the repetition in the last sentence.
4. Dillard relates a childhood event through the eyes of an adult. How does this point of view suggest permanence?
5. Explain the similarities of this seemingly small event in the larger context of human interaction with the natural world.

Writing

1. **Argument** — Write your own description of a similar chain of events focused on another aspect of human interaction with the natural world. Arrange your essay using the Dillard excerpt as a guide. Include specific details, images, and incongruities.
2. **Analysis** — Write an essay in which you analyze how Dillard's rhetorical strategies convey her attitude regarding innocence and interference with natural cycles.

Henry David Thoreau
Walden

In this excerpt from "Brute Neighbors," the author telescopes a very small natural event that parallels human events. Thoreau published *Walden* in 1854.

One day when I went out to my wood-pile, or rather my pile of stumps, I observed two large ants, the one red, the other much larger, nearly half an inch long, and black, fiercely contending with one
5 another. Having once got hold they never let go, but struggled and wrestled and rolled on the chips incessantly. Looking farther, I was surprised to find that the chips were covered with such combatants, that it was not a *duellum*, but a *bellum*, a war between
10 two races of ants, the red always pitted against the black, and frequently two red ones to one black. The legions of these Myrmidons covered all the hills and vales in my wood-yard, and the ground was already strewn with the dead and dying, both red
15 and black. It was the only battle which I have ever witnessed, the only battle-field I ever trod while the battle was raging; internecine war; the red republicans on the one hand, and the black imperialists on the other. On every side they were engaged in
20 deadly combat, yet without any noise that I could hear, and human soldiers never fought so resolutely. I watched a couple that were fast locked in each other's embraces, in a little sunny valley amid the chips, now at noonday prepared to fight till the
25 sun went down, or life went out. The smaller red champion had fastened himself like a vice to his adversary's front, and through all the tumblings on that field never for an instant ceased to gnaw at one of his feelers near the root, having already caused
30 the other to go by the board; while the stronger black one dashed him from side to side, and, as I saw on looking nearer, had already divested him of several of his members. They fought with more pertinacity than bulldogs. Neither manifested the
35 least disposition to retreat. It was evident that their battle-cry was "Conquer or die." In the meanwhile there came along a single red ant on the hillside of this valley, evidently full of excitement, who either had despatched his foe, or had not yet taken part in
40 the battle; probably the latter, for he had lost none of his limbs; whose mother had charged him to return with his shield or upon it. Or perchance he was some Achilles, who had nourished his wrath apart, and had now come to avenge or rescue his Patro-
45 clus. He saw this unequal combat from afar—for the blacks were nearly twice the size of the red—he drew near with rapid pace till be stood on his guard within half an inch of the combatants; then, watching his opportunity, he sprang upon the black war-
50 rior, and commenced his operations near the root of his right fore leg, leaving the foe to select among his own members; and so there were three united for life, as if a new kind of attraction had been invented which put all other locks and cements to shame. I
55 should not have wondered by this time to find that they had their respective musical bands stationed on some eminent chip, and playing their national airs the while, to excite the slow and cheer the dying combatants. I was myself excited somewhat
60 even as if they had been men. The more you think of it, the less the difference. And certainly there is not the fight recorded in Concord history, at least, if in the history of America, that will bear a moment's comparison with this, whether for the numbers
65 engaged in it, or for the patriotism and heroism displayed. For numbers and for carnage it was an Austerlitz or Dresden. Concord Fight! Two killed on the patriots' side, and Luther Blanchard wounded! Why here every ant was a Buttrick—"Fire! for
70 God's sake fire!"—and thousands shared the fate of Davis and Hosmer. There was not one hireling there. I have no doubt that it was a principle they fought for, as much as our ancestors, and not to avoid a three-penny tax on their tea; and the results
75 of this battle will be as important and memorable to those whom it concerns as those of the battle of Bunker Hill, at least.

I took up the chip on which the three I have particularly described were struggling, carried it
80 into my house, and placed it under a tumbler on my window-sill, in order to see the issue. Holding a microscope to the first-mentioned red ant, I saw that, though he was assiduously gnawing at the near fore leg of his enemy, having severed his
85 remaining feeler, his own breast was all torn away, exposing what vitals he had there to the jaws of the black warrior, whose breastplate was apparently too thick for him to pierce; and the dark carbuncles of the sufferer's eyes shone with ferocity such as
90 war only could excite. They struggled half an hour longer under the tumbler, and when I looked again the black soldier had severed the heads of his foes

from their bodies, and the still living heads were hanging on either side of him like ghastly trophies at his saddle-bow, still apparently as firmly fastened as ever, and he was endeavoring with feeble struggles, being without feelers and with only the remnant of a leg, and I know not how many other wounds, to divest himself of them; which at length, after half an hour more, he accomplished. I raised the glass, and he went off over the window-sill in that crippled state. Whether he finally survived that combat, and spent the remainder of his days in some Hotel des Invalides, I do not know; but I thought that his industry would not be worth much thereafter. I never learned which party was victorious, nor the cause of the war; but I felt for the rest of that day as if I had had my feelings excited and harrowed by witnessing the struggle, the ferocity and carnage, of a human battle before my door.

Kirby and Spence tell us that the battles of ants have long been celebrated and the date of them recorded, though they say that Huber is the only modern author who appears to have witnessed them. "Aeneas Sylvius" say they, "after giving a very circumstantial account of one contested with great obstinacy by a great and small species on the trunk of a pear tree," adds that "this action was fought in the pontificate of Eugenius the Fourth, in the presence of Nicholas Pistoriensis, an eminent lawyer, who related the whole, history of the battle with the greatest fidelity." A similar engagement between great and small ants is recorded by Olaus Magnus, in which the small ones, being victorious, are said to have buried the bodies of their own soldiers, but left those of their giant enemies a prey to the birds. This event happened previous to the expulsion of the tyrant Christiern the Second from Sweden." The battle which I witnessed took place in the Presidency of Polk, five years before the passage of Webster's Fugitive-Slave Bill.

First Reading

1. Thoreau relates a closely observed phenomenon and reflects upon its personal meaning. In his examination, he alludes to the war between the Trojans and the Greeks. Write your explanation of the parallels between the ant battle and the battle account written by Homer.

2. Mark your text to note each historical allusion. Add a brief comment about the meaning or the effect of each.

Second Reading

1. Read again the sentence in paragraph 1 that begins, "Looking farther…." Examine the language that makes this sentence precise, especially the words "*duellum*" and "*bellum.*" Explain your understanding of the meaning of this sentence.

2. In paragraph 1, the sentence that begins "The smaller red champion…" signals a series of visual and visceral images. Note these images and explain the effect of each image.

3. Explain how the allusions to several historic battles at the conclusion of paragraph 1 add to Thoreau's metaphoric description and urge his audience to view the ant battle as having momentous significance.

4. In paragraph 2 (lines 78–110), Thoreau continues his observations of the battle by taking a chip of wood inside and observing the combatants through a microscope. Look up the word "berserker" and explain how Thoreau suggests that the ants are the equivalent of human berserkers.

5. Thoreau concludes paragraph 2 as an exhausted observer. Explain how he conveys his exhaustion.

6. In the third paragraph (lines 111–132), Thoreau relates his observations as comparable to more recent historical battles. How does he end this comparison with a mock serious, and humorous, note?

Writing

1. **Exposition** — Write your own account of an aspect of the natural world, and describe that aspect in human terms. This is commonly known as *anthropomorphism*, and it is how humans often view the natural world. Thoreau makes his observation exciting. Make your account exciting.

2. **Analysis** — Write an essay in which you analyze the rhetorical strategies Thoreau uses to convey his view of the natural world, with its seemingly unimportant events, as magnificent to behold.

Gilbert White
The Natural History and Antiquities of Selborne

The author was one of the first English naturalists to make careful observations of his surroundings and record these observations in a systematic way. He developed a deep insight into the interrelationships of living things, and he combined a naturalist's skills with an ability to influence a wider audience through his writing. This letter was written to Thomas Pennant or Daines Barrington about "natural curiosities."

Selborne, May 20, 1777

Dear Sir,

Lands that are subject to frequent inundations are always poor; and probably the reason may be because the worms are drowned. The most insignificant insects and rep-
5 tiles are of much more consequence, and have much more influence in the economy of nature, than the incurious are aware of; and are mighty in their effect, from their minuteness, which renders them less an object of attention; and from their numbers and fecundity. Earth-worms, though in appearance a small and despicable link in the chain of nature, yet, if lost, would make a lamentable chasm. For, to say nothing of half
10 the birds, and some quadrupeds, which are almost entirely supported by them, worms seem to be the great promoters of vegetation, which would proceed but lamely without them. By boring, perforating, and loosening the soil, and rendering it pervious to rains and the fibres of plants, by drawing straws and stalks of leaves and twigs into it; and, most of all, by throwing up such infinite numbers of lumps of earth called worm-casts,
15 which, being their excrement, is a fine manure for grain and grass. Worms probably pro-vide new soil for hills and slopes where the rain washes the earth away, and they affect slopes, probably to avoid being flooded. Gardeners and farmers express their detesta-tion of worms; the former because they render their walks unsightly, and make them much work; and the latter because, as they think, worms eat their green corn. But these
20 men would find that the earth without worms would soon become cold, hard-bound, and void of fermentation; and consequently sterile; and besides, in favour of worm, it should be hinted that green corn, plants, and flowers, are not so much injured by them as by many species of *colioptera* (scarabs), and *tipuloe* (long-legs), in their larva, or grub-state, and by unnoticed myriads of small shell-less snails, called slugs, which silently
25 and imperceptibly make amazing havoc in the field and garden.

These hints we think proper to throw out in order to set the inquisitive and discern-ing to work.

A good monography of worms would afford much entertainment and information at the same time, and would open a large and new field in natural history. Worms work
30 most in the spring; but by no means lie torpid in the dead months; are out every mild night in the winter, as any person may be convinced that will take the pains to examine his grass-plots with a candle; are hermaphrodites, and much addicted to venery, and consequently very prolific.

I am, etc.

First Reading

1. Explain how the first sentence of paragraph 1 is surprising and amusing.
2. Rewrite the second sentence of paragraph 1, and explain the elements of incongruity.
3. Explain the significance of White's references to a "despicable link" and "a lamentable chasm" in paragraph 1, lines 8–9.

4. Paraphrase the remainder of paragraph 1 (lines 9–25) and all of paragraphs 2 and 3 (lines 26–33).

Second Reading

1. Explain how White, like Dillard and Thoreau, examines a closely observed phenomenon and how he reflects upon its personal meaning.
2. How does White's letter mesh his attention to style, form, and ironies of expression with a scientific concern for palpable fact?
3. Explain the effect of White's humorous conclusion.

Writing

1. **Analysis** — Write an essay in which you analyze how White's choices of details and images convey his attitude toward those elements of nature that humans tend to consider insignificant.
2. **Argument** — Write a rebuttal to White's letter in which you argue that the destruction of snails (or another seemingly insignificant creature) is instrumental in causing changes to the natural world. Model your argument on White's letter if you wish, and research any additional facts you might need. Include a bibliography.

Lewis Thomas
The Lives of a Cell

The author was a physician who combined his knowledge and insights into science, especially microbiology and immunology, with meditative reflections on nature and the human body. Thomas's book was published in 1974.

We are told that the trouble with Modern Man is that he has been trying to detach himself from nature. He sits in the topmost tiers of polymer, glass, and steel, dangling his pulsing legs, survey-
5 ing at a distance the writhing life of the planet. In this scenario, Man comes on as a stupendous lethal force, and the earth is pictured as something delicate, like rising bubbles at the surface of a country pond, or flights of fragile birds.

10 But it is illusion to think that there is anything fragile about the life of the earth; surely this is the toughest membrane imaginable in the universe, opaque to probability, impermeable to death. We are the delicate part, transient and vulnerable as
15 cilia. Nor is it a new thing for man to invent an existence that he imagines to be above the rest of life; this has been his most consistent intellectual exertion down the millennia. As illusion, it has never worked out to his satisfaction in the past, any more
20 than it does today. Man is embedded in nature.

The biologic science of recent years has been making this a more urgent fact of life. The new, hard problem will be to cope with the dawning, intensifying realization of just how interlocked
25 we are. The old, clung-to notions most us have held about our special lordship are being deeply undermined.

Item. A good case can be made for our nonexistence as entities. We are not made up, as we had
30 always supposed, of successively enriched packets of our own parts. We are shared, rented, occupied. At the interior of our cells, driving them, providing oxidative energy that sends us out for the improvement of each shining day, are the mi-
35 tochondria, and in a strict sense they are not ours. They turn out to be little separate creatures, the colonial posterity of migrant prokaryocytes, probably primitive bacteria that swam into ancestral precursors of our eukaryotic cells and stayed
40 there. Ever since, they have maintained themselves with their own DNA and RNA quite different from ours. They are as much symbionts as the rhizobial bacteria in the roots of beans. Without them, we would not move a muscle, drum a fin-
45 ger, think a thought.

Mitochondria are stable and responsible lodgers, and I choose to trust them. But what of the other little animals, similarly established in my cells, sorting and balancing me, clustering me to-
50 gether? My centrioles, basal bodies, and probably a good many other more obscure tiny beings at work inside my cells, each with its own special genome, are as foreign, and as essential, as aphids in anthills. My cells are no longer the pure line enti-
55 ties I was raised with; they are ecosystems more complex than Jamaica Bay.

I like to think that they work in my interest, that each breath they draw for me, but perhaps it is they who walk through the local park in the
60 early morning, sensing my senses, listening to my music, thinking my thoughts.

I am consoled, somewhat, by the thought that the green plants are in the same fix. They could not be plants, or green, without chloroplasts, which
65 run the photosynthetic enterprise and generate oxygen for the rest of us. As it turns out, chloroplasts are also separate creatures with their own genomes, speaking their own language.

We carry stores of DNA in our nuclei that may
70 have come in, at one time or another, from the fusion of ancestral cells and the linking of ancestral organisms in symbiosis. Our genomes are catalogues of instructions from all kinds of sources in nature, filed for all kinds of contingencies. As for
75 me, I am grateful for differentiation and speciation, but I cannot feel as separate an entity as I did a few years ago, before I was told these things, nor, I should think, can anyone else.

Item. The uniformity of the earth's life, more as-
80 tonishing than its delivery, is accountable by the high probability that we derived, originally, from some single cell, fertilized in a bolt of lightning as the earth cooled. It is from the progeny of this parent cell that we take our looks; we still share genes
85 around, and resemblance of the enzymes of grasses to those of whales is a family resemblance.

The viruses, instead of being single-minded agents of disease and death, now begin to look like mobile genes. Evolution is still an infinitely
90 long and tedious biologic game, with only winners

staying at the table, but the rules are beginning to look more flexible. We live in a dancing matrix of viruses; they dart, rather like bees, from organism to organism, from plant to insect to mammal to me and back again, and into the sea, tugging along pieces of this genome, strings of genes from that, transplanting grafts of DNA, passing around heredity as though at a great party. They may be a mechanism for keeping new, mutant kinds of DNA in the widest circulation among us. If this is true, the odd virus disease, on which we must focus so much of our attention in medicine today, may be looked on as an accident, something dropped.

Item. I have been trying to think of the earth as a kind of organism, but it is no go. I cannot think of it this way. It is too big, too complex, with too many working parts that lack visible connections. The other night, driving through a hilly, wooded part of southern New England, I wondered about this. If not like an organism, what is it like, what is it *most* like? Then, satisfactorily for that moment, it came to me: it is *most* like a single cell.

First Reading

1. Paraphrase each paragraph in one sentence.
2. Mark diction, images, and paradox, and make marginal notes about meaning or effect.

Second Reading

1. Explain the effect on meaning of the following words in the first paragraph: "surveying," "writhing," "stupendous," and "delicate."
2. In the second paragraph (lines 10–20), how does Thomas's mention of the "illusion" he describes lead to the assumption that we humans consider ourselves "above the rest of life"? How do these rhetorical choices lead to the emphasis of the last sentence of the paragraph?
3. In paragraph 3 (lines 21–27), Thomas claims that we are "interlocked" with nature. How does this continue the emphasis of paragraph 2 and lead us to consider the significance of his claim? Note that he continues the emphasis and explains it in three "items" that constitute the remainder of the essay.
4. Explain the paradoxical qualities of the first sentence of paragraph 4 (lines 28–29).
5. Paragraphs 4 through 8 (lines 28–78) contain explanations with scientific terminology. Explain how this strategy reinforces Thomas's claim at the end of paragraph 2.
6. What do you consider to be the logic of Thomas's reasoning that we need these invaders?
7. Paragraphs 9 and 10 (lines 79–103) constitute Thomas's second "item." Why might he choose to shift from scientific terminology to standard English for this item?
8. Note each aspect of metaphoric language in paragraphs 9 and 10.
9. The final "item" consists of one paragraph (lines 104–112) and constitutes Thomas's conclusion. How does Thomas reconnect with his audience in this paragraph?

Writing

1. **Analysis** — Write an essay in which you analyze how Thomas's rhetorical strategies generate his comparison of Earth to a cell. Consider the following elements: diction, imagery, arrangement, or any other strategies you note.
2. **Synthesis** — Consider the focus of the excerpts from Dillard and Thoreau, Thomas's essay, and the White letter. Write an essay in which you defend, challenge, or qualify the argument that small elements of life on Earth contribute to, or explain some aspect of, human interaction with the natural world. Refer to at least three of the texts for support.

Diane Ackerman
A Natural History of the Senses

Diane Ackerman is a poet, essayist, and naturalist. This essay—"The Round Walls of Home,"
written in 1990—is from a collection exploring the five senses.

Picture this: Everyone you've ever known, everyone you've ever loved, your whole experience of life floating in one place, on a single planet underneath you. On that dazzling oasis,
5 swirling with blues and whites, the weather systems form and travel. You watch the clouds tingle and swell above the Amazon, and know the weather that developed there will affect the crop yield half a planet away in Russia and China.
10 Volcanic eruptions make tiny spangles below. The rain forests are disappearing in Australia, Hawaii, and South America. You see dustbowls developing in Africa and the Near East. Remote sensing devices, judging the humidity in the
15 desert, have already warned you there will be plagues of locusts this year. To your amazement, you identify the lights of Denver and Cairo. And though you were taught about them one by one, as separate parts of a jigsaw puzzle, now you can
20 see that the oceans, the atmosphere, and the land are not separate at all, but part of an intricate, recombining web of nature. Like Dorothy in *The Wizard of Oz*, you want to click your magic shoes together and say three times: "There's no place
25 like home."

You know what home is. For many years you've tried to be a modest and eager watcher of the skies, and of the Earth, whose green anthem you love. Home is a pigeon strutting like a petitioner in the
30 courtyard in front of your house. Home is the law-abiding hickories out back. Home is the sign on a gas station just outside Pittsburgh that reads "If we can't fix it, it ain't broke." Home is springtime on campuses all across America, where students
35 sprawl on the grass like the war-wounded at Gettysburg, Home is the Guatemalan jungle, at times deadly as an arsenal. Home is the pheasant barking hoarse threats at the neighbor's dog. Home is the exquisite torment of love and all the lesser
40 mayhems of the heart. But what you long for is to stand back and see it whole. You want to live out that age-old yearning, portrayed in myths and legends of every culture, to step above the Earth and see the whole world fidgeting and blooming
45 below you.

I remember my first flying lesson, in the doldrums of summer in upstate New York. Push-ing the throttle forward I zoomed down the runway until the undercarriage began to dance;
50 then the ground fell away below and I was airborne, climbing up an invisible *flight* of stairs. To my amazement, the horizon came with me (how could it not on a round planet?). For the first time in my life I understood what a valley was, as I
55 floated above one at 7000 feet. I could see plainly the devastation of the gypsy moth, whose hunger had leeched the forests to a mottled gray. Later on, when I flew over Ohio, I was saddened to discover the stagnant ocher of the air, and to see
60 that the long expanse of the Ohio River, dark and chunky, was the wrong texture for water, even flammable at times, thanks to the fumings of plastic factories, which I could also see, standing like pustules along the river. I began to understand
65 how people settle a landscape, in waves and at crossroads, how they survey a land and irrigate it. Most of all, I discovered that there are things one can learn about the world only from certain perspectives. How can you understand the plan-
70 et without walking upon it, sampling its marvels one by one, and then floating high above it, to see it all in a single eye-gulp.

Most of all, the twentieth century will be remembered as the time when we first began to un-
75 derstand what our address was. The "big, beautiful, blue, wet ball" of recent years is one way to say it. But a more profound way will speak of the orders of magnitude of that bigness, the shades of that blueness, the arbitrary delicacy of
80 beauty itself, the ways in which water has made life possible, and the fragile euphoria of the complex ecosystem that is Earth, an Earth on which, from space, there are no visible fences, or military zones, or national borders. We need to send into
85 space a flurry of artists and naturalists, photographers and painters, who will turn the mirror upon ourselves and show us Earth as a single planet, a single organism that's buoyant, fragile, blooming, buzzing, full of spectacles, full of fascinating hu-
90 man beings, something to cherish. Learning our full address may not end all wars, but it will enrich our sense of wonder and pride. It will remind us that the human context is not tight as a noose, but large as the universe we have the privilege to

95 inhabit. It will change our sense of what a neighborhood is. It will persuade us that we are citizens of something larger and more profound than
mere countries, that we are citizens of Earth, her
joyriders and her caretakers, who would do well
100 to work on her problems together. The view from
space is offering us the first chance we evolutionary toddlers have had to cross the cosmic street
and stand facing our own home, amazed to see it
clearly for the first time.

First Reading

1. Label each paragraph by its rhetorical mode, not necessarily in the order presented: descriptive/definition, exposition, narration, or persuasion.
2. Note Ackerman's shifts in point of view (second person, first person singular, and first person plural). Explain the effect of these shifts.

Second Reading

1. In paragraph 1, Ackerman's images and details create a specific feeling. Choose an adjective that you consider best describes that feeling, and explain why it does so.
2. In paragraph 2 (lines 26–45), Ackerman compares home to several visual aspects of everyday life. What is the effect of this comparison?
3. In paragraph 3 (lines 46–72), Ackerman takes her audience back above the Earth, "floating," but this time in an airplane. How does this paragraph contribute to Ackerman's movement of ideas?
4. Paragraph 4 (lines 73–104) begins with images of delicacy and concludes with images of responsibility. Note the beginning of the persuasive qualities of this paragraph and explain the effect of this movement.

Writing

1. **Analysis** — Write an essay in which you analyze how Ackerman's rhetorical strategies convey her attitude toward human responsibility for the Earth.
2. **Argument/Imitation** — Write an argument for the preservation or the economic development of Earth's natural environment. Model Ackerman's arrangement and attention to visual images.

The photograph is one of several taken by the Apollo 17 astronauts.

First Reading

1. List each detail you can identify in the photograph.
2. Explain what seems to move, and comment about what you know moves but cannot see.
3. What does the photographer's attitude toward the image seem to be?
4. What effect does the medium have on the message of the visual text? Consider, for example, how that message might be different if you were viewing a watercolor or a sculpture.

Second Reading

1. What overall impression does the text create for you?
2. What cultural values does the text suggest?
3. How would Diane Ackerman and Annie Dillard describe the photograph? What about Lewis Thomas?
4. As you read more of the selections in this chapter, consider how Chief Seattle and Vaclav Havel would describe the photograph.

Writing

1. **Exposition/Photo Essay** — Compose a collage of images that present our planet in ways that others might not consider important. Write captions for each image, and write an expository essay that conveys your attitude toward each image in your collection. Document each source, including photographs or other media of your own creation, that you use.

2. **Persuasive** — Write a letter to the editor of your local newspaper or to the editor of a news magazine. Persuade the editor to consider pointing out aspects of human interaction with and human responsibility for the natural world that are often overlooked. You might consider ways the print media can add importance to public awareness of such issues.

Chief Seattle, Suquamish
Respect

In 1854, the "Great White Chief" in Washington made an offer for a large area of Indian land and promised a reservation for the Indian people. The following was Chief Seattle's reply. Translated by Dr. Henry A. Smith, this version of Chief Seattle's speech appeared in the *Seattle Sunday Star* on Oct. 29, 1887. Dr. Smith, who spoke Suquamish, makes it clear that his version is not an exact copy, but rather the best he could put together from notes taken at the time.

How can you buy or sell the sky, the warmth of the land? The idea is strange to us. If we do not own the freshness of the air and the sparkle of the water, how can you buy them? Every part of the earth is sacred to my people. Every shining pine needle, every sandy shore, every mist in the dark woods, every clearing and humming insect is holy in the memory and experience of my people. The sap which courses through the trees carries the memories of the red man.

The white man's dead forget the country of their birth when they go to walk among the stars. Our dead never forget this beautiful earth, for it is the mother of the red man. We are part of the earth and it is part of us. The perfumed flowers are our sisters, the deer, the horse, the great eagle, these are our brothers. The rocky crests, the juices in the meadows, the body heat of the pony, and man—all belong to the same family.

So, when the Great Chief in Washington sends word that he wishes to buy our land, he asks much of us. The great Chief sends word that he will reserve us a place so that we can live comfortably to ourselves. He will be our father and we will be his children. So we will consider your offer to buy our land. But it will not be easy. For this land is sacred to us.

This shining water that moves in the streams and rivers is not just water but the blood of our ancestors. If we sell you land, you must remember that it is sacred, and you must teach your children that it is sacred and that each ghostly reflection in the clear water of the lakes tells of events and memories in the life of my people. The water's murmur is the voice of my father's father. The rivers are our brothers, they quench our thirst. The rivers carry our canoes, and feed our children. If we sell you our land, you must remember, and teach your children, that the rivers are our brothers, and yours, and you must henceforth give the rivers the kindness you would give any brother.

We know that the white man does not understand our ways. One portion of the land is the same to him as the next, for he is a stranger who comes in the night and takes from the land whatever he needs. The earth is not his brother, but his enemy, and when he has conquered it, he moves on. He leaves his father's grave behind, and he does not care. He kidnaps the earth from his children and he does not care. His father's grave and his children's birthright are forgotten. He treats his mother, the earth, and his brother, the sky, as things to be bought, plundered, sold like sheep or bright beads. His appetite will devour the earth and leave behind only a desert.

I do not know. Our ways are different from your ways. The sight of your cities pains the eyes of the red man. But perhaps it is because the red man is a savage and does not understand. There is no quiet place in the white man's cities. No place to hear the unfurling of leaves in spring, or the rustle of an insect's wings. But perhaps it is because I am a savage and do not understand. The clatter only seems to insult the ears. And what is there to life if a man cannot hear the lonely cry of the whippoorwill or the arguments of the frogs around a pond at night? I am a red man and do not understand. The Indian prefers the soft sound of the wind darting over the face of a pond, and the smell of the wind itself, cleaned by a midday rain, or scented with pinion pine. The air is precious to the red man, for all things share the same breath—the beast, the tree, the man, they all share the same breath. The white man does not seem to notice the air he breathes. Like a man dying for many days, he is numb to the stench.

But if we sell you our land, you must remember that the air is precious to us, that the air shares its spirit with all the life it supports. The wind that gave our grandfather his first breath also receives his last sigh. And if we sell you our land, you must keep it apart and sacred, as a place where even the white man can go to taste the wind that it is sweetened by the meadow's flowers.

So we will consider your offer to buy our land. If we decide to accept, I will make one condition:

the white man must treat the beasts of the land as his brothers. I am a savage and do not understand any other way. I have seen a thousand rotting buffaloes on the prairie, left by the white man who shot them from a passing train. I am a savage and I do not understand how the smoking iron horse can be more important than the buffalo that we kill only to stay alive. What is man without beasts? If all the beasts were gone, man would die from great loneliness of spirit. For whatever happens to beasts, soon happens to man. All things are connected.

You must teach your children that the ground beneath their feet is the ashes of your grandfathers. So that they will respect the land, tell your children that the earth is rich with the lives of our kin. Teach your children what we have taught our children, that the earth is our mother. Whatever befalls the earth befalls the sons of the earth. If men spit upon the ground, they spit upon themselves.

This we know: the earth does not belong to man; man belongs to the earth. This we know. All things are connected like the blood which unites one family. All things are connected.

Whatever befalls the earth befalls the sons of the earth. Man did not weave the web of life: he is merely a strand in it. Whatever he does to the web he does to himself. Even the white man, whose God walks and talks with him as friend to friend, cannot be exempt from the common destiny. We may be brothers after all. We shall see.

One thing which we know, which the white man may one day discover—our God is the same God. You may think you own Him as you wish to own our land; but you cannot. He is the God of man, and His compassion is equal for the red man and the white. This earth is precious to him, and to harm the earth is to heap contempt on its Creator.

The whites too shall pass; perhaps sooner than all the other tribes. Contaminate your bed, and you will one night suffocate in your own waste. But in your perishing you will shine brightly, fired by the strength of the God who brought you to this land and for some special purpose gave you dominion over this land and over the red man.

That destiny is a mystery to us, for we do not understand when the buffalo are all slaughtered, the wild horses are tamed, the secret corners of the forest heavy with the scent of many men, and the view of the ripe hills blotted by talking wires. Where is the thicket? Gone. Where is the eagle? Gone. The end of living and the beginning of survival.

First Reading

1. Determine the focus of each paragraph. Annotate the text to identify images and details.
2. Trace the elements of Chief Seattle's focus on the smallest elements of existence.

Second Reading

1. Note the importance of the third sentence in paragraph 1 (lines 2–4). Then consider the statements that follow. For example, the last sentence of paragraph 1 suggests a physical connection between "the red man" and the land. Then, in paragraph 2 (lines 11–19), he emphasizes that connection. Explain how Seattle's emphasis on the physical reflects his view of the earth as family.
2. In paragraph 3 (lines 20–27), Chief Seattle explains the logic of paragraphs 1 and 2. Consider the significance of the word "sacred" in his explanation. Also note his repetition of the word, and explain how the repetition adds emphasis to his logic.
3. In paragraph 4 (lines 28–41), Chief Seattle suggests responsibility for the earth, and this suggestion precedes the condition he describes in paragraph 8 (lines 85–98). How does this early suggestion of responsibility confirm the planned organization of his speech?
4. In paragraph 5 (lines 42–55), Chief Seattle emphasizes the difference in attitudes toward the earth and places a special emphasis on the attitude of the conqueror. Explain what you think might be his reason for including this paragraph.
5. Consider the reasons for and the effect of Chief Seattle's reference to himself as a savage in paragraph 6 (lines 56–76). In this paragraph he also describes what does not exist in cities and repeats the comment about being a savage who does not understand. Consider also the significance of the words "precious" and "numb" in the paragraph.

6. Notice the repetition of "precious" and "sacred" in paragraph 7 (lines 77–84). How does this paragraph confirm a permanence of connection with the Earth? Read again the last two sentences of paragraph 8. Explain the wisdom expressed in these two sentences.

Writing

1. **Argument/Imitation** — Write Chief Seattle's speech in your own words. Craft your appeals to logos, ethos, and pathos suitable for the audience you choose. Consider audiences who may not welcome your ideas.

2. **Synthesis** — Consider this statement from Chief Seattle, "Man did not weave the web of life: he is merely a strand in it." Select from any of the texts in this chapter to defend, challenge, or qualify Chief Seattle's position. Cite evidence from at least three of these sources and refer to each by the author's last name.

Tim Flannery
The Weather Makers

Professor Flannery was named Australian of the Year for 2007. According to the Prime Minister, "He has encouraged Australians into new ways of thinking about our environmental history and future ecological challenges." This essay, entitled "The Slow Awakening," is the first chapter of Professor Flannery's book, published in 2005.

In 1981, when I was in my midtwenties, I climbed Mt. Albert Edward, one of the highest peaks on the verdant island of New Guinea. Although only seventy-four miles from Papua New
5 Guinea's national capital, Port Moresby, the region around Mt. Albert Edward is so rugged that the last significant biological work conducted there was by an expedition from the American Museum of Natural History in the early 1930s.
10 The bronzed grasslands were a stark contrast to the green jungle all around, and among the tussocks grew groves of tree ferns, whose lacy fronds waved above my head. Wallaby tracks threaded from the forest edge to the herbfields that flour-
15 ished in damp hollows, and the scratchings and burrows of yardlong rats and the traces where long-beaked creatures, I later discovered, were unique to such alpine regions.

Downslope, the tussock grassland ended
20 abruptly at a stunted, mossy forest. A single step could carry you from sunshine into the dank gloom, where the pencil-thin saplings on the margin were so festooned with moss, lichens, and filmy ferns that they ballooned to the diameter of
25 my waist. In the leaf litter on the forest floor, I was surprised to find the trunks of dead tree ferns. Tree ferns grew only in the grassland, so here was clear evidence that the forest was colonizing the slope from below. Judging from the distribution
30 of the tree fern trunks, it had swallowed at least thirty yards of grassland in less time than it takes for a tree fern to rot on the damp forest floor—a decade or two at most.

Why was the forest expanding? As I pondered
35 the moldering trunks I remembered reading that New Guinea's glaciers were melting. Had the temperature on Mt. Albert Edward warmed enough to permit trees to grow where previously only grasses could take root? And, if so, was this
40 evidence of climate change? My doctoral studies were in paleontology, so I knew how important changes in climate have been in determining the fate of species. But this was the first evidence I'd seen that it might affect Earth during my lifetime.

45 The experience left me troubled; I knew there was something wrong but not quite what it was.

Despite the good position I was in to understand the significance of these observations, I soon forgot about them. This was partly because,
50 as I studied the various ancient ecosystems that our generation has inherited, seemingly bigger and more urgent issues demanded my attention. And some of the crises did seem dire: The rain forests that I was studying were being felled for tim-
55 ber and to make agricultural land, and the larger animal species living there were being hunted to extinction. In my own country of Australia, rising salt was threatening to destroy the most fertile soils, while overgrazing, degradation of wa-
60 terways, and the logging of forests all threatened precious ecosystems and biodiversity. To me these were the truly pressing issues.

Whether we are crossing the road or paying the bills, it is the big, fast-moving things that com-
65 mand our attention. But seemingly large issues sometimes turn out to be a sideshow. The Y2K bug is one such example. Around the globe many governments and companies spent billions to prepare themselves against the threat, while others
70 spent nothing; and 1999 gave way to 2000 with barely a hiccup, let alone an apocalypse. A skeptical eye is our greatest asset in dealing with this type of "problem." And deep skepticism has a particularly important role to play in science, for
75 a theory is only valid as long as it has not been disproved. Scientists are in fact trained skeptics, and this eternal questioning of their own and others' work may give the impression that you can always find an expert who will champion any
80 conceivable view.

While such skepticism is the lifeblood of science, it can have drawbacks when society is called on to combat real dangers. For decades both the tobacco and asbestos industries found scientists
85 prepared publicly to be doubtful of the discoveries linking their products with cancer. A nonspecialist cannot know whether the view being presented is fringe or mainstream thinking, and so we may

come to believe that there is a real division in the scientific community on these matters. In the case of the asbestos and tobacco, the situation was made worse because cancers often appear years after exposure to carcinogenic products, and no one can say for certain just who, among the many exposed, will be struck down. By creating doubt about the link between their products and cancer, the tobacco and asbestos companies enjoyed decades of fat profits, while millions of people met terrible deaths.

And many people have reacted with rightful caution to news about climate change. After all, we have in the past got things badly wrong.

In the 1972 publication *The Limits to Growth*, the Club of Rome told us the world was running out of resources and predicted catastrophe within decades. In an era of excessive consumption this imagined drought of raw materials gripped the public imagination, even though no one knew with any degree of certainty what volume of resources lay hidden in the earth. Subsequent geological exploration has revealed just how wide of the mark our estimates of mineral resources were back then, and even today no one can accurately predict the volume of oil, gold, and other materials beneath our feet.

The climate change issue is different. It results from air pollution, and the size of our atmosphere and the volume of pollutants that we are pouring into it are known with great precision. The debate now, and the story I want to explore here, concerns the impacts of some of those pollutants (known as greenhouse gases) on all life on Earth.

Is climate change a terrible threat or a beat-up? A bang or a whimper? Perhaps it is something in between—an issue that humanity must eventually face, but not yet. The world's media abound with evidence to support any of these views. Yet perusing that same media makes one thing clear: Climate change is difficult for people to evaluate dispassionately because it entails deep political and industrial implications, and because it arises from the core processes of our civilization's success. This means that, as we seek to address this problem, winners and losers will be created. The stakes are high, and this has led to a proliferation of misleading stories as special interest groups argue their case.

What's more, climate change is a breaking story. Just over thirty years ago the experts were at loggerheads about whether Earth was warming or cooling—unable to decide whether an icehouse or a greenhouse future was on the way. By 1975, however, the first sophisticated computer models were suggesting that a doubling of carbon dioxide (CO_2) in the atmosphere would lead to an increase in global temperature of around five degrees Fahrenheit. Still, concern among both scientists and the community was not significant. There was even a period of optimism, when some researchers believed that extra CO_2 in the atmosphere would fertilize the world's croplands and produce a bonanza for farmers.

But by 1988 climate scientists had become sufficiently worried about CO_2 to establish a panel, staffed with the world's leading experts, to report twice each decade on the issue. Their third report, issued in 2001, sounded a note of sober alarm—yet many governments and industry leaders were slow to take an interest. Because concern about climate change is so new, and the issue is so multidisciplinary, there are few true experts in the field, and even fewer who can articulate what the problem might mean to the general public and what we should do about it.

For years I resisted the impulse to devote research time to climate change. I was busy with other things, and I wanted to wait and see, hoping an issue so big would sort itself out. Perhaps it would be centuries before we would need to think intensively about it. But by 2001, articles in scientific journals indicated that the world's alpine environments were under severe threat. As I read them, I remembered those rotting tree fern trunks in Mt. Albert Edward's forest, and I knew that I had to learn more. This meant teaching myself about greenhouse gases, the structure of our atmosphere, and how the industrialized world powers its engines of growth.

For the last 10,000 years, Earth's thermostat has been set to an average surface temperature of around 57 degrees Fahrenheit. On the whole, this has suited our species splendidly, and we have been able to organize ourselves in a most impressive manner—planting crops, domesticating animals, and building cities. Finally, over the past century, we have created a truly global civilization. Given that in all of Earth's history the only other creatures able to organize themselves on a similar scale are ants, bees, and termites—which are tiny in comparison and have concomitantly small resources requirements—this is quite an achievement.

Earth's thermostat is a complex and delicate mechanism, at the heart of which lies carbon dioxide, a colorless and odorless gas. CO_2 plays a critical role in maintaining the balance necessary to all life. It is also a waste product of the fossil fuels that almost every person on the planet uses for heat, transport, and other energy requirements. On dead planets such as Venus and Mars,

200 CO_2 makes up most of the atmosphere, and it would do so here if living things and Earth's process did not keep it within bounds. Our planet's rocks and water are packed with carbon itching to get airborne and oxidized. As it is, CO_2 makes up
205 around 3 parts per 10,000 in Earth's atmosphere. It's a modest amount, yet it has a disproportionate influence on the planet's temperature. Because we create CO_2 every time we drive a car, cook a meal, or turn on a light, and because the gas lasts
210 around a century in the atmosphere, the portion of CO_2 in the air we breathe is rapidly increasing.

The institutions at the forefront of climate change research are situated half a world away from my home in Adelaide, so for a time I flew
215 frequently across the globe. One night when en route from Singapore to London, as we crossed the great Eurasian landmass, I looked out of the cabin window at a city illuminated below. Its network of lights stretched from horizon to horizon,
220 and the lights burned so bright—with so much energy—as to alarm me. From a height of 33,000 feet the atmosphere seemed so thin and fragile—the breathable part of it lay 16,500 feet below our aircraft. I asked the airline steward where we were.
225 She gave me the name of a city I didn't know. With a jolt I realized that the world is full of such cities, whose fossil-fuel-driven lights cause our planet to blaze into the night sky.

By late 2004, my interest had turned to anxiety.
230 The world's leading science journals were full of reports that glaciers were melting ten times faster than previously thought, that atmospheric greenhouse gases had reached levels not seen for millions for years, and that species were vanishing as
235 a result of climate change. There were also reports of extreme weather events, long-term droughts, and rising sea levels.

For months I tried to fault the new research findings and discussed them at length with
240 friends and colleagues. Only a few people seemed aware of the great changes under way in our atmosphere. And some people I loved and respected continued doing things—such as buying large cars and air conditioners—that I now suspected to
245 be very bad indeed.

By the end of the year, however, glimmers of hope were beginning to emerge, with almost every head of government in the developed world alive to the issue. But we cannot wait for the is-
250 sue to be solved for us. The most important thing to realize is that we can all make a difference and help combat climate change at almost no cost to our lifestyle. And in this, climate change is very different from other environmental issues, such as
255 biodiversity loss and the ozone hole.

The best evidence indicates that we need to reduce our CO_2 emissions by 70 percent by 2050. If you own a four-wheel-drive and replace it with a hybrid fuel car, you can achieve a cut of that mag-
260 nitude in a day rather than half a century. If your electricity provider offers a green option, for the cost of a daily cup of coffee you will be able to make equally major cuts in your household emissions. And if you vote for a politician who has a
265 deep commitment to reducing CO_2 emissions, you might change the world. If you alone can achieve so much, so too can every individual and, in time, industry and government on Earth.

The transition to carbon-free economy is emi-
270 nently achievable because we have all the technology we need to do so. It is only a lack of understanding and the pessimism and confusion generated by special interest groups that is stopping us from going forward.
275 One thing that I hear again and again as I discuss climate change with friends, family, and colleagues is that it is something that may affect humanity in decades to come but is no immediate threat to us. I'm far from certain that that is
280 true, and I'm not sure it is even relevant. IF serious change or the effects of serious change are decades away, that is just a long tomorrow. Whenever my family gathers for a special event, the true scale of climate change is never far from my mind. My
285 mother, who was born during the Great Depression—when motor vehicles and electric lights were still novelties—positively glows in the company of her grandchildren, some of whom are not yet ten. To see them together is to see a chain of the deepest
290 love that spans 150 years, for those grand-children will not reach my mother's present age until late in this century. To me, to her, and to their parents, their welfare is every bit as important as our own. On a broader scale, 70 percent of all people alive
295 today will still be alive in 2050, so climate change affects almost every family on this planet.

A final issue that looms large in discussions is the one of certainty. Four nations are yet to sign the Kyoto Protocol limiting CO_2 emissions: the
300 U.S.A., Australia, Monaco, and Liechtenstein. President George W. Bush has said he wants "more certainty" before he acts on climate change; yet science is about hypotheses, not truths, and no one can absolutely know the future. But this does
305 not stop us from making forecasts and modifying our behavior accordingly. If, for example, we wait to see if an ailment is indeed fatal, we will do nothing until we are dead. And when it comes to more mundane matters, uncertainty hardly de-
310 ters us." We spend large sums on our children's education with no guarantee of a good outcome,

and we buy shares with no promise of a return. Excepting death and taxes, certainty simply does not exist in our world, and yet we often manage our lives in the most efficient manner. I cannot see why our response to climate change should be any different.

One of the biggest obstacles to making a start on climate change is that it has become a cliché before it has even been understood. What we need now is good information and careful thinking, because in the years to come this issue will dwarf all the others combined. It will become the *only* issue. We need to reexamine it in a truly skeptical spirit—to see how big it is and how fast it's moving—so that we can prioritize our efforts and resources in ways that matter.

What follows is my best effort, based on the work of thousands of colleagues, to outline the history of climate change, how it will unfold over the next century, and what we can do about it. With great scientific advances being made every month, this book is necessarily incomplete. That should not, however, be used as an excuse for inaction. We know enough to act wisely.

First Reading

1. Paraphrase each paragraph with one sentence.
2. Note the focus of each paragraph, and identify dates, details, and diction.

Second Reading

1. Explain how the details in paragraph 2 (lines 10–18) expand the meaning of the word "verdant" in paragraph 1.
2. In paragraph 3 (lines 19–33), Flannery continues his description of the region, and in paragraph 4 (lines 34–46) he describes a troubling discovery. Explain why you think he might have included these two paragraphs. What reasons does Flannery give in paragraph 5 (lines 47–62) to explain why he forgets the situation he discovered?
3. Paragraph 6 (lines 63–80) shifts to a different focus. Explain the significance of the anecdote and how it contributes to Flannery's view of global issues.
4. How large a group in the global population would you estimate to be nonspecialists? What should the "nonspecialist" know about global issues? Why might Flannery call our attention to the "skepticism" of the scientist?
5. In paragraph 9 (lines 103–115), Flannery begins his presentation of "predicted catastrophe," but in paragraph 10 (lines 116–122) he states, "The climate change issue is different." The remainder of the first section continues with dates, scientific language, and examples and concludes with his remembrance of "the rotting tree fern trunks." How does this series of paragraphs lead logically to the transitional last sentence of paragraph 14 (lines 175–178)?
6. Paragraphs 15–26 (lines 179–335) complete the essay with more dates, details, and examples. Note the significance of each anecdote and explain how it contributes to Flannery's claim that we cannot resort to "inaction."

Reread the passage, and annotate the essay, carefully noting the impact of particular words, phrases, and details upon your understanding of the text. Then answer these reading comprehension questions. After each one, explain what the question asked you to do or know and why you answered as you did.

1. The essay as a whole is best described as

    (A) a scientific revelation.
    (B) an urgent consideration.
    (C) a reflective chronology.
    (D) an elegant diatribe.
    (E) a considered investigation.

2. In Flannery's reference to Y2K in paragraph 6 (lines 63–80), he states "seemingly large issues sometimes turn out to be a sideshow." He urges

    (A) proscription and caution.
    (B) prevention and preparation.
    (C) concern and urgency.
    (D) calculation and preservation.
    (E) caution and skepticism.

3. In describing his mother and his family, Flannery emphasizes

    (A) permanence.
    (B) humanity.
    (C) evidence.
    (D) prescience.
    (E) fragility.

4. Flannery's attitude toward the actuality of climate change is primarily one of

    (A) disapproval.
    (B) fascination.
    (C) cynicism.
    (D) propitiousness.
    (E) fanaticism.

5. Flannery's tone at the conclusion is primarily one of

    (A) catastrophic skepticism.
    (B) speculative transition.
    (C) cautious urgency.
    (D) calamitous destruction.
    (E) skeptical progression.

Writing

1. **Analysis** — Write an essay in which you analyze Flannery's rhetorical choices in conveying his view that climate change will "become the *only* issue" in the years to come.

2. **Argument** — Conduct your own investigation into the issues of climate. Write a researched argument that defends, challenges, or qualifies Flannery's statement that "We know enough to act wisely."

Vaclav Havel
The Quiver of a Shrub in California

Vaclav Havel is the former prime minister of the Czech Republic. This speech was delivered in 1991 at a university in California.

In my country forests are dying, rivers resemble open sewers, people are sometimes advised not to open their windows, and television advertises gas masks for children to wear on their way to and 5 from school. Mine is a small country in the middle of Europe where the borders between Welds have been destroyed, the land is eroding, the soil is disintegrating and poisoned by chemical fertilizers that in turn contaminate the groundwater, 10 where birds that used to live in the Welds have lost their nesting places and are dying out, while agronomists are forced to combat pests with more chemicals. My country supplies the whole of Europe with a strange export: sulfur dioxide.

15 For years I was one of those who criticized all this; now, I am one of those who are criticized for it. When I think about what has brought about this terrible state of affairs and encounter on a daily basis obstacles that keep us from taking quick action 20 to change it, I cannot help concluding that its root causes are less technical or economic in nature than philosophical. For what I see in Marxist ideology and the communist pattern of rule is an extreme and cautionary instance of the arrogance 25 of modern man, who styles himself the master of nature and the world, the only one who understands them, the one everything must serve, the one for whom our planet exists. Intoxicated by the achievements of his mind, by modern science and 30 technology, he forgets that his knowledge has limits and that beyond these limits lies a great mystery, something higher and infinitely more sophisticated than his own intellect.

I am increasingly inclined to believe that even 35 the term "environment," which is inscribed on the banners of many commendable civic movements, is in its own way misguided, because it is unwittingly the product of the very anthropocentrism that has caused extensive devastation of our 40 earth. The word "environment" tacitly implies that whatever is not human merely envelops us and is therefore inferior to us, something we need care for only if it is in our interest to do so. I do not believe this to be the case. The world is not 45 divided into two types of being, one superior and the other merely surrounding it. Being, nature, the universe—they are all one infinitely complex and mysterious metaorganism of which we are but a part, though a unique one.

50 Everyone of us is a crossroads of thousands of relations, links, influences, and communications— physical, chemical, biological, and others of which we know nothing. While without humans there would have been no *Challenger* space shuttle, there 55 would have been no humans without air, water, earth, without thousands of fortitudes that cannot be fortuitous and thanks to which there can be a planet on which there can be life. And while each of us is a very special and complex network 60 of space, time, matter, and energy, we are nothing more than their network; we are unthinkable without them, and without the order of the universe, whose dimensions they are.

None of us knows how the quiver of a shrub in 65 California affects the mental state of a coal miner in North Bohemia or how his mental state affects the quivering of the shrub. I believe that we have little chance of averting an environmental catastrophe unless we recognize that we are not the 70 masters of Being, but only a part of Being, and it makes little difference that we are the only part of Being known so far that is not only conscious of its own being but is even conscious of the fact that it will one day come to an end.

75 Yet anyone who has said "A" must also say "B." Having recognized that we are no more than a tiny particle in the grand physical structure of things, we must eventually recognize that we are also no more than a speck in the grand metaphysi-80 cal structure of things. We must recognize that we are related to more than the present moment, the present place, that we are related to the world as a whole and to eternity. We must recognize that, by failing to reflect universal, superindividual, 85 and supertemporal interests, we do a disservice to our specific, local and immediate interests. Only people with a sense of responsibility for the world and to the world are truly responsible to and for themselves.

90 The Communist rulers of Czechoslovakia acted according to the principle of *"après nous le deluge."* Hoping that no one would notice, they secured

absolute power for themselves by bribing the entire population with money stolen from future generations. Miners extracting low-quality brown coal from open-face mines—coal that was then burnt without filters or scrubbers—were satisfied because they could easily buy VCRs and then, tired from work, they sat down to watch a video, not noticing that the children watching with them have pus flowing from their eyes.

Their wives noticed. Glad as they were that their husbands were earning relatively decent wages, they began to suspect what those wages represented; they began to realize that had the wages been lower and difference invested in cleaner, more efficient means of generating power, their children would not have chronic conjunctivitis. *"Après nous le deluge"* is the principle of a man who has forgotten that he is only a part of the world, not its owner, of a man who feels no relation to eternity and styles himself a master of space and time.

I believe that the devastation of the environment brought about by the Communist regimes is a warning to all contemporary civilization. I believe that you should read the message coming to you from our part of the world as an appeal to protect the world against all those who despise the mystery of being, whether they be cynical businessmen with only the interest of their corporations at heart, or left-wing saviors high on cheap ideological utopias. Both lack what I would call a metaphysical anchor, that is, a humble respect for the whole of creation, and a consciousness of our obligation to it.

It is not my intention to lecture anyone, but I have felt it necessary to share with you the philosophical experience that I, like so many of my fellow citizens, have gained in the environment I come from. I would say that this experience is the principal article that we can and should expect from my country at this time.

Were I to encapsulate that experience in one sentence, I would probably phrase it as follows: If parents believe in God, their children will not have to go to school wearing gas masks, and their eyes will be free of pus.

First Reading

1. Paraphrase each paragraph with one sentence. Note details and images.
2. Find definitions for any words with which you are unfamiliar.

Second Reading

1. The first paragraph begins with a sentence that startles and follows with images of destruction. Considering his topic, how is this paragraph an effective beginning for Havel's speech?

2. What does Havel suggest is the primary "obstacle" that created the situation he later describes?

3. Explain what you think Havel means by "metaorganism" in paragraph 3 (lines 34–49). How does Havel explain the human connection to the universe in paragraph 4 (lines 50–63)? In paragraph 5 (lines 64–74), Havel comments that we are "only a part of Being." How does this statement lead logically to the following statement from paragraph 6 (lines 75–89): "We must recognize that by failing to reflect universal, superindividual, and supertemporal interests, we do a disservice to our specific, local, and immediate interests"?

4. Explain what you consider Havel's reason for including the shocking image that concludes paragraph 7 (lines 95–101). Havel continues exploring this image in paragraph 8 (lines 102–113). Why does this continued explanation lead logically to his final comment in paragraph 8?

5. Paragraphs 9–11 (lines 114–138) constitute the conclusion of the speech. How does he explain the "warning to all contemporary civilization"? What does he suggest as a recourse, and why does he end by repeating the shocking image?

Read the passage carefully, and annotate the speech, carefully noting the impact of particular words, phrases, and details upon your understanding of the text. Then answer these reading comprehension questions. After each one, explain what the question asked you to do or know and why you answered as you did.

1. Which of the following best describes the rhetorical function of the imagery in the first sentence of paragraph 1?

    (A) It conveys a sense of desperation.
    (B) It provides a specific example of devastation.
    (C) It precludes a criticism.
    (D) It introduces communist ideology.
    (E) It presents an example that conveys attitude.

2. Which of the following words does the author use to illustrate the central idea of the claim?

    (A) "obstacles"
    (B) "ideology"
    (C) "technology"
    (D) "anthropocentrism"
    (E) "metaorganism"

3. In paragraph 5 (lines 64–74), "Being" refers to

    (A) "the one everything must serve" (paragraph 2)
    (B) "commendable civic movements" (paragraph 3)
    (C) "crossroads of thousands of relations" (paragraph 3)
    (D) "nature, the universe" (paragraph 3)
    (E) "thousands of fortitudes" (paragraph 3)

4. The author's observation in the sentence beginning "Only people with a sense…" in paragraph 6 (lines 87–89), is best described as an example of which of the following?

    (A) the speaker's charge against society
    (B) the speaker's claim in the argument
    (C) the speaker's assumption about the audience
    (D) the speaker's appeal to pathos
    (E) the speaker's concession

5. The author's tone in the passage as a whole is best described as

    (A) informal and analytical.
    (B) contemplative and accusative.
    (C) strident and urgent.
    (D) urgent and incisive.
    (E) appealing and respectful.

Writing

1. **Analysis** — Write an essay in which you analyze Havel's rhetorical choices in conveying his view that we have a responsibility to protect the environment and its inhabitants. You might consider Havel's arrangement and images.
2. **Argument/Imitation** — Havel's topic and language are complex. Write an essay in which you defend, challenge, or qualify Havel's claim that "Only people with a sense of responsibility for the world and to the world are truly responsible to and for themselves." Your argument should be as complex in ideas and language as Havel's.

Chapter 7
Boxing

Background

Few humans box, yet few human activities have, over so many centuries and in so many civilizations, generated such intense interest, attention, and controversy as boxing. Its fans passionately celebrate what author A. J. Leibling called "the sweet science," while its detractors relentlessly vilify it as a brutal undertaking. What is clear is that many people are passionately attracted to the ring, its rituals, and its results. Many writers have embraced boxing as a subject, sometimes to extol its benefits, sometimes to bemoan its consequences, sometimes to tell its stories. Boxing presents its audience with contradictions. Some celebrate its graceful, majestic appeal while denying its bitter, brutal truths. Others decry its dangers and destructiveness. In truth, boxing involves commitment, conditioning, endurance of pain, and an understanding of defeat.

An ancient enterprise, boxing is an extreme athletic undertaking. Such extremity makes boxing a particularly exceptional subject of study, even now as its popularity fades. What accounts for its attraction? Why, despite its well-documented dangers, does boxing continue to captivate? What accounts for its special character? Why are representations of and arguments about boxing so compelling and powerful? What about boxing moves us so profoundly to view, read, think, and write about it?

Readings

William Hazlitt
The Fight

Robert Anasi
A Way of Life

Joyce Carol Oates
On Boxing

Neil Leifer
Muhammed Ali vs. Sonny Liston

Mike Lowe
A Picture Perfect Ending

Gordon Marino
Boxing and the Cool Halls of Academe

George Will
Barbarity of Boxing

Hugh McIlvanney
The Case for the Hardest Game

William Hazlitt
The Fight

In December, 1821, William Hazlitt traveled from London and stayed at a Newbury Coaching Inn before continuing to Hungerford, Berkshire, where he watched William Neate fight Thomas Hickman, known as "Gas-Man" to fans. His subsequent essay, "The Fight," was published in the *New Monthly Magazine* in February, 1822. The two excerpts include the essay's introductory paragraph followed by a detailed account of the fight itself.

Where there's a will, there's a way – I said so to my-self, as I walked down Chancery-lane, about half-past six o'clock on Monday the 10th of December, to inquire at Jack Randall's where the fight the
5 next day was to be; and I found "the proverb" nothing "musty" in the present instance. I was determined to see this fight, come what would, and see it I did, in great style. It was my *first fight*, yet it more than answered my expectations. La-
10 dies! it is to you I dedicate this description; nor let it seem out of character for the fair to notice the exploits of the brave. Courage and modesty are the old English virtues; and may they never look cold and askance on one another! Think, ye
15 fairest of the fair, loveliest of the lovely kind, ye practisers of soft enchantment, how many more ye kill with poisoned baits than ever fell in the ring; and listen with subdued air and without shuddering, to a tale tragic only in appearance,
20 and sacred to the FANCY!

***

Reader, have you ever seen a fight? If not, you have a pleasure to come, at least if it is a fight like that between the Gas-man and Bill Neate. The
25 crowd was very great when we arrived on the spot; open carriages were coming up, with streamers flying and music playing, and the country-people were pouring in over hedge and ditch in all direc-tions, to see their hero beat or be beaten. The odds
30 were still on Gas, but only about five to four. Gul-ly had been down to try Neate, and had backed him considerably, which was a damper to the san-guine confidence of the adverse party. About two hundred thousand pounds were pending. The
35 Gas says, he has lost £3,000, which were prom-ised him by different gentlemen if he had won. He had presumed too much on himself, which had made others presume on him. This spirited and formidable young fellow seems to have taken
40 for his motto the old maxim, that "there are three things necessary to success in life – *Impudence! Im-pudence! Impudence!*" It is so in matters of opinion, but not in the *FANCY*, which is the most practical

of all things, though even here confidence is half
45 the battle, but only half. Our friend had vapoured and swaggered too much, as if he wanted to grin and bully his adversary out of the fight. "Alas! the Bristol man was not so tamed!" – "This is the grave digger" (would Tom Hickman exclaim in
50 the moments of intoxication from gin and success, showing his tremendous right hand), "this will send many of them to their long homes; I haven't done with them yet!" Why should he – though he had licked four of the best men within the hour,
55 yet why should he threaten to inflict dishonour-able chastisement on my old master Richmond, a veteran going off the stage, and who has borne his sable honours meekly? Magnanimity, my dear Tom, and bravery, should be inseparable. Or why
60 should he go up to his antagonist, the first time he ever saw him at the Fives Court, and measuring him from head to foot with a glance of contempt, as Achilles surveyed Hector, say to him, "What, are you Bill Neate? I'll knock more blood out of
65 that great carcase of thine, this day fortnight, than you ever knock'd out of a bullock's!" It was not manly, 'twas not fighter-like. If he was sure of the victory (as he was not), the less said about it the better. Modesty should accompany the FANCY
70 as its shadow. The best men were always the best behaved. Jem Belcher, the Game Chicken (before whom the Gas-man could not have lived) were civil, silent men. So is Cribb, so is Tom Belcher, the most elegant of sparrers, and not a man for
75 every one to take by the nose. I enlarged on this topic in the mail (while Turtle was asleep), and said very wisely (as I thought) that impertinence was a part of no profession. A boxer was bound to beat his man, but not to thrust his fist, either actu-
80 ally or by implication, in every one's face. Even a highwayman, in the way of trade, may blow out your brains, but if he uses foul language at the same time, I should say he was no gentleman. A boxer, I would infer, need not be a blackguard
85 or a coxcomb, more than another. Perhaps I press this point too much on a fallen man – Mr. Thomas

Hickman has by this time learnt that first of all lessons, "That man was made to mourn." He has lost nothing by the late fight but his presumption;
90 and that every man may do as well without! By an overly-display of this quality, however, the public has been prejudiced against him, and the knowing-ones were taken in. Few but those who had bet on him wished Gas to win. With my own pre-
95 possessions on the subject, the result of the 11th of December appeared to me as fine a piece of poetical justice as I had ever witnessed. The difference of weight between the two combatants (14 stone to 12) was nothing to the sporting men. Great, heavy,
100 clumsy, long-armed Bill Neate kicked the beam in the scale of the Gas-man's vanity. The amateurs were frightened at his big words, and thought that they would make up for the difference of six feet and five feet nine. Truly, the FANCY are not men
105 of imagination. They judge of what has been, and cannot conceive of anything that is to be. The Gas-man had won hitherto; therefore he must beat a man half as big again as himself – and that to a certainty. Besides, there are as many feuds, fac-
110 tions, prejudices, pedantic notions in the FANCY as in the state or in the schools. Mr. Gully is almost the only cool, sensible man among them, who exercises an unbiassed discretion, and is not a slave to his passions in these matters. But enough of re-
115 flections, and to our tale. The day, as I have said, was fine for a December morning. The grass was wet, and the ground miry, and ploughed up with multitudinous feet, except that, within the ring itself, there was a spot of virgin-green closed in
120 and unprofaned by vulgar tread, that shone with dazzling brightness in the mid-day sun. For it was noon now, and we had an hour to wait. This is the trying time. It is then the heart sickens, as you think what the two champions are about, and
125 how short a time will determine their fate. After the first blow is struck, there is no opportunity for nervous apprehensions; you are swallowed up in the immediate interest of the scene – but

> Between the acting of a dreadful thing
130 > And the first motion, all the interim is
> Like a phantasma, or a hideous dream

I found it so as I felt the sun's rays clinging to my back, and saw the white wintry clouds sink below the verge of the horizon. "So," I thought, "my
135 fairest hopes have faded from my side! – so will the Gas-man's glory, or that of his adversary, vanish in an hour." The swells were parading in their white box-coats, the outer ring was cleared with some bruises on the heads and shins of the rus-
140 tic assembly (for the cockneys had been distanced

by the sixty-six miles); the time drew near, I had got a good stand; a bustle, a buzz, ran through the crowd, and from the opposite side entered Neate, between his second and bottle-holder. He rolled
145 along, swathed in his loose great coat, his knock-knees bending under his huge bulk; and, with a modest cheerful air, threw his hat into the ring. He then just looked round, and began quietly to undress; when from the other side there was a simi-
150 lar rush and an opening made, and the Gas-man came forward with a conscious air of anticipated triumph, too much like the cock-of-the-walk. He strutted about more than became a hero, sucked oranges with a supercilious air, and threw away
155 the skin with a toss of his head, and went up and looked at Neate, which was an act of supererogation. The only sensible thing he did was, as he strode away from the modern Ajax, to fling out his arms, as if he wanted to try whether they would do
160 their work that day. By this time they had stripped, and presented a strong contrast in appearance. If Neate was like Ajax[1], "with Atlantean shoulders, fit to bear" the pugilistic reputation of all Bristol, Hickman might be compared to Diomed, light,
165 vigorous, elastic, and his back glistened in the sun, as he moved about, like a panther's hide. There was now a dead pause – attention was awe-struck. Who at that moment, big with a great event, did not draw his breath short – did not feel his heart
170 throb? All was ready. They tossed up for the sun, and the Gas-man won. They were led up to the scratch – shook hands, and went at it.

In the first round everyone thought it was all over. After making play a short time, the Gas-man
175 flew at his adversary like a tiger, struck five blows in as many seconds, three first, and then following him as he staggered back, two more, right and left, and down he fell, a mighty ruin. There was a shout, and I said, "There is no standing this."
180 Neate seemed like a lifeless lump of flesh and bone, round which the Gas-man's blows played with the rapidity of electricity or lightning, and you imagined he would only be lifted up to be knocked down again. It was as if Hickman held a
185 sword or a fire in the right hand of his, and directed it against an unarmed body. They met again, and Neate seemed, not cowed, but particularly cautious. I saw his teeth clenched together and his brows knit close against the sun. He held out
190 both his arms at full-length straight before him, like two sledge-hammers, and raised his left an inch or two higher. The Gas-man could not get over this guard – they struck mutually and fell, but without advantage on either side. It was the

---

1 **Ajax…. Diomed:** Ajax and Diomed (Diomedes) were heroes in the Trojan War. *Atlantean* refers to Atlas, one of the Titans, condemned by Zeus to support the sky on his shoulders.

same in the next round; but the balance of power was thus restored – the fate of the battle was suspended. No one could tell how it would end. This was the only moment in which opinion was divided; for, in the next, the Gas-man aiming a mortal blow at his adversary's neck, with his right hand, and failing from the length he had to reach, the other returned it with his left at full swing, planted a tremendous blow on his cheek-bone and eyebrow, and made a red ruin of that side of his face. The Gas-man went down, and there was another shout – a roar of triumph as the waves of fortune rolled tumultuously from side to side. This was a settler. Hickman got up, and "grinned horrible a ghastly smile," yet he was evidently dashed in his opinion of himself; it was the first time he had ever been so punished; all one side of his face was perfect scarlet, and his right eye was closed in dingy blackness, as he advanced to the fight, less confident, but still determined. After one or two rounds, not receiving another such remembrancer, he rallied and went at it with his former impetuosity. But in vain. His strength had been weakened, – his blows could not tell at such a distance, – he was obliged to fling himself at his adversary, and could not strike from his feet; and almost as regularly as he flew at him with his right hand, Neate warded the blow, or drew back out of its reach, and felled him with the return of his left. There was little cautious sparring – no half-hits – no tapping and trifling, none of the *petit-maîtreship*[2] of the art – they were almost all knock-down blows: – the fight was a good stand-up fight. The wonder was the half-minute time. If there had been a minute or more allowed between each round, it would have been intelligible how they should by degrees recover strength and resolution; but to see two men smashed to the ground, smeared with gore, stunned, senseless, the breath beaten out of their bodies; and then, before you recover from the shock, to see them rise up with new strength and courage, stand steady to inflict or receive mortal offence, and rush upon each other, "like two clouds over the Caspian" – this is the most astonishing thing of all: – this is the high and heroic state of man! From this time forward the event became more certain every round; and about the twelfth it seemed as if it must have been over. Hickman generally stood with his back to me; but in the scuffle, he had changed positions, and Neate just then made a tremendous lunge at him, and hit him full in the face. It was doubtful whether he would fall backwards or forwards; he hung suspended for about a second or two, and then fell back, throwing his hands in the air, and with his face lifted up to the sky. I never saw anything more terrific than his aspect just before he fell. All traces of life, of natural expression, were gone from him. His face was like a human skull, a death's head, spouting blood. The eyes were filled with blood, the nose streamed with blood, the mouth gaped blood. He was not like an actual man, but like a preternatural, spectral appearance, or like one of the figures in Dante's "Inferno." Yet he fought on after this for several rounds, still striking the first desperate blow, and Neate standing on the defensive, and using the same cautious guard to the last, as if he had still all his work to do; and it was not till the Gas-man was so stunned in the seventeenth or eighteenth round, that his senses forsook him, and he could not come to time, that the battle was declared over. Ye who despise the FANCY, do something to show as much pluck, or as much self-possession as this, before you assume a superiority which you have never given a single proof of by any one action in the whole course of your lives! – When the Gas-man came to himself, the first words he uttered were, "Where am I? What is the matter!" "Nothing is the matter, Tom – you have lost the battle, but you are the bravest man alive." And Jackson whispered to him, "I am collecting a purse for you, Tom." – Vain sounds, and unheard at that moment! Neate instantly went up and shook him cordially by the hand, and seeing some old acquaintance, began to flourish with his fists, calling out, "Ah, you always said I couldn't fight – What do you think now?" But all in good humour, and without any appearance of arrogance; only it was evident Bill Neate was pleased that he had won the fight. When it was all over, I asked Cribb if he did not think it was a good one? He said, "Pretty well!" The carrier-pigeons now mounted into the air, and one of them flew with the news of her husband's victory to the bosom of Mrs. Neate. Alas, for Mrs. Hickman!

---

2 **Petit-maîtreship**: A French-English coinage. A *grand-maître* was an expert; a *petit-maître* is a pretentious, affected person who assumes the manner of an expert.

First Reading

1. Think about the rhetorical triangle. Hazlitt provides his audience with a narrative of his experience. What do you think is his aim in doing so?
2. What indications of audience are particularly prominent in Hazlitt's text?
3. By contemporary standards, Hazlitt's sentences are long. How does their length affect and enhance the reader's experience of his account?
4. Specify two sentences that strike you as particularly effective. Identify elements of language (such as diction, syntax, and the arrangement and selection of detail) in the sentences that affect your reading.
5. What is Hazlitt's focus? Identify particular passages that convey his primary interests.
6. What is Hazlitt's view of boxing and how does he establish it? What relevance does his representation of the sport have for us today?
7. In the second paragraph, Hazlitt sets the stage for the coming fight. What does his attention to these particular details suggest about his knowledge of his audience?
8. What features of Hazlitt's account distinguish it from a contemporary account of such an event?

Second Reading

Annotate the essay, carefully noting how he uses the resources of language to achieve his aims. Then answer these reading comprehension questions. After each one, explain what the question asked you to do or know and why you answered as you did.

1. A prominent characteristic of the opening paragraph is its

   (A) representation of action.
   (B) description of women.
   (C) declaration of intent.
   (D) recapitulation of past experience.
   (E) analysis of perspective.

2. Paragraph 2 contains each of the following EXCEPT

   (A) rhetorical question.
   (B) parenthetical intrusion.
   (C) direct comparison.
   (D) considered prediction.
   (E) detailed description.

3. The overall tone of Hazlitt's essay is best described as

   (A) reserved and aloof.
   (B) reflective and measured.
   (C) energetic and detailed.
   (D) distressed and alert.
   (E) vexed and frustrated.

4. Through his references to Ajax and Diomed in lines 158–164, the author

   (A) debates each fighter's prospects.
   (B) interrupts his account of events.
   (C) signals his regard for the past.
   (D) characterizes each fighter.
   (E) illustrates previous observations concerning vanity.

5. In line 258, the reference to Dante

   (A) further establishes the author's credentials.
   (B) breaks the tedium of the description.
   (C) concludes a lengthy debate.
   (D) provides anecdotal evidence.
   (E) emphasizes the importance of the moment.

1. **Summary and Paraphrase** — Summarize the action of the fight between Bill Neate and the Gas-man. Then write your own account, purposefully conveying the action to a person of our own time who has never attended a boxing match.

2. **Analysis** — Read the last paragraph of the selection carefully. Then write an essay that analyzes how Hazlitt uses diction, syntax, imagery, allusion, and tone to convey his experience of a boxing match to his audience.

Robert Anasi
A Way of Life

During his early 30s, while he was still eligible to participate, Robert Anasi chose to train for and enter the Golden Gloves competition, a major amateur boxing event. His subsequent memoir, *The Gloves: A Boxing Chronicle*, published in 2002, provides a participating fighter's view of boxing and its realm. What follows is the book's first chapter.

The gym becomes a way of life. Arrive on 14th Street at 5:30 P.M., and there might be a few fighters left from the first wave, the ones too young for day jobs, the ones who work odd hours or who don't work at all. You shake hands with your teammates (boxing culture requiring a certain formality) and take your gear into the bathroom. Off with the shirt, shoes, pants and, after a quick glance in the mirror to see how you're cutting up, on with the T-shirt, shorts and high-lace boxing shoes. Back in the gym, if no one else is around, Milton may be dozing. He lies on the upholstered bench, long legs bent off the end and touching the floor. A padded trainer's mitt is set over his eyes. He is only half asleep and will make lazy comments or stir to answer his cell phone. His energy ebbs and flows with the activity in the gym. If fully awake, he might have a hand in a packet of cheese curls or wrapped around a candy bar, interchangeable components of the toxic flow of junk food that sustains him.

You sit on the varnished planks of the wood floor and begin your workout, lengthening hamstrings, flexors, adductors, gluts and lats, the rubbery sheath of your skeleton. Stretching is somewhat abstract to Milton's fighters; some of the best seem to do without it altogether. Milton certainly doesn't emphasize it. Stretching isn't very street, isn't very...*tough*. Stretching seems abstract, seems abstract until the day you step forward in the ring and have your quadriceps seize or you wrench your back and can't train for weeks. Perhaps Milton's best fighters know the limits of their bodies better than you (certainly they move with a loping looseness that you envy), or perhaps they don't and are putting bodies and dream careers to risk.

After ten minutes of floor stretches, you rise and begin to loosen your arms and back. A boxer needs flexibility in his waist, is always ducking, bending, rotating on the axis of his hips. The wall mirrors watch you as you twist, a presence doubling the scene so that you can follow whatever happens through the length and depth of the room. The mirrors knit the gym together; always scanning with some part of your attention, you are immediately aware when anyone enters. As you stretch, your body quickens to the rhythm of the music—hip-hop, generally, on the radio, old tapes or new CDs. Along with old school stuff like Wu-Tang and Biggie, this year's big sellers are DMX, Jay-Z and Nas, the harder the better for the young toughs, murder, robbery, shooting and looting while you bounce. The music is loud enough to make conversation difficult, loud enough to make Milton scream, "Turn this shit down!" The boom box bass dictates the boxers' rhythm. Those times a white person tries to slip on a rock CD the other fighters shake their heads and ask, "How can you people train to this shit?"

Next comes the rope, slip-slap cadence of which takes at least a few months to negotiate (awkward leaps of novices as the rope tangles feet and limbs, as the plastic band scalds bare skin). The rope for balance, for coordination and to raise energy for the workout to come. All sorts of pretty tricks come with dexterity on the rope: running in place, double passes under each jump, and perhaps most impressive, the crossover, in which the wrists cross as the rope goes beneath you, very smooth. Milton has his own warm-up drills as well, custom-designed to make the leadfoot fleet, for the good boxer dances as well as hits. You hop back and forth across a tapeline on one foot, back and forth along the hallway forward and back, then run crisscross up the tapeline and return backpedaling. After a few minutes of this, you step into the ring with a pair of dumbbells. You circle the ring in a fighter's shuffle while punching the dumbbells straight into the air, then circle rotating the weights before you, elbows bent, all toward a further dexterity in moving the hands and feet together. Next is Milton's patented "dunh, dunh-duh," his own waltz, two steps sideways and then a pivot off the leading foot to bring you back into stance and facing your opponent. "Dunh, dunh-duh," to get out of trouble and pivot on an opponent who may be following too close, to pivot and *counter* with a hook or cross. You move and circle, breath coming faster, the faintest dappling of sweat on your forehead and staining your shirt. The day grind, the coffee and greasy lunch burn out of you as you move. This evening, like so many others, you barely dragged yourself to the gym. A thousand obstacles, a million rationalizations presented themselves. You were up late last night. You had a headache. You wanted to go out for dinner instead, see a movie, you have a deadline at your day job.... As you climbed the stairs and dressed, those obstacles evaporated, and as you move now, their last traces break and fade in the air. The obstacles seem so insignificant, in fact, that if you even think of them, you can't understand why they so hindered you. You are alive in your body, now. Your eyes open wide. Looking around, you see the gym has filled, people in conversation clusters, in various states of dress. You leave the ring and shake more hands. With an audience present, Milton no longer dozes but is up and talking. Not just talking but expressing, directing, edifying, illuminating, the impresario of this shadowed room.

"Hey, Gumby! What is that? You're punching handicapped."

"So when I was in camp with Shannon Briggs, I told him, 'They have you standing straight up, fighting like a white guy. That's not what got you here. You have to start moving your head again and breaking at the waist.'"

"Hey, somebody get my phone. Hello, Supreme. Yeah, I'm here every day starting at eight in the morning, and we close at ten at night. So come on down and be our next contestant."

"Julian! Are you working out, or cutting out?"

The bell (bell in name only—not a bell but a buzzing electric clock) marks rounds, the base unit measure of gym time. Rounds last three minutes with a warning buzz at two minutes thirty and another buzz at round's end for a rest of a minute, work/rest, work/rest, work/rest. "I did five rounds on the heavy bag, five on the rope." "How many rounds have we been sparring?" "One more round!" From your gym bag you draw the length of cloth that will protect those most delicate of weapons, the hands. Scrupulous fighters always draw perfectly rolled wraps from their bags, wraps rewrapped after drying from their last use so that they will roll on smooth and unwrinkled, but you, maybe you threw yours in the bag after pulling them off and forgot about them until now. They come to daylight, crumpled cotton lengths white, yellow or faded red, a little stiff with dried sweat, smelling of the same. A not unpleasant smell, you think, the salty must that permeates boxing, a combination of sweat with the glove leather it soaks. Boxers cultivate sweat, for sweat reduces them, makes them lean, symbolizes necessary exertion. All serious athletes sweat heavily, but in boxing sweat is the essential element, the sea in which the boxer is born and through which he swims.

After the rope and the warm-ups comes shadowboxing, the heavy bags, exercises and more shadowboxing. Milton may have you work pads with him as well, directing you to strike the oversize gloves on his hands while he shouts instructions and corrects your movement, using such choice idioms as "retarded," "robotic," "paraplegic," "idiot" and "bullshit," among others, punctuated with little smacks to your head. All this training, however, diminishes beside sparring. Sparring is the psychic center of the gym, as the ring is its actual material center. Milton's gym is a fighters' gym, not a health club or "fitness center." Fighters fight. To prepare to fight, fighters must spar. "We'll go with anybody," Milton states as a point of pride, that's how tough he believes his "Supreme Team" to be, and in point of proof, boxers, professional and amateur, come from all over the city to match up against his team. So sparring remains the center, and the other life in the gym revolves around it. People halt their workouts to watch. Milton insists that you watch ("That's how you learn," he says, "by imitation"). People come in just *to* watch. In the old days, tickets were sold for sparring sessions at the big gyms near Times Square or at the camps of champions as they prepared for title fights. Milton dreams of opening a streetfront gym to attract clientele.

"That would be the way to do it," he says. "Have it behind big windows right on Fourteenth Street. There'd be a crowd watching us twenty-four/seven. Once they saw how you guys spar, we'd be getting new people walking in all the time, begging us to teach them."

Your regular sparring partners have arrived and ask you if you want to work, or you ask them. "We'll go light," they say, or, "Just a couple of rounds," or, "I'm sore today, so we'll take it slow." Whatever they say, it's a decision of moment. A whole new set of excuses and escapes present themselves: You're tired; you want to avoid a headache; you have a date; you've sparred too much this week already....

Milton presses the issue. "Hey, you want to go in with...?" A zeal for contact drives him. He wants more! Now! And will throw all willing or semi-willing bodies together, heavyweight and featherweight, man and woman. Milton seems to love his gym work best when it comes to the threshold of real combat, when he can stand with his arms on the ropes shouting instructions. "Two-three! Slip, then pull back! Throw more jabs. Sit down in your punches!" Or he jumps up and down with a hand in the air, his fingers semaphoring the number of the punch he wants thrown (to conceal it from the boxer whose back is turned).

Sparring alters the normal routine on the floor. Milton will advise you to stop hitting the heavy bag or to go easy with the dumbbells. You do not want to get arm-weary. To agree to spar is a momentous decision and is nothing at all. Simply life in the gym. After nodding agreement, you shadowbox a few rounds in the mirror, skip rope, shake out your shoulders. Milton wants the show to begin. "Are you ready yet? Come on. Today. Hurry up and get the gear on." Finally, you accept that you are ready. Slip in your mouthpiece, the molded plastic to prevent your teeth from slicing your lips. You pull up the groin protector, draw the headgear over your ears, slather Vaseline around your eyes, across your nose, cheeks, lips (not too good for the skin, that, but it keeps the glove leather from chafing). Someone girds you with the fourteen- or sixteen-ounce sparring gloves and you step through the ropes. The preparation has a ritual air; though it's possible to pull on your gloves and fasten your chin strap yourself, it's better to have someone else do it for you. The care sanctifies you, helps separate this activity from all others. You dance about in the ring, throw a few flurries, jaw with your partner until Milton commands, "BOX!"

Two opposed philosophies dominate sparring. One states that sparring should always be light, not combat simulation but a venue for excising flaws and polishing technique. The famous Irish trainer Brendan Ingle (whose pupils include such champions as Johnny Nelson, Hero Graham and, of course, "Prince" Naseem Hamed) will allow his students to throw only body punches, thereby protecting the tender, skull-cased brain. Signs posted on his gym walls read: BOXING CAN DAMAGE YOUR HEALTH. IMPORTANT, NO SPARRING WITHOUT SUPERVISION. FOR YOUR OWN SAFETY, GUMSHIELDS AND HEADGUARDS MUST BE WORN. This Ingle approach emphasizes such terms as "light" and "easy" and "work." The other philosophy states that the sparring should be hard (hard but not wild). Most trainers will claim to belong to the first school. Most trainers actually belong to the second. The reason for this duplicity, conscious or not, is the doubling that serves to cloak the realities of pugilism. Boxing is a combat sport, and fighters are directed to inflict, within the rules, a maximum amount of damage.

This truth must be concealed to some extent. Few trainers will say to each other before their fighters spar, "I hope my guy kills your guy." Although they want exactly that: a demonstration of their students' prowess in the clearest manner possible. The trainers cannot make such a statement; the challenge would raise the stakes from sparring to a gym war. Instead they mention "good rounds," "going easy," "working with" someone. As in the romance around sex, the stereotyped, delicate language serves to cloak a more brutal reality.

As a trainer Milton stands completely in the second school. He will overmatch his fighters and watch as they sustain real beatings (one of his tricks is to turn off the bell near the end of the round so that the fighters' endurance will be tested). The result for you, in the first months, is headaches, bruises, pain. This sparring serves a purpose. Endure those first months and you will have little to fear.

When the bell buzzes, you smack leather with your partner by way of salute and then begin to circle. You are boxing. A thousand times you've done this and still the tension, pressing and binding. Moments ago you were talking to a friend about work and telling jokes. Now…In the distortions of mouthpiece and headgear, your partner loses his human characteristics and becomes half monster. The first round moves slowly as you warm to the action, building up until, bang! A shot stings your face, ricochets from your headgear, crushes your lips. It's a good morning cup of coffee; you begin to accelerate, clear and rising. Now you will hit back. This is not your friend. The person facing you has become a series of problems to solve, a greater or lesser degree of intimidation. Things you try work or don't work. Depending on his mood, gym occupancy, activity on his cell, Milton becomes more or less involved. "Feint two-three!" "One to the body, one to the body, then something else." "Think out there! You've got to think!" "Use your defense!" You try to act on his commands and keep your eyes focused on the man trying to kill you.

When the buzzer ends the round, you take water, listen to Milton's promptings and circle the ring, shaking out your arms. This continues for three rounds, or six, or ten. Sweat runs; sweat streams, flows, pools. You are an aquatic animal. Sweat drenches your brow, burns your eyes, renders your white T-shirt translucent and drowns your socks. All your training does not prepare you for the ocean. You gasp but there is never enough air; your gloves become anchors dragging you to the bottom. As the rounds progress, you may gain confidence, put together combinations, slip

and pivot like at pro, drive your partner back. Or your confidence may flag; you may retreat, thrash
315 tire air with wild punches as thunderbolts split your head. The two of you may forget that this is "work" and tend toward murder. There is no fellowship then. Your partner is a thing to be broken. "Good hook," Milton shouts, leaping from
320 his bench as the action boils. The tension slows time. You must stay focused. Break concentration for an instant, and the result is not embarrassment (the other team scores, you lose the beat in music or dance) but pain. The tension frets your energy,
325 erodes it. "Relax your shoulders," Milton shouts. "Think!" The water rises over your thighs, your neck, your mouth.

Suddenly it ends. Either you quit or your partner quits, or Milton wants the ring for somebody
330 else. The alien landscape that you sped through vanishes. You gear down and step through the ropes back to a gym different from the one you left. A fog obscures the room, even if you haven't taken any shots to the head. You return to a lesser
335 place, less vivid, less encompassing. Someone has to unlace your gloves for you. The boxer with gloves on is helpless for anything except striking. He must be fed water. He cannot scratch an itch on his shoulder and asks his trainer to do it. Your
340 hands emerge, small and swaddled. You wander around the floor for a minute, acclimating. You wipe the traces of Vaseline from your face with a shirtsleeve, look in the mirror to see if you are scraped or bruised. You drop gear here and there
345 across the room. Sometimes it's not until days later that you realize your helmet and cup have gone missing and you return to the gym to find them hanging from pegs on the wall.

After another few hits of water, you pull on bag
350 gloves and go to work on the heavy bags. You've thrown thousands of punches in your months at the gym but they never seem good enough for Milton. "You're still punching retarded," he says. Punching too high ("Who are you trying to hit,
355 the Green Giant?") or too low ("Stop hitting those midgets"). "You're punching handicapped. Let your hands go. Let them be free." Milton might not notice you for a week or more, but just when you think he has forgotten you, you're laved by such
360 words of love. Through the circuit you go: heavy bags and hook bags and the jumpy little double-end bag that snaps back after being struck. Then shadow boxing, the rope again and exercises: sit-ups, crunches, push-ups, dips and the little weight
365 lifting fighters allow themselves. The muscle that comes from weights tightens the body, reducing range and speed. Boxers need to stay loose and quick; a good punch snaps at the maximum arm extension. "Power thrills but speed kills" is a box-
370 ing maxim; the faster man will beat the stronger man. Boxers also don't want to add bulk because bulk is weight and changes one's class. As you cool down, you say goodbye and arrange your next sparring session. You've been in the gym for
375 nearly three hours. On the way home, your body crashes, even after Gatorade and energy bars. Sluggish, sullen and starving, you're good for little more than television for the next hour or two.

First Reading

1. Distinguish Anasi's perspective from that of Hazlitt in the essay on pages 112–114. What authority is Anasi able to claim as a result?

2. Why does Anasi adopt the second-person point of view? Evaluate the effectiveness of this tactic after rewriting a portion of the selection in the first person.

Second Reading

Identify shifts in the focus and changes in the pace of this text. Note specific locations in the text where such changes occur. What indicates a shift in focus? What indicates a change in pace? How do these shifts and changes affect your experience of Anasi's account?

Writing

Exposition — Writing in the second person, represent an experience you have had that others have not. Imagine your audience to be one interested in knowing about the experience. Identify and consider adopting some of the rhetorical strategies evident in Anasi's account that allow his readers access to his experience. As you draft and revise, consider how you are conveying "what it feels like to…" for your audience.

Joyce Carol Oates
On Boxing

Oates's original essay about boxing has evolved into an entire book on the subject, as her interest in the sport persists. The following passage, taken from the beginning of her original essay, is not rooted in any particular match or event. Consequently, Oates provides a perspective on the larger subject that is distinctive from that of an observer (Hazlitt) or a participant (Anasi). Oates published *On Boxing* in 1987.

Each boxing match is a story—a unique and highly condensed drama without words. Even when nothing sensational happens: then the drama is "merely" psychological. Boxers are there to
5 establish an absolute experience, a public accounting of the outermost limits of their beings; they will know, as few of us can know ourselves, what physical and psychic power they possess—of how much, or how little, they are capable. To enter the
10 ring near-naked and to risk one's life is to make of one's audience voyeurs of a kind: boxing is so intimate. It is to ease out of sanity's consciousness and into another, difficult to name. It is to risk, and sometimes to realize, the agony of which *agon*
15 (Greek, "contest") is the root.

In the boxing ring there are two principal players, overseen by a shadowy third. The ceremonial ringing of the bell is a summoning to full wakefulness for both boxers and spectators. It sets into
20 motion, too, the authority of Time.

The boxers will bring to the fight everything that is themselves, and everything will be exposed—including secrets about themselves they cannot fully realize. The physical self, the male-
25 ness, one might say, underlying the "self." There are boxers possessed of such remarkable intuition, such uncanny prescience, one would think they were somehow recalling their fights, not fighting them as we watch. There are boxers who
30 perform skillfully, but mechanically, who cannot improvise in response to another's alteration of strategy; there are boxers performing at the peak of their talent who come to realize, mid-fight, that it will not be enough; there are boxers—including
35 great champions—whose careers end abruptly, and irrevocably, as we watch. There has been at least one boxer possessed of an extraordinary and disquieting awareness not only of his opponent's every move and anticipated move but of
40 the audience's keenest shifts in mood as well, for which he seems to have felt personally responsible—Cassius Clay / Muhammad Ali, of course. "The Sweet Science of Bruising" celebrates the physicality of men even as it dramatizes the limi-
45 tations, sometimes tragic, more often poignant, of the physical. Though male spectators identify with boxers no boxer behaves like a "normal" man when he is in the ring and no combination of blows is "natural." All is style.

50 *Every talent must unfold itself in fighting.* So Nietzsche speaks of the Hellenic past, the history of the "contest"—athletic, and otherwise—by which Greek youths were educated into Greek citizenry. Without the ferocity of competition, without, even,
55 "envy, jealousy, and ambition" in the contest, the Hellenic city, like the Hellenic man, degenerated. If death is a risk, death is also the prize—for the winning athlete.

In the boxing ring, even in our greatly human-
60 ized times, death is always a possibility—which is why some of us prefer to watch films or tapes of fights already past, already defined as history. Or, in some instances, art. Most of the time, however, death in the ring is extremely unlikely; a sta-
65 tistically rare possibility like your possible death tomorrow morning in an automobile accident or in next month's headlined airline disaster or in a freak accident involving a fall on a stairs or in the bathtub, a skull fracture, subarachnoid hem-
70 orrhage. Spectators at "death" fights often claim afterward that what happened simply seemed to happen—unpredictably, in a sense accidentally. Only in retrospect does death appear to have been inevitable.

75 If a boxing match is a story it is an always wayward story, one in which anything can happen. And in a matter of seconds. Split seconds! (Muhammad Ali boasted that he could throw a punch faster than the eye could follow, and he
80 may have been right.) In no other sport can so much take place in so brief a period of time, and so irrevocably.

Because a boxing match is a story without words, this doesn't mean that it has no text or lan-
85 guage, that it is somehow "brute," "primitive," "inarticulate," only that the text is improvised

in action; the language a dialogue between the boxers of the most refined sort (one might say, as much neurological as psychological: a dialogue of split-second reflexes) in a joint response to the mysterious will of the audience which is always that the fight be a worthy one so that the crude paraphernalia of the setting—ring, lights, ropes, stained canvas, the staring onlookers themselves—be erased, forgotten. (As in the theater or the church, settings are erased by way, ideally, of transcendent action.) Ringside announcers give to the wordless spectacle a narrative unity, yet boxing as performance is more clearly akin to dance or music than narrative.

First Reading

1. Annotate the passage by Oates.
2. Write a *says/does analysis* of the essay.
3. Identify the central argument of the passage.
4. Oates employs a metaphor to account for the nature of boxing. What makes this metaphor appropriate?
5. How does Oates's diction convey her attitude toward boxing?
6. How would Oates respond if boxing were banned? What makes you think so?

Second Reading

Review your annotation of Oates' text from the first reading, carefully noting the impact of particular words, phrases, and details upon your understanding of the text. Then answer these reading comprehension questions. After each one, explain what the question asked you to do or know and why you answered as you did.

1. With the phrase "without words" in paragraph 1, the author

   (A) introduces a sustained paradox.
   (B) denies a common metaphor.
   (C) appeals to logos.
   (D) presents a causal relationship.
   (E) initiates a elaborate chronology.

2. In the context of the entire passage, the reference to "the authority of Time" (lines 19–20) suggests each of the following EXCEPT

   (A) the duration of each round.
   (B) the irrevocable progress of a boxing match.
   (C) the freak possibility of sudden death.
   (D) the unfolding of each fighter's talent.
   (E) the potential brevity of action.

3. The most prominent organizing device of paragraph 3 (lines 21–49) is

   (A) narration.
   (B) explanation.
   (C) refutation.
   (D) comparison.
   (E) speculation.

4. In paragraph 5 (lines 59–74), the author discusses the possibility of death by

   (A) comparing occurrences.
   (B) understating its importance.
   (C) presenting relevant statistics.
   (D) dismissing its inevitability.
   (E) offering a generalization.

5. The content of this passage effectively conveys the author's _____ her subject.

   (A) disinterest in
   (B) intrigued attention to
   (C) skeptical viewpoint toward
   (D) alarmed presence concerning
   (E) unapologetic defense of

Analysis — Explore and explain the ways in which the texts by William Hazlitt, Robert Anasi, and Joyce Carol Oates intersect with and diverge from one another. Consider the aim and tactics of each author, citing text that supports and illustrates your thinking as you distinguish and connect the texts.

Neil Leifer's photograph captures Muhammad Ali's moment of triumph over Sonny Liston at the 1965 heavyweight boxing championship. The following article by sports writer Mike Lowe appeared in the *Maine Sunday Telegram* in 2005, forty years after Ali seized the championship from Liston in Lewiston, Maine. Lowe made Leifer's photograph the subject of his article.

"Get up!"

"Get up and fight!"

You don't need to know who the boxers are in the photo you're looking at.

5 Yet, you know exactly what is happening. The action shouts at you.

You see one boxer on his back, his arms over his head. You see the other boxer looking down at him, snarling something—"Get up!"—his gloved 10 right hand up by his left shoulder as if he had just gestured to the fallen boxer to get up off the floor.

The boxers are, of course, Muhammad Ali and Sonny Liston. Ali is the one snarling. Liston is the one on his back.

15 The photo was taken 40 years ago Wednesday. The site was the Central Maine Youth Center—

now known as the Colisée—in Lewiston. The fight was for the heavyweight championship of the world.

20   The moment was captured by two photographers: the late John Rooney of the Associated Press and Neil Leifer for *Sports Illustrated*.

Forty years ago it was simply regarded as a good photo. Now it is considered one of the great-25 est sports photos ever taken.

"I knew it was a good picture," said Leifer, who has had his photos on more than 200 covers of *Sports Illustrated* and *Time* magazines. "But I never imagined it would take on the life that it did.

30   "Why? Well, I think first because people have come to love Muhammad. Even his worst detractors, after he lit the (Olympic) torch in Atlanta, turned around."

The 62-year-old Leifer considers that photo 35 "the most fortuitous thing that ever happened to me in my life."

Not professionally—Leifer was already regarded as one of the best sports photographers in the world—but because it forever linked him to Ali, 40 who would become a friend.

"As I got to know him well, I think he is one of the great human beings of all time," said Leifer in a phone interview from his New York City home. "He is such a special individual, unlike any ath-45 lete you'll ever meet."

Leifer is returning to Lewiston this week to recreate the scene in the Colisée. It is part of an assignment he is doing for *Sports Illustrated*, which he left in 1978. Leifer is returning to all the great 50 events he shot for *SI*—the Rose Bowl, the Super Bowl, the Final Four, the Kentucky Derby, etc.—to shoot them one more time, but not necessarily from an action perspective.

As part of it, he thought it would be great to 55 return to Lewiston.

"I thought it would be fun to go back on the 40th anniversary and shoot the ghost of Ali and Liston in an empty ring," he said. "This is not my strong suit as a photographer, still life, but the 60 idea of seeing the arena again was something that I liked."

Leifer remembers that Tuesday evening 40 years ago very well. He had arrived in Lewiston several days earlier, along with the rest of *SI*'s 65 staff, to set up his equipment.

There were usual problems—not enough power for his strobe lights, for one, so they had to figure out how to divert some extra amps to the lights—and he needed the time to check the lighting in the 70 building and set up his two remote cameras.

He also learned that he was sitting in Liston's corner, which turned out to be a huge stroke of luck. Leifer was pleased with that seat. He would be looking into Ali's corner and he liked the 75 thought of capturing Ali as a gladiator, ready to come out and fight.

But that seat also put him in position to get the shot.

"Luck, luck, luck," said Leifer. "I don't know 80 what percentage it plays, but the fact is, you have to be lucky to be in the right spot. No photographer could have predicted where the knockout would happen.

"Believe me, I've been in the wrong seat many 85 times."

Leifer was there for *SI* along with Herbie Scharfman, who had first choice of seats. Scharfman took his traditional spot—right next to the judge, where he would have to contend with only 90 one other photographer, on his left.

Leifer had photographers to his left and right and it can get tight during fights. Sometimes you think you've got the shot only to have a photographer's arm in the picture.

95   The fight began and, very shortly, ended.

Ali's quick right dropped Liston to the canvas. Right where Leifer wanted.

"There is a perfect spot in the ring for photographers," he said, "a spot where, had I put an `x' 100 on the ring, if we were making a movie I would say, 'This is where I want Sonny to fall down and Ali, I want you standing here.'

"Not only was I on the right side of the ring, but they were exactly where I wanted them."

105   He focused and clicked.

The next morning, Leifer raced out to get the morning papers, any that he could find. There, on the front page of every one of them, was Rooney's photo.

110   "I saw it," he said. "My hope was that I had gotten something that good."

He did. Rooney's photo is different than Leifer's. It is taken from a different angle—to Leifer's left—and was part of a four-frames-per-second 115 action sequence Rooney shot. Leifer had one shot to get it right.

"I knew I was on the right side," said Leifer. "I knew I had a clear shot, I knew I was in the right spot."

120   But he didn't know what he had until he returned to New York the next day to process the film:

Ali standing over Liston, taunting him; the right arm bent with the glove up by his left shoulder; Scharfman framed by Ali's legs; a white light—125 from Leifer's strobe—reflected on Ali's left shoulder, separating his body from the bluish backdrop (caused by the strobe light reflecting off the smoke in the building).

The shot was spectacular, even more so because of the timing. Leifer's strobe lights took three seconds to recycle. Had he clicked his shutter one second earlier, he doesn't get the shot.

"I had assumed for years that Muhammad had stood over Liston for two, three seconds, taunting him," said Leifer. "I never realized until the last five or six years that it was an instant. Ali did it once and it was over.

"I marvel that I got that picture."

Surprisingly, that photo did not grace *SI*'s cover the following week. *SI* used one from George Silk, a *Life* magazine photographer, on the cover. It wasn't even used on the lead page of the article.

It didn't win any awards. Now the photo is cherished and one of the most valued of Ali.

"It's the way people want to remember him," said Leifer. "That's the only explanation I have. You always know if you've got something extraordinary when you start hearing what a great picture it was from your peers. My recollection is that they said, `Nice shot.' Nothing more.

"I think it began to take on a life of its own at the end of the decade, when every publication was doing a (decade-ending) issue. It got played prominently there. By the mid-1970s, after his comeback and the three (Joe) Frazier fights and the Zaire fight (with George Foreman), Ali was always in the news and this picture kept getting used.

"By 1990, it was the Ali picture. My feeling is that it's because it's a heroic look, a heroic image, of one of the greatest athletes of our time."

And it captured Ali perfectly.

First Reading

1. Describe the photograph in your own words.
2. Relate the photograph to comments made by at least two of the authors that preceded it.

Second Reading

1. Distinguish between a caption for the photo and Lowe's story of how it came to be. How does Lowe's account enrich the audience's experience of the picture?
2. How does the passage of four decades alter the photograph? What happens to a picture when it is no longer current or newsworthy?

Writing

Argument — Study "A Picture Perfect Ending" by Mike Lowe and "Muhammed Ali vs. Sonny Liston" by Neil Leifer. Then write an essay in which you analyze the combined impact of the texts and develop a position on Lowe's claim that "You don't need to know who the boxers are in the photo you're looking at."

Gordon Marino
Boxing and the Cool Halls of Academe

A former boxer, Gordon Marino is a professor of philosophy, curator of the Kierkegaard Library, and assistant football coach at St. Olaf College. He also trains amateur boxers. Marino published this article in 2004.

"Know thyself" was the Socratic dictum, but Tyler Durden, the protagonist in the movie *Fight Club*, asks, "How much can you know about yourself if you've never been in a fight?" Although trainers of the bruising art wince at the notion that boxing equals fighting, there can be no doubt that boxing throws you up against yourself in revealing ways. Take a left hook to the body or a trip to the canvas, and you soon find out whether you are the kind of person who will ever get up.

For a decade, I have been teaching both boxing and philosophy. My academic colleagues have sometimes reacted to my involvement with the sweet science with intellectual jabs and condescension. A few years ago at a philosophy conference, I mentioned that I had to leave early to go back to the campus to work with three of my boxers from the Virginia Military Institute who were competing in the National Collegiate Boxing Association championships. Shocked to learn that there was such a college tournament, one professor scolded, "How can someone committed to developing minds be involved in a sport in which students beat one another's brains out?" I explained that the competitors wore protective headgear and used heavily padded 16-ounce gloves in competition as well as in practice, but she was having none of it. "Headgear or not," she replied, "your brain is still getting rattled. Worse yet, you're teaching violence."

I countered that if violence is defined as purposefully hurting another person, then I had seen enough of that in the philosophical arena to last a lifetime. At the university where I did my graduate studies, colloquia were nothing less than academic gunfights in which the goal was to fire off a question that would sink the lecturer low. I pointed out, "I've even seen philosophers have to restrain themselves from clapping at a comment that knocked a speaker off his pins and made him feel stupid." I followed up by arguing that getting and taking punches makes you feel safer in the world, and that people who do not feel easily threatened are generally less threatening. She wasn't buying any of it. Then I made the mistake of making myself an object lesson by noting that I had boxed for years and still seemed to be able to put my thoughts together. That earned me a smile and a pat on the wrist.

If I were thrown in the ring today and had to defend the art of self-defense against the sneering attitude of some academicians, I would have at least two colleagues in my corner. In *Body & Soul: Notes of an Apprentice Boxer* (Oxford University Press, 2004) the MacArthur-award-winning Loïc Wacquant, a sociology professor at New School University, described the sentimental education that he received training for three years at a boxing gym in Chicago's South Side. Professor Wacquant, who earned his red badge of courage by competing in the famous Chicago Golden Gloves tournament, insists that boxing clubs are sanctuaries of order, peace, and tranquility in a helter-skelter world. According to Wacquant, whose ring name was "Busy Louie," the gym is *"a school of morality* in Durkheim's sense of the term, that is to say a machinery designed to fabricate the spirit of discipline, group attachment, respect for others as for self, and autonomy of the will that are indispensable to the blossoming of the pugilistic vocation." The machinery often works so well that it forges a kind of mutual affection that is absent from the cool halls of academe. When he left Chicago for a postdoctoral position at Harvard, Wacquant fell into a terrible funk about leaving his fistic family. He writes, "In the intoxication of my immersion, I even thought for a while of aborting my academic career to 'turn pro' and thereby remain with my friends from the gym and its coach, DeeDee Armour, who had become a second father to me."

Carlo Rotella, an associate professor of English and director of American studies at Boston College and the author of *Cut Time: An Education at the Fights* (Houghton Mifflin, 2003), spent a year taking notes in the gym of the former heavyweight champion Larry Holmes. Rotella contends that life is all about hurting and getting hurt, and that there are few courses in life that prepare you for the whirring blades outside your door like boxing. In the introduction to one of the best boxing books ever written, Rotella remarks:

"The deeper you get into the fights, the more you may discover about things that would seem at first blush to have nothing to do with boxing. Lessons in spacing and leverage, or in holding part of oneself in reserve even when hotly engaged, are lessons not only in how one boxer reckons with another but also in how one person reckons with another. The fights teach many such lessons—about virtues and limits of craft, about the need to impart meaning to hard facts by enfolding them in stories and spectacle, about getting hurt and getting old, about distance and intimacy, and especially about education itself: Boxing conducts an endless workshop in the teaching and learning of knowledge with consequences."

Still, I think the best defense of boxing is Aristotelian. In his *Nichomachean Ethics*, Aristotle offers his famous catalog of the moral virtues. Whenever I teach this section of the *Ethics* I always begin by asking students what they think are the ingredients of moral virtue. Respect, compassion, honesty, justice, and tolerance always fly quickly up onto the board, often followed by creativity and a sense of humor. I usually need to prod to elicit "courage." And so I hector, "How can you be consistently honest or just if you don't have the mettle to take a hit?"

Aristotle writes that developing a moral virtue requires practicing the choices and feelings appropriate to that virtue. Accordingly, colleges today often offer a smorgasbord of workshop-like events to help develop the virtue of tolerance, for example, by making students more comfortable with people from diverse backgrounds. But where are the workshops in courage, a virtue that Nelson Mandela, John McCain, and others have claimed to have found in boxing?

According to Aristotle, courage is a mean between fearlessness and excessive fearfulness. The capacity to tolerate fear is essential to leading a moral life, but it is hard to learn how to keep your moral compass under pressure when you are coseted from every fear. Boxing gives people practice in being afraid. There are, of course, plenty of brave thugs. Physical courage by no means guarantees the imagination that standing up for a principle might entail. However, in a tight moral spot I would be more inclined to trust someone who has felt like he or she was going under than someone who has experienced danger only vicariously, on the couch watching videos.

In fact, boxing was a popular intercollegiate sport until the early 1960s, when a fatality and problems with semiprofessionals' posing as students counted the sport out. In 1976 college boxing was resurrected as a club sport, and now, under the umbrella of USA Boxing (the governing body for amateur boxing in the United States), the National Collegiate Boxing Association includes about 30 college teams. Every April sectional, regional, and national championships are held. I recently chatted with Maja Cavlovic, a female boxer from Estonia who graduated from the Virginia Military Institute this spring. A power puncher, Ms. Cavlovic reflected, "Boxing helped me learn how to control my emotions. You get in there and you are very afraid, and then all of your training takes over."

The two-time heavyweight champion George Foreman concurs with Ms. Cavlovic. In addition to being an immensely successful businessman, Mr. Foreman directs a large youth club outside of Houston with a vibrant boxing program. Since Mr. Foreman also is a preacher I asked him, "How do you reconcile teaching kids to deliver a knockout blow with Jesus' injunction that we should turn the other cheek?" Mr. Foreman chuckled and explained, "To be successful in the ring you have to get control of your emotions—that includes anger. And the kids who stick with it in the gym are much less violent than when they came in through the door."

Americans for the most part live in a culture of release in which passion and spontaneity are worshipped. Beyond being told that troublesome feelings are medical problems, our young people receive scant instruction in modulating their emotions. As a result, there are very few opportunities to spar with heavyweight emotions such as anger and fear. In the ring, those passions constantly punch at you, but if you keep punching, you learn not to be pummeled by your emotions. Keeping your guard up when you feel like leaping out of the ring can be liberating. After he won his first bout, I asked Karl Pennau, a St. Olaf student whom I trained, what he had gleaned from his study of the sweet science. He replied, "Learning boxing has given me a lot more than just another sport to play. It is a tough, tough game, but having trained and been in the ring, I won't ever think that I can't do something again."

First Reading

1. State Marino's purpose. Restate, in your own words, the central argument of his essay.
2. Identify Marino's most prominent claims and assertions. How do these claims relate to his central argument? Does he consistently back up his assertions?
3. What do his argument and its presentation indicate about Marino's regard for his audience? What assumptions does he make about his readers?
4. Where and how does Marino claim, and then establish, his authority over his subject? What portions of the text empower him to take a stand?
5. What counts as evidence in this essay?

Second Reading

1. Complete a *says/does analysis* of Marino's writing. Drawing upon your analysis, answer the following questions.
2. Where does Marino use the authority of others in support of his argument?
3. Where does the author rely on his own observations?
4. How does Marino draw upon anecdote to make his argument?
5. Where does he draw upon experience (both his own and that of others) in order to develop his argument?
6. Identify and examine Marino's use of each of the three appeals.
   a. Where in the essay is ethical appeal most prominent?
   b. Where in the essay is logical appeal most prominent?
   c. Where in the essay is emotional appeal most prominent?
7. Characterize each of the following statements and then explain how each functions in Marino's essay:
   a. "…you soon find out whether you are the kind of person who will ever get up." (lines 9–10)
   b. "…life is all about hurting and getting hurt…" (line 88)
   c. "I usually need to prod to elicit 'courage'." (lines 116–117)
   d. "Boxing gives practice in being afraid." (lines 135–136)
   e. "Beyond being told that troublesome feelings are medical problems, our young people receive scant instruction in modulating their emotions." (lines 176–179)

The following essay is by George Will, who regularly comments, in both print and electronic media, on global and American events, society, values, ethics, and politics. It was published in 1982.

For 150 years people have been savoring Macauley's judgment that the Puritans hated bear-baiting not because it gave pain to the bear but because it gave pleasure to the spectators. However, there are moments, and this is one, for blurting out the truth: The Puritans were right. The pain to the bear was not a matter of moral indifference, but the pleasure of the spectators was sufficient reason for abolishing that entertainment.

Now another boxer has been beaten to death. The brain injury he suffered was worse than the injury to the loser in a boxing match is supposed to suffer. It is hard to calibrate such things—how hard an opponent's brain should be banged against the inside of his cranium—in the heat of the battle.

From time immemorial ways, men have been fighting for the entertainment of other men. Perhaps in a serene temperate society boxing would be banned along with other blood sports—if, in such a society, the question would even arise. But a step toward the extinction of boxing is understanding why that is desirable. One reason is the physical injury done to young men. But a sufficient reason is the quality of the pleasure boxing often gives to spectators.

There is no denying that boxing like other, better sports, can exemplify excellence. Boxing demands bravery and, when done well, is beautiful in the way that exercise of finely honed physical talents is. Furthermore, many sports are dangerous. But boxing is the sport that has as its object the infliction of pain and injury. Its crowning achievement is the infliction of serious trauma on the brain. The euphemism for boxing is "the art of self-defense." No. A rose is a rose is a rose, and a user fee is a revenue enhancer is a tax increase, and boxing is aggression.

It is probable that there will be a rising rate of spinal cord injuries and deaths in football. The force of defense players (a function of weight and speed) is increasing even faster than the force of ball carriers and receivers. As a coach once said, football is not a contact sport—dancing is a contact sport—football is a collision sport. The human body, especially the knee and spine, is not suited to that. But football can be made safer by equipment improvements and rules changes such as those proscribing certain kinds of blocks. Boxing is fundamentally impervious to these.

Such an argument cuts no ice in a society where the decayed public philosophy teaches that the pursuit of happiness is a right sovereign over all other considerations; that "happiness" and "pleasure" are synonyms, and that there is no hierarchy of values against which to measure particular appetites. Besides, some persons will say, with reason, that a society in which the entertainment menu includes topless lady mud wrestlers is a society past worrying about.

Sports besides boxing attract persons who want their unworthy passions stirred, including a lust for blood. I remember Memorial Day in the Middle West in the 1950s, when all roads led to the Indianapolis Speedway, where too many fans went to drink Falstaff beer and hope for a crash. But boxing is in a class by itself.

Richard Hoffer of the *Los Angeles Times* remembers the death of Johnny Owen, a young 118-pound bantamweight who died before he had fulfilled his modest ambition of buying a hardware store back home in Wales. Hoffer remembers that "Owens was put in a coma by a single punch, carried out of the Olympic (arena) under a hail of beer cups, some of which were filled with urine."

The law cannot prudently move far in advance of mass taste, so boxing cannot be outlawed. But in a world in which many barbarities are unavoidable, perhaps it is not too much to hope that some of the optional sorts will be outgrown.

First Reading

1. On a paragraph-by-paragraph basis, complete a *says/does analysis* of Will's essay.
2. What is George Will's central argument? What assumptions does Will make in his argument?
3. How does Will use comparison in support of his argument? How does he use selection of detail?

Second Reading

1. Why does the placement of the assertion, "But boxing is in a class by itself" at the end of paragraph 7 (line 67) matter?
2. Characterize the tone of Will's essay. Identify words and phrases that indicate the essay's attitude.
3. Speculate: why doesn't Will argue for an outright ban on boxing?

Writing

Dialog — Write the dialog of a conversation that Gordon Marino (see pages 127–128) and George Will would have with each other about boxing and American society. What portion of this essay would Will use to challenge Marino? How do you think Marino would respond?

A British sports journalist for *The Sunday Times*, Hugh McIlvanney has also been published in *Sports Illustrated* and other major publications. The following text, written in 1982, introduces an extensive collection of his articles on boxing.

Now that the British Medical Association has added its influential voice to the fluctuating clamour for the abolition of boxing, some people may feel that a book like this should carry a gov-
5 ernment health warning. Many millions around the world believe that the fight game is so far from being a legitimate sport that it should be disowned by every civilised society. As someone who not only finds the greatest performers in box-
10 ing irresistibly thrilling but has been writing about them professionally for more than 20 years, I am bound to challenge that view. However, I have too much respect for the abolitionists' argument to try to ignore or belittle their central objections. Any
15 supporter of boxing who does not admit to some residual ambivalence about its values, who has not wondered in its crueller moments if it is worth the candle, must be suspect. But many of the attacks made on it are fairly dubious, too. Talking,
20 as a few members of the BMA have done, about 'organised brain damage' and 'legalised grievous bodily harm' is gimmicky sloganising, a case of going into the debating ring with a horseshoe in the glove.
25   Among doctors themselves there is a conspicuous lack of unanimity about how seriously the brain cells are affected by prolonged involvement in boxing and how the risk compares with that created by less heavily criticised contact sports such
30 as rugby and American football, which might be held responsible for paralysing a higher percentage of those who take part in them. Just as it is natural that fist-fighting should be a profoundly emotive issue, so it is essential that some of the
35 more generalised condemnations of it should be scrutinised. The first point that must be stressed is that deaths in the ring do not make the most powerful argument against professional boxing. If opposition is based on the ratio of fatalities to
40 the numbers participating, boxing is left trailing by motor racing, to name just one other hazardous game. It may be pointed out, too, that fighters don't run amok and kill spectators, as racing cars sometimes do. Motives, not statistics, call pugi-
45 lism into question.

The most damaging element in the case to be made against it is that it is the one sport in which the fundamental aim of a contestant is to render his immediate opponent unconscious. No matter
50 how you dress it up, that's the tune they're playing in there. Ninety-nine times out of a hundred even the fanciest mover would rather forget about accumulating points and take the early bus home. A sport with such apparently primitive objectives
55 is bound to be seen by many as being morally reprehensible as well as having intolerable physical dangers. Their moral indignation is intensified when they consider the huge sums of money that are often generated by the professional game and
60 the proliferation of non-combatants who insist on grabbing a share of the spoils. Add to that the widespread assumption that most of the spectators at boxing shows are at worst sadists vicariously satisfying a blood lust, or at best benighted
65 souls who somehow feel that they can acquire virility by osmosis in a fight crowd, and it becomes clear that defenders of the sport cannot look for an easy passage. Some civilised men have, when asked to justify their enthusiasm for it, fallen back
70 on facetiousness. One such was the late A. J. Liebling, who wrote about fights and fighters with as much distinction as anyone since Hazlitt (and rather more often than William did). Liebling suggested that if any fighter had gone as batty as
75 Nijinsky there would have been a public outcry. 'Well, who hit Nijinsky?' he asked. And why, he wanted to know, wasn't there a campaign against ballet? It gave girls fat legs.
    However, at the end of the day boxing does
80 not have to hide behind jokes or macho bluster. It is an activity so basic that ultimately its best defense is human nature, a flawed argument at any time but one that is not easily trampled underfoot. Aggression is central to all competitive
85 sports and it would be astonishing if there were not many young men left dissatisfied with the sublimation of it involved in ball games, in track and field athletics, in adventure pursuits such as mountaineering or in the racing of horses or ma-
90 chines. Such natures hunger for the rawest form

of competition and that means boxing. We may regret that our species has not progressed beyond that appetite but to introduce legislation prohibiting consenting adults from satisfying it would, conceivably, be out of step with recent trends in our liberal society.

Of course, it is a constant, if not always honestly articulated, part of the abolitionists' case that the fighters are hapless victims pressed into reluctant service in the ring by the mercenary and corrupt forces that control professional boxing. It is a view of the business learned mainly from B-movies....

The point being made here is not that boxing is free of mercenary and corrupt forces. It has a huge variety of doubtful operators, ranging from a minority of outright villains to a much larger group of promoters who blinker themselves against the harsh implications of the deals they make. But what must be said is that in this area, as almost everywhere else. The abolitionists over-simplify to the extent of serious distortion. Certainly some boxers are badly used, but the modern fighter in a country like Britain is usually as much his own man as any professional sportsman is. Anyone who imagines that Johnny Owen was under any kind of duress when he went into the ring for the world bantamweight championship match with Lupe Pintor of Mexico that led to Owen's death in that same autumn of 1980 simply did not know the boy. He was, as it happens, an extreme example of someone who desperately wanted to box. His personality was a small cloud of reticence until he entered the ambience of boxing, in a gym or an arena. Once there, he was transformed from a 24-year-old virgin whose utterances tended to come in muffled monosyllables into a confident, skilled practitioner of a rough but exciting trade. It may be—as I suggested in the hours after seeing him disastrously injured at the Olympic Auditorium in Los Angeles—that Johnny Owen's tragedy was to find himself articulate in such a dangerous language. But the people who say he should have been denied access to that language run the risk of playing God.

Some will declare that only the psychologically inadequate could ever need boxing and there might be some sense in the claim if anyone cares to define psychological inadequacy in the age of the neutron bomb. At a more obvious level of comparison, it seems to many of us that the motorcycle has not only demonstrated an infinitely greater capacity to kill and maim young men than boxing ever did but is rather more readily identified with coarser spirits. Hell's Angels have caused more public havoc than the members of boxing clubs. To touch on that is not to fall in with those who believe that exchanging blows with padded gloves builds character. The game may have saved thousands of hard-case youngsters from the worst excesses of the street, but few of those salvaged had the instincts of muggers to start with. Most boys who go in for boxing have a deep, combative urge to test themselves and there isn't much of the test about battering an old-age pensioner and legging it with her purse.

Mentioning nobility in connection with boxing is chancy, but exposure to men like Joe Frazier has encouraged such boldness. And Frazier still itched to fight the best heavyweights in the world long after he had retired with a pile of dollars. 'All right,' say the critics, 'tell us what is ennobling about years of having the cranium pummelled, about the absorption of so many blows that the functioning of the brain is almost certain to be impaired.' Reference to all the thousands who have emerged from long hard careers without any evident cerebral damage, such as Gene Tunney (who fought some of the most destructive punchers imaginable and survived stinking rich and intimidatingly sharp into his 80s) or our own Henry Cooper, is no more a conclusive answer that are the greatly improved safety measures and medical supervision. The blatant truth is that there are genuine risks. The relevant question is whether our society considers those risks acceptable in relation to other sports. There is no doubt that fighters consider them so. Naturally, they don't dwell on the possibility of being knocked punchy, any more than a Grand Prix driver thinks of being minced or barbecued in his cockpit. The per capita likelihood on the second is probably much greater than of the first. Jackie Stewart, whose genius was reinforced by marvellous luck, came through a magnificently successful career as a driver unscathed. But Stewart has pertinent things to say about why he put himself in danger so often. He thinks that too much of modern life is wrapped in cotton-wool. 'People who are allowed to live life to the full, to its outer edges, are a blessed group,' he says. The exhilaration of his sport was vastly different from the excitement of a boxer's, but that too is an outer edge.

Fighters are a long way from being wrapped in cotton-wool and further measures could be taken to reduce the threat of major injuries. Perhaps a limited form of headguard should be introduced. But it must be admitted that if the game loses its rawness, it is nothing. If it ever became a kind of fencing with fists, a mere trial of skills, reflexes and agility, and not the test of courage, will and resilience that it is now, then it would lose its appeal for many who are neither sadists nor seekers after the trappings of virility. For some of us boxing, with all its thousand ambiguities, offers in its best moments a thrill as pure and basic as a heartbeat.

Maybe I should not be drawn to it, but I am, and I acknowledge no hypocrisy in deciding in 1980 that I could be at a graveside service in Mer-thyr Tydfil when Johnny Owen was buried and at the ringside in New Orleans a fortnight later when Roberto Duran met Sugar Ray Leonard. Our society will have to become a lot more saintly before the abolition of boxing qualifies as an urgent priority.

(London, August, 1982)

First Reading

1. McIlvanny states in lines 12–14, "I have too much respect for the abolitionists' argument to try to ignore or belittle their central objections." Does the tone of McIlvanney's essay suggest that he takes opposition to boxing seriously, or is he actually dismissive of his opponents?

2. This essay preceded George Will's by several months. Did Will appear to give credence to any of McIlvanney's arguments? Explain.

Second Reading

1. Both Will and McIlvanney refer to the sport of automobile racing. How does each one make a comparison that serves their respective arguments?

2. Johnny Owen was a Welsh fighter who was killed in a 1980 championship fight in Los Angeles. Both McIlvanny and Will refer to him in their essays. Contrast McIlvanney's reference and use of Owen's death with Will's. How does the comparison reflect the different approaches taken by the authors to their subject and to their respective audiences?

Writing

Synthesis

Research, Preparation and Writing Time one week following final reading assignment

Directions The following task is based on the preceding three texts by Gordon Marino, George Will, and Hugh McIlvanney. Before you begin to plan your own essay, reread these texts. Then take some time to carefully compare and contrast the texts in light of each other.

Introduction In the aftermath of the 1962 death of Benny Paret in a boxing match with Emile Griffith, Norman Cousins wrote: "The crowd wants the knockout; it wants to see a man hurt."

Assignment After careful consideration of the introduction, **write an essay in which you either defend or question the social mores that give rise to sporting events that feature the possibility of grievous injury or sudden death**. Cite Marino, Will, and McIlvanney in your essay in ways that serve your own argument. In addition, extend the support for your argument by using at least two other sources. Use Modern Language Association style to document your sources.

Prewriting As you plan your essay, use the following scenario to guide you: Imagine you have been invited into a discussion of the issues raised by the assignment while in the presence of each author. What would the conversation include? What would you hear in the way of response? How would you then enter into the discussion?

Prepare a draft for a teacher or peer conference, and then write and submit a final version. Your essay will run from 5 to 7 pages.

Chapter 8

Genes

Background

Genetic engineering, in its many forms, attracts global attention. It is the subject of film, essays, editorials, speeches, cartoons, and heated debate. Few among us understand the technicalities of the science or the methods of investigation involved. Many of us know of the possible decisions for physicians, the consequences for patients, or the responsibilities for lawmakers. We read texts and hear talk of the benefits and dangers. How do we know if the texts and the talk are reliable? How can we withhold judgment when the issues are so controversial? But sound thinking requires we do exactly that. Do we wish to be, as Vaclav Havel said, "masters of being," controlling all that is in our power to control? How much control should we exercise? Or do we as consumers, scientists, and lawmakers consider ourselves contributors to a harmonious community of informed citizens who make decisions that benefit all members? What is our responsibility, and how do we make sound decisions about such elements of and possibilities for our being? Some argue that genetic engineering manipulates and threatens nature. Others believe that such activity offers boundless and unforeseen benefits to humanity. What should be the limits of genetic engineering, and who should decide? These issues suggest it is our duty as citizens of the global community to know more.

Readings

Robert Wright
Who Gets the Good Genes?

Eric Cohen
The Real Meaning of Genetics

Laurie Zoloth
Embryonic Stem Cell Research Is Ethical

C. Ben Mitchell
The Return of Eugenics

Michael J. Sandel
The Case Against Perfection

Human Genome Project
Impacting Many Disciplines

Jonathan Rhodes
Building a Public Conversation on the Meaning of Genetics

The Hinxton Group, an International Consortium on Stem Cells, Ethics and Law
Consensus Statement

William P. Cheshire, Jr.
Small Things Considered: The Ethical Significance of Embryonic Stem Cell Research

This essay appeared in the January 11, 1999, issue of *Time* magazine. The writer is a senior fellow at the New America Foundation and the author of *Nonzero: The Logic of Human Destiny* and *The Moral Animal: Evolutionary Psychology and Everyday Life*. He has also written for *The Atlantic Monthly*, *The New Yorker*, and *The New York Times Magazine*.

In the 1932 novel *Brave New World*, Aldous Huxley envisioned future childbirth as a very orderly affair. At the Central London Hatchery and Conditioning Center, in accordance with orders
5 from the Social Predestination Room, eggs were fertilized, bottled and put on a conveyor belt. Nine months later, the embryos—after "decanting"—were babies. Thanks to state-sponsored brainwashing, they would grow up delighted
10 with their genetically assigned social roles—from clever, ambitious alphas to dim-witted epsilons.

Ever since publication of Huxley's dystopian novel, this has been the standard eugenics nightmare: government social engineers subverting
15 individual reproductive choice for the sake of an eerie social efficiency. But as the age of genetic engineering dawns, the more plausible nightmare is roughly the opposite: that a laissez-faire eugenics will emerge from the free choices of millions of
20 parents. Indeed, the only way to avoid Huxleyesque social stratification may be for the government to get into the eugenics business.

Huxley's scenario made sense back in 1932. Some American states were forcibly sterilizing
25 the "feebleminded," and Hitler had praised these policies in *Mein Kampf*. But the biotech revolution that Huxley dimly foresaw has turned the logic of eugenics inside out. It lets parents choose genetic traits, whether by selective abortion, selec-
30 tive reimplanting of eggs fertilized in vitro or—in perhaps just a few years—injecting genes into fertilized eggs. In Huxley's day eugenics happened only by government mandate; now it will take government mandate—a ban on genetic tinker-
35 ing—to prevent it.

An out-and-out ban isn't in the cards, though. Who would try to stop parents from ensuring that their child doesn't have hemophilia? And once some treatments are allowed, deciding where to
40 draw the line becomes difficult.

The Bishop of Edinburgh tried. After overseeing a British Medical Association study on bioethics, he embraced genetic tinkering for "medical reasons," while denouncing the "Franken-
45 stein idea" of making "designer babies" with good looks and a high IQ. But what is the difference? Therapists consider learning disabilities to be medical problems, and if we find a way to diagnose and remedy them before birth, we'll
50 be raising scores on IQ tests. Should we tell parents they can't do that, that the state has decided they must have a child with dyslexia? Minor memory flaws? Below-average verbal skills? At some point you cross the line between handi-
55 cap and inconvenience, but people will disagree about where.

If the government does try to ban certain eugenic maneuvers, some rich parents will visit clinics in more permissive nations, then come home to
60 bear their tip-top children. (Already, British parents have traveled to Saudi Arabia to choose their baby's sex in vitro, a procedure that is illegal at home.) Even without a ban, it will be upper-class parents who can afford pricey genetic technolo-
65 gies. Children who would in any event go to the finest doctors and schools will get an even bigger head start on health and achievement.

This unequal access won't bring a rigid caste system a la *Brave New World*. The interplay be-
70 tween genes and environment is too complex to permit the easy fine-tuning of mind and spirit. Besides, in vitro fertilization is nobody's idea of a good time; even many affluent parents will forgo painful invasive procedures unless horrible hered-
75 itary defects are at stake. But the technology will become more powerful and user friendly. Sooner or later, as the most glaring genetic liabilities drift toward the bottom of the socioeconomic scale, we will see a biological stratification vivid enough to
80 mock American values.

Enter the government. The one realistic way to avoid this nightmare is to ensure that poor people will be able to afford the same technologies that the rich are using. Put that way, it sounds inno-
85 cent, but critics will rightly say it amounts to subsidizing eugenics.

State involvement will create a vast bioethical quagmire. Even if everyone magically agrees that

improving a child's memory is as valid as avoid-
90 ing dyslexia, there will still be things taxpayers
aren't ready to pay for—genes of unproven benefit, say, or alterations whose downsides may ex-
ceed the upside. (The tendency of genes to have
more than one effect—pleiotropy—seems to be
95 the rule, not the exception.) The question will be
which techniques are beyond the pale. The answers will change as knowledge advances, but the
arguments will never end.

In *Brave New World*, state-sponsored eugenics
100 was part of a larger totalitarianism, a cultural war
against family bonds and enduring romance and
other quaint vestiges of free reproductive choice.
The novel worked; it left readers thinking that
nothing could be more ghastly than having gov-
105 ernment get into the designer-baby business. But
if this business is left to the marketplace, we may
see that government involvement, however messy,
however creepy, is not the creepiest alternative.

First Reading

1. Find Wright's assumption in paragraph 4 (lines 36–40), and explain who would disagree with him.
2. Paraphrase Wright's if/then reasoning in paragraph 5 (lines 41–56).
3. Does Wright answer the question asked in his title? If yes, what evidence does he offer that convinces? If no, how would you answer it?

Second Reading

1. In paragraph 2, Wright explains "the standard eugenics nightmare" and "the more plausible nightmare." How does the word "nightmare" affect your understanding of contemporary issues of eugenics?
2. Based on your reading of paragraphs 1–6 (lines 1–67), explain the term "social stratification." Then explain the term "bioethical quagmire" in paragraph 9 (lines 87–98).
3. What are the effects of Wright's reference to Hitler in paragraph 3 (lines 23–35) and his reference to the Bishop of Edinburgh in paragraph 5 (lines 41–56)?
4. Explain why you agree or disagree with Wright's definition of "totalitarianism" in the concluding paragraph.

Writing

1. **Analysis** — Write an essay in which you analyze the rhetorical strategies Wright uses to convey his view of "the more plausible nightmare."
2. **Argument** — Write an essay in which you agree or disagree with Wright's idea that government involvement in bioethics is "not the creepiest alternative."

Eric Cohen
The Real Meaning of Genetics

This essay was originally delivered as the inaugural lecture of the Genomics Forum at the University of Edinburgh, in Scotland. Its author, Eric Cohen, is editor of *The New Atlantis* and director of the Project on Bioethics and American Democracy at the Ethics and Public Policy Center, a think tank in Washington, D.C.

With a subject as large and as profound as modern genetics, we face a major question from the start about how to approach it. We could take a *scientific approach*, examining the use of infor-
5 mation technology in genomic research, or the latest advances in identifying certain genetic mutations, or the transfer of genetic knowledge into useful medical technologies. We could take a *social scientific approach*, seeking to understand
10 the economic incentives that drive the genetic research agenda, or surveying public attitudes toward genetic testing, or documenting the use of reproductive genetic technology according to socioeconomic class. We could take a *public safety*
15 *approach*, reviewing different genetic tests and therapies for safety and efficacy, and ensuring that sound regulatory procedures are in place to protect and inform vulnerable patients undergoing gene therapy trials. As we think about the ge-
20 netic future, all of these approaches are valuable, but none of them is sufficient.

The reason we care so much about the new genetics is that we sense that this area of science will touch on the deepest matters of human life—such
25 as how we have children, how we experience freedom, and how we face sickness and death. Like no other area of modern science and technology, genetics inspires both dreams and nightmares about the human future with equal passion: the dream
30 of perfect babies, the nightmare of genetic tyranny. But as usual, the dream and the nightmare are not the best guides to understanding the real meaning of genetics. We need a more sober approach—one that confronts the real ethical dilemmas we face,
35 without constructing such a monstrous image of the future that our gravest warnings are ignored like the bioethics boy who cried wolf.

Possibility and Prediction
In thinking about the new genetics, we seem to
40 commit two errors at once: worrying too much too early and worrying too little too late. For decades, scientists and science-fiction writers—and it is sometimes hard to tell the difference—have predicted the coming of genetic engineering:
45 some with fear and loathing, some with anticipatory glee. But when the gradual pace of technological change does not seem as wonderful as the dream or as terrible as the nightmare, we get used to our new powers all too readily. Profound
50 change quickly seems prosaic, because we measure it against the world we imagined instead of the world we truly have. Our technological advances—including those that require overriding existing moral boundaries—quickly seem insuffi-
55 cient, because the human desire for perfect control and perfect happiness is insatiable.

Of course, sometimes we face the opposite problem: Scientists assure us that today's breakthrough will not lead to tomorrow's nightmare.
60 They tell us that what we want (like cures for disease) is just over the horizon, but that what we fear (like human cloning) is technologically impossible. The case of human cloning is indeed instructive, revealing the dangers of both over-
65 prediction and under-prediction. So permit me a brief historical digression, but a digression with a point.

In the 1970s, as the first human embryos were being produced outside the human body, many
70 critics treated *in vitro* fertilization and human cloning as equally pregnant developments, with genetic engineering lurking not far behind. James Watson testified before the United States Congress in 1971, declaring that we must pass laws about
75 cloning now before it is too late. In one sense, perhaps, the oracles were right: Even if human cloning did not come as fast as they expected, it is coming and probably coming soon. But because we worried so much more about human cloning
80 even then, test-tube babies came to seem prosaic very quickly, in part because they were not clones and in part because the babies themselves were such a blessing. We barely paused to consider the strangeness of originating human life in the labo-
85 ratory; of beholding, with human eyes, our own human origins; of suspending nascent human life in the freezer; of further separating procreation

from sex. Of course, IVF has been a great gift for many infertile couples. It has answered the biblical Hannah's cry, and fulfilled time and again the longing most individuals and couples possess to have a child of their own, flesh of their own flesh. But it has also created strange new prospects, including the novel possibility of giving birth to another couple's child—flesh *not* of my flesh, you might say—and the possibility of picking-and-choosing human embryos for life or death based on their genetic characteristics. It has also left us the tragic question of deciding what we owe the thousands of embryos now left-over in freezers— a dilemma with no satisfying moral answer.

But this is only the first part of the cloning story. Fast-forward now to the 1980s. By then, IVF had become normal, while many leading scientists assured the world that mammals could never be cloned. Ian Wilmut and his team in Scotland proved them all wrong with the birth of Dolly in 1996, and something similar seems to be happening now with primate and human cloning. In 2002, Gerald Schatten, a cloning researcher at the University of Pittsburgh, said "primate cloning, including human cloning, will not be in our lifetimes." By 2003, he was saying that "given enough time and materials, we may discover how to make it work." And by 2005, Schatten and his South Korean colleagues had reliably cloned human embryos to the blastocyst stage, the very biological moment when they might be implanted to initiate a pregnancy. In all likelihood, the age of human reproductive cloning is not far off, even if the age of full-blown genetic engineering may never come.

Looking at where the science of genetics is heading, we must beware the twin vices of over-prediction and under-prediction. Over-prediction risks blinding us to the significance of present realities, by inebriating us with distant dreams and distant nightmares. Under-prediction risks blinding us to where today's technological breakthroughs may lead, both for better and for worse. Prediction requires the right kind of caution—caution about letting our imaginations run wild, and caution about letting science proceed without limits, because we falsely assume that it is always innocent and always will be. To think clearly, therefore, we must put aside the grand dreams and great nightmares of the genetic future to consider the moral meaning of the genetic present—the meaning of what we can do now and why we do it. And we need to explore what these new genetic possibilities might mean for how we live, what we value, and how we treat one another.

Humanly speaking, the new genetics seems to have five dimensions or meanings: (1) genetics as a route to self-understanding, a way of knowing ourselves; (2) genetics as a route to new medical therapies, a way of curing ourselves; (3) genetics as a potential tool for human re-engineering, a prospect I find far-fetched; (4) genetics as a means of knowing something about our biological destiny, about our health and sickness in the future; and (5) genetics as a tool for screening the traits of the next generation, for choosing some lives and rejecting others.

First Reading

1. Cohen begins his remarks by examining a variety of approaches to the subject of modern genetics. What reasons would you give to confirm his statement at the end of the first paragraph, "but none of them is sufficient"?

2. In paragraph 2 (lines 33–34), Cohen comments that we need a "sober approach—one that confronts the real ethical dilemmas we face." What reasons might he have for choosing the words "sober" and "dilemmas"?

3. In paragraphs 5, 6, and 7 (lines 68–142), Cohen presents a brief history of some advances in genetic engineering beginning with the 1970s and ending with the present. How does this description support his argument?

4. Find Cohen's biblical, mythological, and literary allusions. Explain the effect of each.

Second Reading

1. Read paragraph 2 carefully, paying particular attention to the last two sentences. What do Cohen's comments suggest about contemporary society?

2. In paragraph 5 (lines 68–101), what is the effect of the juxtaposition of the idea of something "prosaic" with "test-tube babies"?

3. Near the end of paragraph 5, Cohen comments about the possibility of a birth that is "flesh *not* of my flesh." Explain the paradoxical qualities of Cohen's comment.

4. Explain how, in paragraph 6 (lines 102–122), Cohen de-emphasizes the assurances of some scientists.

5. In paragraph 7 (lines 123–142), Cohen explains "over-prediction" and "under-prediction." Rewrite this paragraph in your own words.

Writing

1. **Argument** — In paragraph 8 (lines 143–153), Cohen names five dimensions of genetics. Consider your ideas about the advantages and disadvantages of each dimension as it applies to your understanding of "the new genetics." Then write an essay in which you examine both sides of one dimension and its importance as a consideration for patients, medical professionals, or lawmakers.

2. **Argument** — Consider the advantages and disadvantages of each dimension Cohen names in paragraph 8 as it applies to your understanding of "the new genetics." Then write a researched and documented essay in which you agree or disagree with Cohen's statement that each dimension is important to the global society.

Embryonic stem cell research is an issue where politics, religion, and science collide. In September 2004, the U.S. Senate Committee on Commerce, Science, and Transportation invited experts to give testimony at a hearing entitled "Embryonic Stem Cell Research: Exploring the Controversy." Laurie Zoloth, professor of bioethics and religion at Northwestern University, addressed the ethical implications of this research.

My name is Laurie Zoloth, and I am a professor of bioethics and religion in the Medical Humanities and Bioethics program, and director of bioethics at the Center for Genetic Medicine at the Feinberg School of Medicine, Northwestern University in Illinois. I want to thank the committee for asking us to testify about the ethical issues in human embryonic cell research, and tell you why my University and many of the organizations in which I serve—the Howard Hughes Medical Institute, the International Society for Stem Cell Research, the AAAS [American Association for the Advancement of Science], the NAS [National Academy of Sciences]—support and encourage human embryonic stem cell research. First, for it is part of our broad commitment to the translation of basic medical research into the great moral enterprise of healing—serving the public's health is the core moral gesture of the medicine we teach. Second, we support stem cell research as a free academic activity, like free speech, that must be protected and sustained in our University and that must be both funded and regulated in full view of the public.

As I wrote this speech, my 10th grader was also writing a speech about stem cells—I note this not tangentially, nor merely to remind that I am a mother of five, and I, like each of you, worry about the sort of moral universe I will leave to my children, but to stress how central this debate has become in our American democracy—it is the subject of how we speak of healing and our duty to heal, and it is the subject when we speak of human dignity, and it is how we express our hope and our fear of the future. Stem cells are important in this way because of the serious rumor of hope they carry for millions of yearning patients and families. As an early watcher of the science of stem cells, I have listened carefully to the excitement of the researchers, and while ethicists urge caution and avoid hyperbolic claims, most ethicists are convinced that the sincerity and veracity of a growing body of evidence about how these cells can be coaxed into useful tissue, and how these cells can explain the very nature of how cells grow, change and divide and die—in short, how disease plays out at the cellular level—is stunningly important. If even some of what we are told to hope for is correct, then how we think about illness and injury will be transformed.

The Duty of Just Medicine

So why do ethical considerations stop full funding of this science? I would argue that there are three issues: where we get the cell, how we get the cell and what we use them for. First, is the issue of the origins of the cells, which means the moral status of the human blastocyst—can we destroy blastocysts, made in the lab, for any purpose? Can we do it for medical research and why or why not? Second is the process that researchers need to get eggs and sperm donated fairly and safely and responsibly, and handled with dignity. How are women's special needs protected? How do we protect human subjects in the first stages of this research? Finally, if researchers can find successful therapies, how will good goals of medicine be protected, and access to the therapies be fair? Can we come to agreement on the proper ends of medicine?

Stem cells are interesting to ethicists for precisely the same reason that they are intriguing to the market—they represent a therapeutic intervention that, unlike heart transplants, could be universally available, replicable and scaleable. If the daunting problems of histocompatibility can be overcome, embryonic stem cells could be made universally acceptable to any body. Unlike adult stem cells, which would have to be created each time for each particular user, the premise of application is the wide use. Bioethicists defend high intensity interventions like organ transplant, which have saved, albeit at high cost, thousands of individuals. But organ transplants are terribly expensive, and always rationed, and the risks considerable. Stem cell research is aimed at a wider community of vulnerable patients, and at no one particular category, age, ethnicity, or class. The sort of injury and diseases that stem cells are indicated for are not boutique, or rare—cell death and cell growth is at the core of nearly all disorders. Research into these essential causes would be precisely the sort of research we ought to insist on. Further, understanding how embryonic cells are programmed and reprogrammed might allow us to understand how to de-program cells, allowing adult cells to regenerate, teaching the body to heal itself. The demand for justice and the scrutiny to which genetic medicine is given are indications that we understand the power of genetics to reconfigure the self, and the society—in this way, the very debate about stem cells forces precisely the justice considerations that I would argue must be a part of medicine. The principle of justice places a priority on the public aspects of research—on public funding and on public oversight review boards for protocols.

Theological Differences

I think we can come to some agreement—around the duties of just medicine, and just science, and we have in the past come to agree on the how we must treat human research subjects and regulate that process, but I think we cannot come to some sort of agreement on what most divides us today—when human life begins, for this is a profoundly religious question in a profoundly religious country, profoundly dedicated to the proposition that our freedom to faithfully interpret our faith is the core of American life. For nearly all Jews, most Muslims, many Buddhists, and many Protestants, it is not only permissible to use human blastocysts to create stem cell lines, it is morally imperative—it must be done if it can lead to saving lives or healing. As an orthodox Jew, I understand the blastocyst, made in the lab, at the very first stages of division, prior to the time it could even successfully be transferred to a woman's body as just what it is at that moment: a cluster of primitive cells. It does not have the moral status of a human child—it lacks a mother's womb, its existence is only theoretical without this, and even in the course of a normal pregnancy a blastocyst at 3 days is far before our tradition considers it a human person. While I respect that this is a difference in theology, and while I understand the passion and the conviction of those for whom the blastocyst is a person from the moment of fertilization, I do not believe this, and it is matter of faith for me as well. My passion and my conviction are toward the suffering of the one I see in need, ill, or wounded—for Jews and Muslims, the commandment to attend to this suffering is core to our faiths. Jewish organizations from Hadassah to the rabbinic and lay boards of all national Jewish denominations speak in one voice on this matter: human embryonic stem cell research is an activity of *pekuah nefesh*, saving and healing broken lives, and of *tikkun olam*—repairing an unfinished natural world.

What are you to do, as leaders of our polity when we will not compromise faith positions? I suggest we must learn to compromise our faith policies—we do for other deeply felt issues and we must in this case as well. For example: we did not agree when life ended, but when heart transplants became a possibility, Harvard convened a committee to set criteria for "brain death"—an imperfect, biologically ragged, but useable compromise that allowed transplant research to develop. The US leads the world in successful transplant surgical techniques—and yet some faiths do not agree on these criteria. We do not agree on prenatal diagnosis, yet this is widely done, as is IVF [in vitro fertilization] even if it means embryos are destroyed to get one successful pregnancy. We do not agree, but we publicly fund and publicly go forward with research about these polices and we allow each family and physician to make private choices. We do this by a combination of courage and compromise—you shape our policy in different ways: Republicans in one way, Democrats in another, but both allow for research to go forward with limits, based in time, or geography. Now it is time to revisit these limits.

The Courage to Compromise

[In the first half of 2004] I have traveled to three countries to look at their stem cell research and meet with their scientists: Israel, England and Korea. In each of these places, I also met with the bioethicists, philosophers, legal scholars and theologians who reflect on the research—who have demanded the same sort of careful, national, and public oversight I would think ethically important. What I saw was impressive—and for this committee in particular, critical. I saw that these countries understood that basic research in biology would be a core driver of their economy, that the knowledge, wisdom and energy that inspired that research would open the door to a world of new possibilities, some false starts, to be sure, but perhaps—just perhaps—some new starts. These countries understand that turning their full attention to science is not only prudent in our competitive global world, it is compassionate—it is the right thing to do to shape your country's future toward healing the needs of the suffering. In

South Korea's labs, they meet at dawn to begin the work every single day, working with the same passion and government support we give to our Mars Rover programs, for example.

Ought we to tremble when we cross such a threshold of human knowledge? Ought we to worry that we may be going too far or too fast? Of course, for we are being asked to understand the world differently, the self differently, what it means to be human and to be unique, differently—to know and to see things which were impossible to know or see a decade ago. Of course we need to think soberly about the possibility that the research may fail utterly, or that it may succeed but lead us into a place of great unpredictability—that is the very nature of research—that is why the future is what makes us free, this uncertainty.

Courage to face the problem will mean a compromise that can be regulated, as we did with recombinant DNA, as we did in organ transplantation. I would urge a far broader and more open policy than our American scientists face now, for it is far too late to stop, ban, or have a moratorium on the basic science of human embryonic stem cells—it not only will proceed, it has proceeded, in Asia, Israel, Europe and England. Stem cell research will now clearly be a possible road. Where that road might turn us is unknown—but what is certain is that if we turn off the road, we will watch others pass us by. Our challenge—and this means each of us—scientist, citizen, congregant, critic and enthusiast—most of all Senator—will be how to live bravely and decently and fairly in a complex world of difficult moral choices. Can stem cell research yield therapies that could help millions who now suffer? Will it yield cures for diabetes, Parkinson's, spinal cord injury? Who can yet know? If it were able to help even some, that might be light enough in the storm filled world. I tell my son that he must raise these questions, the core questions of ethics and of biology—How are we human? How will we be free? What must I do about the suffering of the other person? And that stem cell science can remind us that we are most human when we act as healers, we are the most free when we explore what we don't yet know, and we are bound to a duty to shape our work to care always for the person in need.

First Reading

1. Annotate Zoloth's testimony and specifically note the movement of ideas.
2. Also note and explain the effects of Zoloth's use of diction, anecdotes, and examples.
3. Consider the effect of Zoloth's personal references and use of questions. How do these strategies engage or connect the speaker with her audience?

Second Reading

1. In paragraph 1, Zoloth expresses the commitment of the medical community to stem cell research as "the great moral enterprise of healing." Then she explains what that statement means. Examine her explanation and explain the meaning of "core moral gesture."
2. Also in paragraph 1, Zoloth compares stem cell research to free speech and states that it must be "protected," "sustained," "funded," and "regulated." What is the effect of this comparison and these word choices?
3. In paragraph 2, how does Zoloth explain that the debate is "central" to American democracy?
4. In paragraphs 5 and 6 (lines 108–173), Zoloth addresses and explains issues of disagreement. Explain her reasoning in paragraph 5. In paragraph 6, she suggests that compromise is necessary. Note the example she provides and explain what she asks the Committee to consider.
5. Zoloth concludes paragraph 6 with the suggestion that compromise requires courage and then moves to state that oversight of stem cell research is "ethically important." How does her description of those with whom she met add to her credibility? What might be her reason for stating that "attention to science" is important?

6. What is the effect of her comparison of the passion of the South Korean stem cell researchers to that of Americans for the Mars Rover programs (lines 196–199)?

7. In paragraph 8 (lines 200–212), Zoloth confronts another objection. Explain how she expresses that uncertainty is the nature of research and that it is desirable.

8. According to Zoloth, what is "our challenge"?

9. Explain why you agree or disagree with the importance of each of Zoloth's "core questions" of ethics and biology that she identifies in the concluding paragraph.

Writing

1. **Argument/Imitation** — Write a speech in which you agree or disagree with Zoloth. In your speech, imitate her pattern of arrangement.

2. **Analysis** — Write an essay in which you analyze how Zoloth's rhetorical strategies express her belief that stem cell research is ethical.

3. **Comparison** — After you read the Cheshire essay on pages 156–160, analyze the persuasive qualities of both Zoloth's speech and Cheshire's essay. Then write an essay in which you examine the qualities of each text and explain which one presents a more persuasive argument regarding stem cell research.

Eugenics is a social philosophy that advocates the improvement of human hereditary traits. C. Ben Mitchell, associate professor of Bioethics and Contemporary Culture at Trinity International University in Deerfield, Illinois, is the editor of *Ethics & Medicine.* The following editorial appeared in the summer 2005 issue of that journal.

Author of the Father Brown mysteries and political essayist G. K. Chesterton perceptively said, "We can be almost certain of being wrong about the future, if we are wrong about the past'." The American eugenics movement is one of those historical epochs which we can ill afford to repeat. Yet we are inching increasingly close to doing so.

5   With the power of contemporary genetic technology a new eugenic enthusiasm has emerged. Our culture's emphasis on the genetically "fit" and our difficulty embracing those who are "less fit" fuels this enthusiasm.

The quest for genetic enhancement of our offspring is the most virulent form of the new eugenics. James Hughes, one of the architects of so-called transhumanism, has ar-

10   gued: "The right to a custom made child is merely the natural extension of our current discourse of reproductive rights. I see no virtue in the role of chance in conception, and great virtue in expanding choice. If women are to be allowed the 'reproductive right' or 'choice' to choose the father of their child, with his attendant characteristics, then they should be allowed the right to choose the characteristics from a catalog. It will be con-

15   sidered obsessive and dumb to give your kids only parental genes."

Similarly, James Watson, who with Francis Crick discovered the doublehelical nature of the DNA molecule, told *The Guardian* in 2003, "If you really are stupid, I would call that a disease… So I'd like to get rid of that… It seems unfair that some people don't get the same opportunity. Once you have a way in which you can improve our children, no

20   one can stop it. It would be stupid not to use it because someone else will. Those parents who enhance their children, then their children are going to be the ones who dominate the world."

It may be unlikely in our age of reproductive freedom that the new eugenics will be enforced through mandatory sterilization – as in the past. There are, however, other,

25   more subtle forms of coercion. Personal choice and consumerism are much more likely to fuel eugenics today. One day, when genetic tests are more widely available, it might even become illegal to bring a child into the world with a genetic disability.

Discrimination against persons because of their race, gender, or disabilities is an ugly reality. Discrimination based on genetic identity is even uglier. If we would preserve a

30   truly human future for ourselves and for our children we must value individuals for who they are, not for what they can do. The laudable goal of treating human disease and relieving human suffering must not be allowed to become a tool for exercising "quality control" over our offspring. To do so would be to use the good gift of genetic knowledge for evil ends. Only vigilance on the part of all of us can prevent a bleak genetic future.

First Reading

1. Explain your understanding of the Chesterton quote in paragraph 1.
2. Mitchell presents the Hughes argument in paragraph 3 (lines 8–15). What is the effect of his reference to Hughes's comments in connection with "the most virulent form of the new eugenics"?
3. Paragraph 4 (lines 16–22) is a reference to comments by James Watson. Explain Watson's comments.

Second Reading

1. If Chesterton focused on the past and future, Hughes on expanding choice, and Watson on enhancement, what is your explanation of Mitchell's focus?
2. Read paragraphs 5 and 6 (lines 23–34) closely. Examine the positive and negative connotations. Explain how Mitchell's word choice contributes to emotional appeals.

Writing

1. **Argument/Imitation** — Write a rebuttal to Mitchell's argument. Imitate Mitchell's organization and find three references to introduce your argument effectively.
2. **Analysis** — Write an essay in which you analyze how Mitchell's rhetorical strategies convey his values regarding genetic knowledge.

Michael J. Sandel
The Case Against Perfection

This article appeared in the April 2004 issue of *The Atlantic Monthly*. Its author teaches political philosophy at Harvard University, where he is the Anne T. and Robert M. Bass Professor of Government. This article reflects his personal views.

Breakthroughs in genetics present us with a promise and a predicament. The promise is that we may soon be able to treat and prevent a host of debilitating diseases. The predicament is that our newfound genetic knowledge may also enable us to manipulate our own nature—to enhance our muscles, memories, and moods; to choose the sex, height, and other genetic traits of our children; to make ourselves "better than well." When science moves faster than moral understanding, as it does today, men and women struggle to articulate their unease. In liberal societies they reach first for the language of autonomy, fairness, and individual rights. But this part of our moral vocabulary is ill equipped to address the hardest questions posed by genetic engineering. The genomic revolution has induced a kind of moral vertigo.

***

In a social world that prizes mastery and control, parenthood is a school for humility. That we care deeply about our children and yet cannot choose the kind we want teaches parents to be open to the unbidden. Such openness is a disposition worth affirming, not only within families but in the wider world as well. It invites us to abide the unexpected, to live with dissonance, to rein in the impulse to control. A *Gattaca*-like world in which parents became accustomed to specifying the sex and genetic traits of their children would be a world inhospitable to the unbidden, a gated community writ large. The awareness that our talents and abilities are not wholly our own doing restrains our tendency toward hubris.

Though some maintain that genetic enhancement erodes human agency by overriding effort, the real problem is the explosion, not the erosion, of responsibility. As humility gives way, responsibility expands to daunting proportions. We attribute less to chance and more to choice. Parents become responsible for choosing, or failing to choose, the right traits for their children. Athletes become responsible for acquiring, or failing to acquire, the talents that will help their teams win.

One of the blessings of seeing ourselves as creatures of nature, God, or fortune is that we are not wholly responsible for the way we are. The more we become masters of our genetic endowments, the greater the burden we bear for the talents we have and the way we perform. Today when a basketball player misses a rebound, his coach can blame him for being out of position. Tomorrow the coach may blame him for being too short. Even now the use of performance-enhancing drugs in professional sports is subtly transforming the expectations players have for one another; on some teams players who take the field free from amphetamines or other stimulants are criticized for "playing naked."

The more alive we are to the chanced nature of our lot, the more reason we have to share our fate with others. Consider insurance. Since people do not know whether or when various ills will befall them, they pool their risk by buying health insurance and life insurance. As life plays itself out, the healthy wind up subsidizing the unhealthy, and those who live to a ripe old age wind up subsidizing the families of those who die before their time. Even without a sense of mutual obligation, people pool their risks and resources and share one another's fate.

But insurance markets mimic solidarity only insofar as people do not know or control their own risk factors. Suppose genetic testing advanced to the point where it could reliably predict each person's medical future and life expectancy. Those confident of good health and long life would opt out of the pool, causing other people's premiums to skyrocket. The solidarity of insurance would disappear as those with good genes fled the actuarial company of those with bad ones.

The fear that insurance companies would use genetic data to assess risks and set premiums recently led the Senate to vote to prohibit genetic discrimination in health insurance. But the bigger danger, admittedly more speculative, is that genetic enhancement, if routinely practiced, would make it harder to foster the moral sentiments that social solidarity requires.

Why, after all, do the successful owe anything to the least-advantaged members of society? The best answer to this question leans heavily on the notion of giftedness. The natural talents that enable the successful to flourish are not their own doing but, rather, their good fortune—a result of the genetic lottery. If our genetic endowments are gifts, rather than achievements for which we can claim credit, it is a mistake and a conceit to assume that we are entitled to the full measure of the bounty they reap in a market economy. We therefore have an obligation to share this bounty with those who, through no fault of their own, lack comparable gifts.

A lively sense of the contingency of our gifts—a consciousness that none of us is wholly responsible for his or her success—saves a meritocratic society from sliding into the smug assumption that the rich are rich because they are more deserving than the poor. Without this, the successful would become even more likely than they are now to view themselves as self-made and self-sufficient, and hence wholly responsible for their success. Those at the bottom of society would be viewed not as disadvantaged, and thus worthy of a measure of compensation, but as simply unfit, and thus worthy of eugenic repair. The meritocracy, less chastened by chance, would become harder, less forgiving. As perfect genetic knowledge would end the simulacrum of solidarity in insurance markets, so perfect genetic control would erode the actual solidarity that arises when men and women reflect on the contingency of their talents and fortunes.

Thirty-five years ago Robert L. Sinsheimer, a molecular biologist at the California Institute of Technology, glimpsed the shape of things to come. In an article titled "The Prospect of Designed Genetic Change" he argued that freedom of choice would vindicate the new genetics, and set it apart from the discredited eugenics of old.

To implement the older eugenics…would have required a massive social programme carried out over many generations. Such a programme could not have been initiated without the consent and co-operation of a major fraction of the population, and would have been continuously subject to social control. In contrast, the new eugenics could, at least in principle, be implemented on a quite individual basis, in one generation, and subject to no existing restrictions.

According to Sinsheimer, the new eugenics would be voluntary rather than coerced, and also more humane. Rather than segregating and eliminating the unfit, it would improve them. "The old eugenics would have required a continual selection for breeding of the fit, and a culling of the unfit," he wrote. "The new eugenics would permit in principle the conversion of all the unfit to the highest genetic level."

Sinsheimer's paean to genetic engineering caught the heady, Promethean self-image of the age. He wrote hopefully of rescuing "the losers in that chromosomal lottery that so firmly channels our human destinies," including not only those born with genetic defects but also "the 50,000,000 'normal' Americans with an IQ of less than 90." But he also saw that something bigger than improving on nature's "mindless, age-old throw of dice" was at stake. Implicit in technologies of genetic intervention was a more exalted place for human beings in the cosmos. "As we enlarge man's freedom, we diminish his constraints and that which he must accept as given," he wrote. Copernicus and Darwin had "demoted man from his bright glory at the focal point of the universe," but the new biology would restore his central role. In the mirror of our genetic knowledge we would see ourselves as more than a link in the chain of evolution: "We can be the agent of transition to a whole new pitch of evolution. This is a cosmic event."

There is something appealing, even intoxicating, about a vision of human freedom unfettered by the given. It may even be the case that the allure of that vision played a part in summoning the genomic age into being. It is often assumed that the powers of enhancement we now possess arose as an inadvertent by-product of biomedical progress—the genetic revolution came, so to speak, to cure disease, and stayed to tempt us with the prospect of enhancing our performance, designing our children, and perfecting our nature. That may have the story backwards. It is more plausible to view genetic engineering as the ultimate expression of our resolve to see ourselves astride the world, the masters of our nature. But that promise of mastery is flawed. It threatens to banish our appreciation of life as a gift, and to leave us with nothing to affirm or behold outside our own will.

First Reading

1. Paraphrase each paragraph into one sentence in order to create a summary of the essay.
2. Explain the meaning of "moral vertigo" in paragraph 1. What is the effect of Sandel's use of the term?
3. In paragraph 2, Sandel examines the dispositions of hubris and humility in regard to genetics. Explain his position. What values does he reject?
4. What would Sandel's supporters say about "the chanced nature of our lot" (lines 59–60)? What would Sandel's opponents say?

Second Reading

1. How does Sandel's use of the anecdote in paragraph 4 (lines 44–58) contribute to his idea of responsibility?
2. Consider the reasons Sandel might have for including paragraphs 5 and 6 (lines 59–80) about insurance markets. How would you counter this evidence?
3. Carefully read again paragraphs 10–13 (lines 123–170). Consider Sandel's presentation of the Sinsheimer article, and explain how it leads logically to Sandel's conclusion.
4. Re-examine Sandel's final paragraph. Then complete the following statement:

    Sandel claims that _____, because _____.

Writing

1. **Analysis** — Write an essay in which you analyze how Sandel's rhetorical strategies convey his values regarding genetic engineering.
2. **Argument** — Write an essay in which you evaluate the advantages and disadvantages of genetic engineering and present your view of the aspect you consider most critical to the global community.

Human Genome Project
Impacting Many Disciplines

Completed in 2003, the Human Genome Project (HGP) had as its goals to identify all the genes in human DNA, determine the sequences of the chemical base pairs that are components of DNA, create a database of the results, improve tools for data analysis, transfer technology to the private sector, and address ethical, legal, and social issues. The HGP was conducted by the U.S. Department of Energy and the National Institutes of Health, in partnership with scientific organizations around the world. Analysis of the data will continue for many years. To view a large color image, go to http://genomics.energy.gov/gallery/basic_genomics/detail.np/detail-32.html

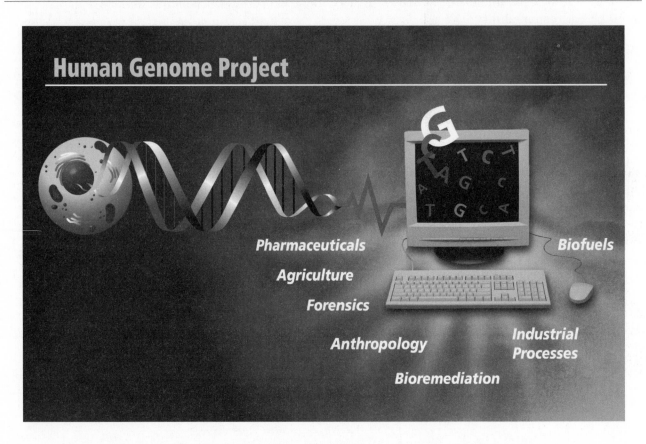

     Almost everyone will be affected by applications of information and technologies derived from the Human Genome Project. Entirely new approaches will be implemented in biological research and the practice of medicine and agriculture. Genetic data will provide the foundation for research in many fields, leading to an unprecedented un-
5 derstanding of the inner workings of whole biological systems. The benefits of genomic research are, or soon will be, realized in such areas as forensics and identification science, ecology and environmental science, toxic-waste cleanup, creation of new bioenergy sources and more efficient industrial processes, and in understanding the mysteries of evolution, anthropology, and human migration. Among the fields that HGP research
10 will impact are engineering, computer science, mathematics, counseling, sociology, ethics, religion, law, agriculture, education, pharmaceuticals, instrumentation, nuclear medicine, forensics, bioremediation, biofuels, and journalism. Cross-disciplinary students with solid backgrounds in science and in one or more other fields such as journalism, law, and computer science will be needed to tackle the issues and applications
15 arising from the HGP.

First Reading

1. Upon what do you first focus in the poster? What directed your focus to that element?
2. Describe your idea about the purpose of this poster.
3. Consider several titles for the poster and choose one you find most suitable. Does your title change the way a viewer might consider the image? Explain why or why not.
4. How does the poster convey information? If you had not read the paragraph, what could you determine from reading the poster?

Second Reading

1. To what issues or controversy do you think the poster responds?
2. Explain your ideas about the intended audience. Be specific in your description.
3. What elements unify the visual text? Write a list of everything you see before you decide.
4. Decide how the whole can be divided into parts.
5. How did this designer manipulate the contrasts, images, and light to shape the composition?
6. What seems most important in the poster? Why? Consider the elements that are included and those elements that may have been left out.

Writing

1. **Analysis** — Write an analysis of the details that generated your response to the poster. Consider such elements as contrasts of dark and light, point of view, and details. To introduce your analysis, present your thesis, and to conclude, defend it.
2. **Argument** — Write an argument from the point of view of an opponent of genetic engineering. Your audience is the general reading public, not specialists, so anticipate the range of values and knowledge. Choose your evidence and arrange your argument carefully. You might consider a Toulmin or Rogerian arrangement. You might also write the rebuttal to your argument or work with a partner and take opposing positions.

Jonathan Rhodes
Building a Public Conversation on the Meaning of Genetics

This article appears on the Web site of the Institute on Biotechnology and the Human Future, which is affiliated with the Illinois Institute of Technology. At the time of publication of the article, the author was a student at IIT's Chicago-Kent College of Law and a research assistant at both the Institute and the Center on Nanotechnology and Society.

Why Should We Care About Genetics?

Town hall meetings are commonplace during election cycles, as politicians roll up their shirtsleeves to get out and meet the people in a community
5 forum. In the spirit of bringing the community together to share ideas, the Illinois Humanities Council (IHC) has commenced a year-long project designed to increase public knowledge of genetics. The initiative, entitled Future Perfect: Conversa-
10 tions on the Meaning of the Genetics Revolution, has been designed to engage citizens in conversations about advances in genetics and their impact on the individual and society. During the kick-off event, the IHC brought together experts and lay-
15 persons in an exploration of the basic question: "Why should we care about genetics?"

The Possibility of an Informed Debate

Jon D. Miller, professor of integrative studies at Michigan State University, opened the discussion
20 by setting out the challenges. Chief among them is the difficulty of having an informed public debate on important scientific developments.

Miller framed the issue by asserting that the 20th century was "the century of physics," with
25 Einstein's theories transforming the way we live in and think about the world. He then proclaimed that the 21st century will be "the century of biotechnology," during which scientific developments in biotechnology and nanotechnology will
30 have the same potential to radically shift how we view the world and how we function within it.

During the biotech century, advances in genetics will alter the definition of health. And, over time, as these advances are assimilated into every-
35 day discussions about health and well being, they will become fixtures in the public policy debate.

As the human foray into the 21st century commences, the current landscape of public knowledge, understanding, and engagement must be assessed.
40 Over the past three decades, Miller's research has focused on measuring the general biomedical and genetic literacy in the United States and Europe. In town-hall-meeting spirit, Miller's presentation involved the audience in an interactive dialogue
45 by way of a series of true-false questions testing scientific literacy in the area of genetics.

Two-thirds of the audience received a "passing" score. This "passage rate" was significantly higher than the "passage rate" Miller found in his studies
50 of public scientific literacy. In these studies, Miller found such literacy highest in Denmark, with 47% of the Danish participants "passing." The United States came in at the middling rank of 28th among the 34 countries studied.
55 Such an outcome, Miller argued, is far too low for a democratic society. Informed debate about genetics or other complex scientific developments cannot occur if citizens do not have a basic understanding of the principles, issues, and terms
60 involved. To achieve this, Miller advocated for a fundamental change in scientific education. The requisite changes include: teaching children the core skill sets - including analysis and critical thinking - that will enable them to grapple with
65 the science and technologies of tomorrow; and offering ongoing, just-in-time, continuing education on science and technology for adults throughout their lifetime.

Taking the Good with the Bad?

70 Today, however, a classical understanding of genetics may not be sufficient to effectively manage health in a complicated scientific landscape. Rex Chisholm, director of the Center for Genetic Medicine at Northwestern University and the second
75 presenter during the town hall meeting, articulated his belief that the public is ready for a more fully developed understanding of genetics.

According to Chisholm, modern-day genetics likely mean that drugs can be selected for effec-
80 tiveness based on one's genetic makeup, but this will also likely mean that governments or corporations have access to this most personal information. Such information could lead to discrimination on many fronts. Chisholm asked the audience
85 to consider whether the potential benefits of tailor-made drugs outweigh the potential stigmas.

Art as a Medium for Contemplating Science

Big questions about the role of genetics in public health need to be approached from diverse perspectives across disciplines. Liz Lerman, founding artistic director of the Liz Lerman Dance Exchange and closing speaker, suggested that the arts could serve as a bridge between the complexities of science and culture. In proving of this potential role for the arts, Lerman set out to explore genetics through dance and other media. Through her contemporary dance work, entitled Ferocious Beauty: Genome, Lerman studied the effects of genetic disease on the body, including the unique movements of those affected by Huntington's disease.

The key to an informed debate about genetics turns upon understanding, and the key to achieving understanding is recognition of the different ways in which learning occurs. By utilizing novel approaches to learning, the arts can prove enriching in a way that other disciplines are not, according to Lerman. As a result, the arts offer an avenue for cultural exploration and meaningful exchange that is essential to public discourse on genetics and other emerging technologies.

Seizing the Opportunity

When science changes its mind, everyone is affected. And science changes its mind all the time, because that is what science is supposed to do in light of new knowledge. As humanity embarks on what might be a genetics revolution, the ability to improve health will only be matched by the potential for the misuse of the technology. Developments in technology will inevitably cause disruption and change, impacting humankind on an unmatched global scale and in unprecedented, and likely permanent, ways. Thus, prospective and ongoing public discourse about the ethical, legal, societal implications of genetics is essential.

First Reading

1. Read and annotate the text, noting paragraph focus and historical and cultural references.
2. Examine and explain Rhodes's pattern of arrangement.

Second Reading

1. How does Professor Miller's reference to the 20th century as "the century of physics" (line 24) and your knowledge of that time period contribute to your understanding of his reference to the 21st century as "the century of biotechnology" (lines 27–28)?
2. What is the effect of Miller's presentation of statistics in paragraph 6 (lines 47–54)?
3. Explain the merits of Miller's proposal of "a fundamental change in scientific education" (line 61).
4. Explain why, in lines 76–77, the second presenter, Rex Chisolm, believes that the public wants to know more about genetics.
5. Explain how closing speaker Liz Lerman's suggestion for the arts to be a possible "bridge between the complexities of science and culture" (lines 93–94) might work in contemporary society.
6. Find Rhodes's specific claim in paragraph 12 (lines 112–125) and explain the advantages and disadvantages of his ideas for "ongoing public debate."

Writing

1. **Argument** — Write a letter to the editor of your local newspaper explaining the importance of public knowledge of the sciences, especially in the area of genetics. Choose your evidence from historical or current examples and recent statistics.
2. **Persuasion** — Write a speech about the importance of public forums to promote a more precise understanding of the ethical issues of genetics. Plan to deliver it to your student body or to one of your classes.

The Hinxton Group is an international, interdisciplinary group of experts who meet to explore ethical and policy challenges related to embryo research and stem cell science. Following is the opening portion of the consensus statement of the group's 2006 meeting. Members of the Stem Cell Ethics and Policy Program at the Johns Hopkins Berman Institute of Bioethics founded the Hinxton Group in 2004.

Stem cell and related research holds out immense promise for good. This research has the potential to dramatically increase our understanding of human biology from which may come new treatments for many serious diseases and injuries. The moral reason to conduct stem cell and nuclear reprogramming research thus comes from both the pos-
5   sibility of advancing knowledge and the values of relieving suffering and promoting human welfare. Furthermore, intra- and international scientific collaboration are vital to the success and advancement of science.

While we strive for consensus on a fundamental ethical framework for stem cell research, we acknowledge the reality of cultural diversity and moral disagreement about
10   some elements of stem cell research. Inconsistent and conflicting laws prevent some scientists from engaging in this research and hinder global collaboration. Societies have the authority to regulate science, and scientists have a responsibility to obey the law. However, policy makers should refrain from interfering with the freedom of citizens unless good and sufficient justification can be produced for so doing. As scientists, phi-
15   losophers, bioethicists, lawyers, clinicians, journal editors and regulators involved in this field, we have reached consensus that if humankind is to have the very best chance of realizing the benefits of stem cell research in an ethically acceptable manner, the following principles should govern the ethical and legal regulation and oversight of stem cell and related research and its clinical applications. This is by no means a comprehen-
20   sive list of principles, but rather a declaration of those discussed and agreed upon by our group:

1.   Stem cell research should seek to minimize harm, and any risk of harm should be commensurate with expected overall benefit. Scientists and clinicians should conduct research according to ethically acceptable norms. For example, research
25   should be conducted so as to protect the well-being, liberty and rights of cell and tissue donors as well as research participants. Research participants and donors of human materials must provide valid informed consent, and conflicts of interest should be appropriately addressed.

2.   The law carries great power to facilitate or restrict scientific exploration in the area
30   of stem cell research. Law makers should be circumspect when regulating science. When enacted, laws or regulations governing science nationally and internationally ought to be flexible, so as to accommodate rapid scientific advance.

3.   Scientists and clinicians have a responsibility to obey the law. However, they also have the right to know through clear and explicit laws, what is and is not permit-
35   ted with respect to their research, the jurisdiction of any prohibitions, and related penalties, so that they can regulate their behavior accordingly.

4.   In countries with laws that restrict elements of human embryonic stem cell (hESC) research but that do not expressly prohibit international collaborations, research institutions should neither discriminate against nor restrict the freedom of their
40   investigators who want to travel to do work that is undertaken with scientific and ethical integrity.

5. Lawmakers should be similarly circumspect in restricting citizens' conduct extraterritorially with regard to stem cell research. So long as scientifically and ethically defensible hESC research is undertaken in a country in which it is legally permissible, scientists should be free to participate in that research without fear of being liable to prosecution, restriction, or discrimination in another jurisdiction.

6. It is essential that scientists and policy makers consult each other and the public in the attempt to develop regulatory regimes for stem cell research that strike the best possible balance between free scientific inquiry and social values.

7. Journal editors should encourage authors to include in manuscripts explicit descriptions of their roles in the published research so as to clarify the appropriateness of their participation, in particular for researchers residing in countries with more restrictive laws and collaborating with researchers residing in countries with more permissive laws.

First Reading

Paraphrase each declaration in one sentence.

Second Reading

1. Explain how Laurie Zoloth's speech on pages 141–143 reflects the importance of the second principle.

2. Explain how William Cheshire's essay on pages 156–160, or Michael Sandel's essay on pages 147–148, reflects the importance of the fifth principle.

3. Choose which of the seven declarations best expresses the ethical framework for Robert Wright's essay on pages 136–137, and explain how the essay reflects that principle.

Writing

1. **Debate** — Select one of the principles and plan a debate. Write the arguments for both sides, or articulate the debate with a classmate. Plan your claims and counterarguments using evidence from any of the texts in this chapter.

2. **Argument** — Write a speech about "the fundamental ethical framework for stem cell research." Plan to deliver your speech to the U.S. Senate Committee on Commerce, Science, and Transportation.

William P. Cheshire, Jr.

Small Things Considered: The Ethical Significance of Embryonic Stem Cell Research

This paper was presented on November 19, 2004, at the *New England Law Review* Symposium on the topic "Stem Cell Research to Human Cloning: Where Do We Draw the Line?" Its author, William P. Cheshire, Jr., M.D., M.A., F.A.A.N., is an associate professor of neurology at the Mayo Clinic College of Medicine and the director of biotechnology ethics at the Center for Bioethics and Human Dignity.

Weighty matters sometimes concern the very small. In physics, for example, splitting the atom changed the world. In biology, mutation of a single nucleotide base pair can give rise to diseases such as sickle cell anemia.[1] In music, melody reaches the brain by way of the body's smallest bones positioned within the middle ear.[2] In religion, by omitting from one word in *Deuteronomy* the smallest Hebrew letter *yod*—a jot of ink the size of a comma—King Solomon altered the meaning of the text to justify polygamy.[3] In law, on the basis of a solitary semicolon, the San Francisco Superior Court this year rejected a proposed court order that would have halted same-gender marriage.[4] In literature, the detective Sherlock Holmes solved difficult cases by applying his intellect to the analysis of small yet significant, ordinarily unnoticed details.[5] And today, scholars from many disciplines are assembled here to consider the obligations of science, society, and the law with regard to nascent human life.

The human embryo, likewise, is a small detail of vast importance. To consider the embryo vis-à-vis the preceding analogies is to encounter an entity endowed with potential, compactness, fragility, dynamic linkage to a harmonious continuum, givenness, and particularity. The embryo, indeed, is a living clue to the mystery of emerging humanity. To this, one naturally responds in awe. Regardless of what one's views may be on politics, jurisprudence, stem cell research, or cloning, thoughtful people generally agree that the beginning of human life marks something special.[6] The initiation of human form during embryogenesis is a phenomenon unlike any other in biology.[7] From this humble beginning emerge the minds of scientists, physicians, poets, philosophers, and lawyers alike. And yet, within our shared sense of awe, there is a small difference of great consequence. The disparity to which I refer lies in divergent judgments about the purpose for which embryos exist, and hence leads to conflicting views

of how biotechnology ought to be regulated. One form of awe, to which I will refer as "practical awe," marvels at the scientific discoveries and potential medical applications latent within the embryo that possesses the very secrets of cellular differentiation. Practical awe looks to embryonic stem cell research and human embryo cloning in the hope of finding revolutionary advances in science and medicine.

Another form of awe, to which I will refer as "sacred awe," respects the embryo as the biological beginning of a new human life. Sacred awe recognizes the embryo's membership within the human family and appreciates that the embryo is a living organism of the species *Homo sapiens* who is actively unfolding her genetic blueprint along the developmental trajectory of a unique and gifted individual. This view does not depend on religious revelation and need not confer on nascent life the full legal status accorded humans born. It simply appreciates an implicit dignity and inviolability about human life in its continuity across all stages of development that science reveals in wondrous detail.

Practical awe regards the embryo as morally similar to any other bodily tissue sample, that is, deserving a measure of respect as a human specimen. Practical awe aspires to unrestricted access to embryos for research projects aimed at understanding early human development and generating potential medical therapies. Practical awe delights in the anticipated fruits of embryonic stem cell research and may tolerate exaggeration where claims promote moving beyond what is currently a limited degree of knowledge in this new field. Trusting in scientific progress above all else, practical awe risks overlooking the potential for abuse of technology in the hands of fallible people.[8]

Sacred awe maintains that all human life is created with immeasurable dignity. Sacred awe reveres the amazing potential innate to existing embryonic life. Sacred awe thus welcomes research

85 on stem cells derived from adult tissue and um-
bilical cord blood, which has shown considerable
scientific promise, having already moved into
clinical applications without depending on the
destruction of human life. Sacred awe cannot in
90 good conscience, however, countenance propos-
als to harvest embryonic stem cells by sacrificing
nascent human lives for biotechnology projects.
To do so would violate the special respect owed
innocent human life. To conscript some of the
95 youngest of our kind for research entailing their
destruction would transgress the ethical line of
nonmaleficence and profoundly distort the meaning of human procreation.

It is sometimes argued that public policy should
100 balance medical and ethical considerations. As
important as medical benefits are, it would be
perilous to place medical and ethical interests on
the same scale. Medicine has a positive obligation
to promote scientific research to benefit suffering
105 patients, and there are many ways available in
which to pursue such research. From the time of
Hippocrates, medicine also has the obligation to
"first, do no harm."[9] This negative obligation can
be satisfied only by refusing to violate the norm
110 that one should not harm or exploit human life in
the service of positive interests. Whereas the ways
of beneficence have no upper limit, in that there
will always be more that could be done to improve
medical knowledge and the human condition, the
115 requirement of nonmaleficence represents a lower limit for ethically acceptable research. It sets a
critical constraint on the manner in which we may
ethically pursue the obligations of beneficence.

Western civilization inherits a rich history of
120 efforts to protect human subjects from research
abuse. Among these, the Nuremberg Code speci-
fies that no experiment should be conducted
where there is an "*a priori* reason to believe that
death or disabling injury will occur."[10] It is impor-
125 tant to note that the Code does not discriminate
on the basis of age. It imposes no threshold of
developmental maturation below which vulnerable human subjects are denied protection. Fundamental protection is assumed to be owed to all
130 human beings equally.[11] It is sometimes argued
that ethical codes for human research subjects
should not apply in this case because the human
embryo is too small an entity to qualify as a human form. In response, it must be remembered
135 that this is exactly what every human being looks
like at the earliest stage of development along the
biologic lifespan. As Nigel Cameron points out,
"[t]o suggest that the size of the embryo—or of
any object—is its most significant aspect implies
140 a thoroughly pre-scientific view of the world."[12]

Quite apart from the breathtaking cellular detail
that can be seen through the lens of the electron
microscope, genetics and embryology reveal the
astonishing complexity of the self-organizing,
145 complete, and integrated organism classified as
the human embryo. Some of the most expensive
and elaborate scientific research today concerns
nanotechnology and subatomic physics, which
explore the complexities of nature on a scale much
150 smaller than that of even the embryo. The relevant
question is not what size is the embryo, but rather
what kind of being is the embryo?

The goals which flow out of sacred awe and
practical awe are thus incommensurable. The
155 sense of practical awe invites science to pursue
foremost the laudable goal of beneficence, while
the sense of sacred awe awakens society to the
moral imperative of nonmaleficence. Practical
awe and sacred awe may coexist at the moment
160 a new human embryo comes into existence, but
they soon part company. For although peeling
open the embryo and exposing her stem cells to
scientific investigation gratifies the practical awe,
that same act annihilates the subject of the sacred
165 awe. Even at the small scale, medical ethics provides limits beyond which science must not go.
At stake in this debate over small things, therefore, are matters of enormous importance. In the
remainder of this paper, three key questions will
170 be considered.

First is whether science should be granted unlimited liberty so long as the anticipated benefits
are judged to be proportionately appealing. Scientific inquiry is one of the highest goods, but it
175 is not the total good, nor is scientific freedom absolute. Responsible oversight of the scientific enterprise should foster excellent research while taking care not to overrate the promise of science nor
to underrate its potential for misuse. Arguments
180 in favor of human embryonic stem cell research
frequently appeal to utilitarian ethical reasoning, which in its most basic formulation seeks the
greatest good for the greatest number. Although
useful in particular applications, utilitarianism is
185 an incomplete ethical theory that, if applied vigor-
ously, unravels at both ends. At one end it renders
judgments on the basis of consequences which in
reality are complex and unpredictable. At the other end, it balances dissimilar categories of good
190 that should not legitimately be compared on the
same scale. Utilitarian analysis, to the point, is
flawed in its treatment of the primary good of human life, in that universal application of its logic
would justify serious harm if the potential ben-
195 efits to others in terms of secondary goods were
seen to be sufficiently great.

Absolute scientific freedom would entail authorization to engage in research known to be unethical, yet done anyway. A science guided only by utilitarian reasoning and freed to conduct research destructive to human embryos would turn the Nuremberg Code upside down. Science, to prosper, need not forsake or attempt to redefine ethics. Violating fundamental ethical principles learned from the difficult lessons of history is an unnecessary compromise that, in the final analysis, cannot secure human flourishing.

The second question is whether human life should be subjected to instrumental use. The stem cell debate has moved beyond discussions about taking human life to plans for making life explicitly destined for destruction. Before us lies the unprecedented prospect of a research agenda that would create a class of human life existing solely for instrumental manipulation and exploitation. It is a small task to recognize the huge moral leap of such a project. Those who cherish the founding principles of our country should appreciate that the instrumentalization of human life would cast aside the affirmation set forth in this nation's Declaration of Independence, that all human beings have intrinsic worth and dignity.[13] To codify in law a provision for destructive research on human embryos would mean that the protection of the law would be withheld from certain categories of human life intended to serve merely instrumental roles in society.

Federal bioethics advisory groups serving under both Democratic[14] and Republican[15] presidents have affirmed that the human embryo is a developing form of human life deserving of respect. To reduce the meaning of respect to treating the embryo as a means to others' ends is an odd use of language.[16] Perhaps the dictionary, like Pinnochio's nose, will lengthen in response. *The American Heritage Dictionary of the English Language*, published here in Boston, defines *human resources* as "[t]he persons employed in a business or organization."[17] Embryonic stem cell research programs would need to solicit the addition of a new word usage. Human resources could also mean, depending on one's view of ethics, human embryos intended as stem cell donors for biomedical research projects.

Third is the question of whether the conscience of a nation, as reflected in its laws, in its professional codes of ethical conduct, and in the values of its diverse communities, will effectively confront scientific misbehavior while the moral conflict is yet small. There is a growing public uneasiness about what many of my patients perceive to be a runaway train of scientismic hubris. One

need only glance at the daily newspaper to find regularly occurring reports of attempts at human cloning,[18] creation of bizarre embryo variations combining male and female cells[19] or human and animal cells,[20] patchwork pregnancies with human offspring having as many as five parents,[21] and just this month a proposal abroad to engineer headless humans as organ donors.[22] Some of these projects evade federal oversight administered to research sponsored by the National Institutes of Health by proceeding quietly under private funding. Others locate where the laws are more accommodating. But in most cases the legislative process simply has not caught up to the technology. For the sake of science and the benefits it yields for all, wisely crafted regulations are needed to preserve public confidence in the ethical uses of biotechnology. Even better would be more effective ethical self-regulation from within the scientific community.

There is, of course, disagreement over what constitutes ethical biotechnology, as well as how stringently scientific research should be curtailed so that scientific creativity is not stifled. Countless goals are negotiable, but some are so essential that they cannot be compromised without agonizingly disrupting the moral basis of a society and provoking enduring contention. One such example may well be human embryonic stem cell research and its co-conspirator, human cloning research. Promises of cures have fueled the campaign for genres of research that would have previously been unthinkable. Although promotion of these projects has won the consent of many, it is no small matter that they would also violate the deeply held convictions of a considerable segment of society.

Increasing economic commitments to such research would more likely escalate than relax passionate controversy as more and more people would be asked to participate in its projects. Once medical products were developed or tested using embryonic stem cells, Americans who objected on moral grounds to the destruction of embryos would be expected to become complicit with the taking of life and to breach their consciences in order to have access to the evolving standard of medical care. Not only would innovative treatments be ethically tainted, but also the production of vaccines, the testing of new drugs and the refinement of existing treatments might upgrade to stem cell methodologies once available. The occasional failures of such research could potentially stir up further contention over such questions as to whom would fall the social and financial cost of caring for those who, in the rush to receive developing treatments, suffered complications such as hyperfunctioning stem cell grafts or tumors. Efficacious medical products could also provoke contention if they turned out to be too costly to be distributed to all eligible patients or if their manufacture necessitated recruiting large numbers of women to serve as oocyte donors.

From a prudential perspective, research programs that do not raise moral problems are more likely to achieve their goals rapidly and be sustainable over the long term. Noncontentious research offers opportunities for people to work together toward medical progress that all can support with an untroubled conscience. Steering clear of highly controversial research paths is the surest way to avoid conflicts between science and law, between science and religion, or between medicine and ethics.

Imposing upon the American people a contentious program permitting human embryo research and cloning and risking the intensification of moral division is unnecessary. Claims of the alleged superiority of embryonic stem cells over adult-derived stem cells rely on a very thin scientific veneer. The scientific evidence has not at this time established which stem cell type has greater clinical potential, and the case for adult-derived stem cells has not received a fair hearing. Rather, the most visible sources of public information too often have been politically motivated rhetoric[23] or assertions made in seemingly objective scientific language from those with sizeable or undisclosed financial conflicts of interest.[24] To channel resources into controversial research on embryos would also divert precious resources from ethically noncontentious research. Further efforts at serious and open discussion are needed. In conclusion, it gives me pause to consider that our descendants will one day read in schoolbooks about the biotechnology challenges faced in the early days of the twenty-first century. History will judge how we meet the challenge of human embryonic stem cell research. It falls to our generation to choose which path science will take. Our decisions, our policies, our legislation, our rulings, and our willingness to participate in the debate will determine whether the history books will record experiments on human embryos as a full-blown blunder or a footnote of folly.

In the interest of the common good, we must not permit scientific advances to be secured by any means possible. In medicine, as in law, it matters whether we treat the smallest of our kind instrumentally or humanely. To grow accustomed to viewing early human life as little more than the means to others' ends would ultimately threaten vulnerable human beings at all stages of life, once it was believed that others would benefit from their harm. Good ends do not justify immoral means.[25]

My great-grandfather grew up in North Carolina during an era when, under the law, African-Americans were not considered persons. Imagine how our nation's history might have played out if, instead of being installed as a pillar of the Southern economy, the institution of slavery had been rejected from the start. The morality of a culture can, if its citizens exercise courage, rise above the blinding interests of material wealth, sheer power, and prejudicial suspicion. He often remarked, I am told, that in life it is "the little things that count."[26] The little lives also matter.

1. *See* MAYO CLINIC STAFF, MAYO CLINIC, *Sickle Cell Anemia* (July 8, 2003), *at* http://www.mayoclinic.com/invoke.cfm?id=DS00324.

2. *See* MAYO CLINIC, *Audiological Testing Services*, *at* http://www.mayoclinic.org/audiology-jax/hearingtests.html (last visited Mar. 23, 2005).

3. MIDRASH RABBAH: EXODUS 103-04 (S.M. Lehrman trans., The Soncino Press 1983) (Midrash on *Deuteronomy* 17:17; *Matthew* 5:17-19).

4. *See* Lisa Leff, *Sides Files Briefs in Gay Marriage Legal Showdown*, VENTURA COUNTY STAR, Feb. 17, 2004, at 5.

5. *See* William P. Cheshire, *Inevitable Human Cloning as Viewed from 221-B Baker Street*, 20 ETHICS & MED. 141-49 (2004).

6. Jose B. Cibelli et al., *The First Human Cloned Embryo*, SCI. AM., Jan. 2002, at 44-51; *see also*, PRESIDENT'S COUNCIL ON BIOETHICS, BIOTECHNOLOGY AND PUBLIC POLICY: BIOTECHNOLOGIES TOUCHING THE BEGINNINGS OF HUMAN LIFE (Staff Working Paper Oct. 2003), *available at* http://bioethics.gov/background/bpp_defend_dig.html.

7. *See* JAN LANGMAN, MEDICAL EMBRYOLOGY 1 (4th ed. 1981).

8. *See* C. S. LEWIS, THE ABOLITION OF MAN 67 (Simon & Schuster 1996) ("[W]hat we call Man's power over Nature turns out to be a power exercised by some men over other men with Nature as its instrument.").

9. HIPPOCRATES, EPIDEMICS, *in* 1 HIPPOCRATES 165 (W.H.S. Jones trans., Harvard Univ. Press 1923) (Book I, § XI).

10. Leonard H. Glantz, *The Influence of the Nuremberg Code on U.S. Statutes and Regulations*, *in* THE NAZI DOCTORS AND THE NUREMBERG CODE: HUMAN RIGHTS

IN HUMAN EXPERIMENTATION, 183, 184 (George J. Annas & Michael A. Grodin eds., Oxford Univ. Press 1992).

11. *See* William P. Cheshire, Jr. et al., *Stem Cell Research: Why Medicine Should Reject Human Cloning*, 78 MAYO CLINIC PROC. 1010, 1018 (2003), *available at* http://www.mayoclinicproceedings.com/pdf/7808/7808c2.pdf.

12. Nigel M. de S. Cameron, *You Were a "Dot" Once, Too*, (Oct. 19, 2004), *available at* http://www.tothesource.org/10_20_2004/10_20_2004_printer.htm.

13. THE DECLARATION OF INDEPENDENCE para. 2 (U.S. 1776) ("We hold these truths to be self-evident, that all men are created equal, that they are endowed by their Creator with certain unalienable Rights, that among these are Life, Liberty and the pursuit of Happiness.").

14. *See* NAT'L BIOETHICS ADVISORY COMM'N, *Ethical Issues in Human Stem Cell Research*, at ii (Sept. 1999), *available at* http://www.georgetown.edu/research/nrcbl/nbac/stemcell.pdf.

15. *See* PRESIDENT'S COUNCIL ON BIOETHICS, HUMAN CLONING AND HUMAN DIGNITY: AN ETHICAL INQUIRY (July, 2002), *available at* http://bioethics.gov/reports/cloningreport/ terminology.html.

16. William P. Cheshire, Jr., *Human Embryo Research and the Language of Moral Uncertainty*, AM. J. BIOETHICS, Winter 2004, at 1-5.

17. THE AMERICAN HERITAGE DICTIONARY OF THE ENGLISH LANGUAGE 855 (4th ed. 2002).

18. *See, e.g.*, Dennis Kelly, *Company Claims World's First Human Clone*, USA TODAY, Dec. 27, 2002, *available at* http://www.usatoday.com/news/health/2002-12-27-babyclone_x.htm; Laura Ungar, *Doctor Claims He Has Cloned 2 Embryos: Medical Ethicists Denounce Efforts*, COURIER-J. (Louisville, Ky.), Sept. 1, 2004, at 1B.

19. *See, e.g.*, Martin Hutchinson, *Mixed-Sex Human Embryo Created*, BBC NEWS, July 3, 2003, *at* http://news.bbc.co.uk/2/hi/health/3036458.stm.

20. *See, e.g.*, Eugene Russo, *Cow-Human Cell News Raises Ethical Issues*, THE SCIENTIST, Dec. 7, 1998, at 1; *U.K. Law Allows Human-Animal Hybrid Work*, BIGNEWSNETWORK.COM, June 2, 2004, *at* http://feeds.bignewnetwork.com/?sid=b1f6b14a430bd579; Ying Chen et al., *Embryonic Stem Cells Generated by Nuclear Transfer of Human Somatic Nuclei into Rabbit Oocytes*, 13 CELL RES. 251 (2003), *available at* http://www.cell-research.com/20034/251.pdf.

21. Tim Utton, *The IVF Twins Who Have Five Parents*, DAILY MAIL (London), Sept. 13, 2004, *available at* http://www.dailymail.co.uk/pages/text/print.html?in_article_id=317667&in_page_id=1799.

22. *Science's New Frontier—A Headless Human?*, INDO-ASIAN NEWS SERVICE, Oct. 29, 2004, *available at* http://www.hindustantimes.com/news/72421080368,00180007.htm.

23. Leon R. Kass, *Playing Politics with the Sick*, WASH. POST, Oct. 8, 2004, at A35.

24. Cibelli et al., *supra* note 6, at 51; Paul Elias, *Biotech Shares Rise Before Stem Cell Vote*, ASSOCIATED PRESS, Oct. 25, 2004, *available at* http://www.rgj.com/news/stories/html/2004/10/25/83617.php; Steven Milloy, *Stem Cell Panel Has Vested Interest in Research*, FOX NEWS CHANNEL, Jan. 25, 2002, *available at* http://www.foxnews.com/printer_friendly_story/0,3566,43880,00.htm.

25. Literature provides welcome guidance on this point. Consider, for example, Gandalf's reply in J. R. R. Tolkien's, *The Fellowship of the Ring*: "A new Power is rising.... We may join with that Power. It would be wise, Gandalf. There is hope that way. Its victory is at hand; and there will be rich reward for those that aided it. As the Power grows, its proved friends will also grow; and the Wise, such as you and I, may with patience come at last to direct its courses, to control it. We can bide our time, we can keep our thoughts in our hearts, deploring maybe evils done by the way, but approving the high and ultimate purpose: Knowledge, Rule, Order; all the things that we have so far striven in vain to accomplish, hindered rather than helped by our weak or idle friends. There need not be, there would not be, any real change in our design, only in our means." "Saruman," [Gandalf] said, "I have heard speeches of this kind before, but only in the mouths of emissaries sent from Mordor to deceive the ignorant. I cannot think that you brought me so far only to weary my ears." J. R. R. TOLKIEN, THE FELLOWSHIP OF THE RING 340 (Ballantine Books 1982).

26. LAWRENCE FOUSHEE LONDON, BISHOP JOSEPH BLOUNT CHESHIRE: HIS LIFE AND WORK 81 (Univ. of N.C. Press 1941).

First Reading

1. Annotate Cheshire's essay, noting paragraph focus, pattern of arrangement, and figurative language.
2. Carefully read the footnotes and consider what information each contributes to the essay and to your understanding of the ideas Cheshire presents.

Second Reading

1. How does Cheshire's chronicle of examples of the importance of small things in paragraph 1 contribute to the presentation of his argument?
2. Examine and explain the paradoxical qualities of the first sentence of paragraph 2.
3. Paraphrase your understanding of "practical awe" and "sacred awe" based on Cheshire's descriptions.
4. At the conclusion of paragraph 8 (lines 153–170), Cheshire presents the idea that three key questions should be considered. Paraphrase the three questions that begin in paragraph 9 (lines 171–196). Note Cheshire's position on each question, and explain whether or not you agree.
5. What does Cheshire propose in the last sentence of paragraph 16 (lines 321–325)?
6. Cheshire's concluding paragraph begins with an anecdote. Read it again to determine whether the anecdote provides final convincing evidence to support his claim. If so, how? If not, why?

Revisit your annotations of Cheshire's text from your first reading, making additional notes as needed. Then answer these reading comprehension questions. After each one, explain what the question asked you to do or know and why you answered as you did.

1. Which of the following best states the subject of the passage?

   (A) Humans share a sense of awe for all aspects of the beginning of life.
   (B) Nascent human life must be described ethically and legally.
   (C) Cellular differentiation determines the beginning of new human life.
   (D) Society owes all members fundamental protection from abuse.
   (E) Human embryos are the beginnings of human life.

2. Which of the following best explains the abstract term "harmonious continuum" (line 26)?

   (A) "mystery of emerging humanity"
   (B) "a phenomenon unlike any other"
   (C) "secrets of cellular differentiation"
   (D) "unfolding her genetic blueprint"
   (E) "human life in its continuity"

3. The reference to Hippocrates in paragraph 6 (lines 106–108) serves to

   (A) introduce the idea of a "negative obligation."
   (B) suggest that researchers "exploit human life."
   (C) confirm that "the ways of beneficence have no upper limit."
   (D) reiterate that " more could be done to improve medical knowledge."
   (E) elucidate the idea of constraints.

4. The tone of paragraph 7 (lines 119–152) can best be described as

   (A) laconic.
   (B) didactic.
   (C) ironic.
   (D) prosaic.
   (E) elegiac.

5. The statement, "Responsible oversight of the scientific enterprise should foster excellent research while taking care not to overrate the promise of science nor to underrate its potential for misuse" (lines 176–179), implies that an important human quality is that of thinking

(A) pejoratively.
(B) perceptively.
(C) perspicaciously.
(D) pedantically.
(E) proscriptively.

6. All of the following elements are included in paragraph 13 (lines 245–272) EXCEPT

(A) anecdote.
(B) hyperbole.
(C) metonymy.
(D) metaphor.
(E) tricolon.

7. The purpose of footnote 25 is to inform the reader that

(A) power in the hands of a few is dangerous.
(B) a fictional reference substantiates effective evidence.
(C) the speaker of the passage compares himself to Gandalf.
(D) order accomplishes high purposes.
(E) Gandalf would discount abuse of power.

8. The author's tone at the conclusion of the essay, in paragraph 19 (lines 368–379), is primarily

(A) grandiose and condescending.
(B) serious and judicious.
(C) formal and respectful.
(D) acerbic and unsympathetic.
(E) prosaic and uncompromising.

9. Taken as a whole, the footnotes suggest that

(A) the author relies primarily on his own writing.
(B) the author refers primarily to literature.
(C) legal texts are not the writer's preferred sources.
(D) medical references are most reliable.
(E) varied sources complicate the issues.

Writing

1. **Analysis** — Write an essay in which you analyze the rhetorical strategies Cheshire uses to present his position about the importance of small things in considering issues of stem cell research.

2. **Argument** — Write an argument to rebut or support Cheshire's claim. Document your sources and prepare your own footnotes.

3. **Synthesis** — Reconsider several of the texts presented in this chapter. Develop a position that defends, challenges, or qualifies the claim that public understanding of the aspects of genetic engineering is critical to the nation or the global society. Then write an essay that synthesizes at least three of the texts for support. Refer to the sources by the author's last name or the title of the text.

Chapter 9
Food

Background

In order for us to live, food *must* be part of our lives, but its necessity only suggests its compelling importance. For some, including those who work in farming and fishing, in the grocery industry, or in restaurants, food defines their livelihoods. For many, food is taken for granted, part of a quick routine, while for others, food and the dining experience are a revered passion, one of life's great pleasures. Meanwhile, those who face starvation must scramble and scrounge for food. Still others, ironically, turn away from the act of eating. Food is central at family and social events and is often associated with emotions. Food also involves ethical considerations. Who gets to eat what? How much does it cost? What food is safe to eat and who gets to say so? Where should we buy it? Do I dare to eat a peach, a whoopie pie, a slice of bacon, or must I make a beeline for some broccoli?

The selections in this chapter are concerned with several facets of our lives with food. What are the associations between food and family? How does food help define a culture? What are some of the ethical dimensions around eating? What are proper public policies in regard to the availability and sale of food?

Readings

M. F. K. Fisher
The Measure of My Powers

Ruth Reichl
The Queen of Mold

Claire Brassil
Cake Walk

Samuel L. Johnson
Coriatachan in Sky

Elizabeth M. Williams
The Sixth Deadly Sin

Peter Singer and Jim Mason
Food is an Ethical Issue—But You Don't Have to Be Fanatical About It

**United States Department of Health and Human Services
and United States Department of Agriculture**
Dietary Guidelines for Americans 2005: Key Recommendations
for the General Population

Cynthia Tucker
Broad-based Effort Needed to Attack Americans' Obesity

Greg Beato
How Big Nutrition Destroys Your Will to Fatness

Rob Rogers
Trans Fat

Alan Miller
A Transitional Phase

M. F. K. Fisher
The Measure of My Powers

Mary Frances Kennedy Fisher made food her subject. The author of 20 books, including several memoirs and numerous essay collections, she has been credited with turning food writing into a genre. In this essay, taken from *The Gastronomical Me* (1943), Fisher recreates the joy associated with childhood memories of food and her family.

The first thing I remember tasting and then wanting to taste again is the grayish-pink fuzz my grandmother skimmed from a spitting kettle of strawberry jam. I suppose I was about four.

Women in those days made much more of a ritual of their household duties than they
5 do now. Sometimes it was indistinguishable from a dogged if unconscious martyrdom. There were times for This, and other equally definite times for That. There was one set week a year for "the sewing woman." Of course, there was Spring Cleaning. And there were other periods, almost like festivals in that they disrupted normal life, which were observed no matter what the weather, finances, or health of the family.
10 Many of them seem odd or even foolish to me now, but probably the whole staid rhythm lent a kind of rich excitement to the housebound flight of time.

With us, for the first years of my life, there was a series, every summer, of short but violently active cannings. Crates and baskets and lug-boxes of fruits bought in their prime and at their cheapest would lie waiting with opulent fragrance on the screened
15 porch, and a whole battery of enameled pots and ladles and wide-mouthed funnels would appear from some dark cupboard.

All I knew then about the actual procedure was that we had delightful picnic meals while Grandmother and Mother and the cook worked with a kind of drugged concentration in our big dark kitchen, and were tired and cross and at the same time oddly
20 triumphant in their race against summer heat and the processes of rot.

Now I know that the strawberries came first, mostly for jam. Sour red cherries for pies and darker ones for preserves were a little later, and then came the apricots. They were for jam if they were very ripe, and the solid ones were simply "put up." That, in my grandmother's language, meant cooking with little sugar, to eat for breakfast or des-
25 sert in the winter which she still thought of in terms of northern Iowa.

She was a grim woman, as if she had decided long ago that she could thus most safely get to Heaven. I have the feeling that my Father might have liked to help with the cannings, just as I longed to. But Grandmother, with that almost joyfully stern bowing to duty typical of religious women, made it clear that helping in the kitchen was a bitter
30 heavy business forbidden certainly to men, and generally to children. Sometimes she let me pull stems off the cherries, and one year when I was almost nine I stirred the pots a little now and then, silent and making myself as small as possible.

But there was no nonsense anyway, no foolish chitchat. Mother was still young and often gay, and the cook too...and with Grandmother directing operations they all
35 worked in a harried muteness...stir, sweat, hurry. It was a pity. Such a beautifully smelly task should be fun, I thought.

In spite of any Late Victorian asceticism, though, the hot kitchen sent out tantalizing clouds, and the fruit on the porch lay rotting in its crates, or readied for the pots and the wooden spoons, in fair glowing piles upon the juice-stained tables. Grandmother, sav-
40 ing always, stood like a sacrificial priestess in the steam, "skimming" into a thick white saucer, and I, sometimes permitted and more often not, put my finger into the cooling froth and licked it. Warm and sweet and odorous. I loved it, then.

First Reading

1. Describe the tone of the essay.
2. In paragraph 2, why does Fisher capitalize the words "This" and "That" and the phrase "Spring Cleaning"?
3. Indicate where Fisher's use of descriptive detail is most prominent.
4. Whose presence is particularly prominent in the essay? Where is this presence introduced, and how is it subsequently developed?
5. What is the impact of the accumulation of detail upon Fisher's intended audience?

Second Reading

1. Where in the essay do Fisher's childhood experiences carry the text? Where in the essay do her subsequent reflections on those experiences predominate? Why are both elements important to the essay as a whole?
2. In the first paragraph, after emphasizing "tasting" and "wanting to taste again" along with a description of "grayish-pink fuzz" and a "spitting kettle," Fisher writes, "I suppose I was about four." How do these features establish her point of view? Why is point of view so important in this essay?
3. How do you account for the brevity of paragraph 3 (lines 10–11)? What subject does the content of the paragraph emphasize?
4. Identify where the following rhetorical tactics and moves are effectively employed: parallelism, oxymoron, simile, repetition, and sensory detail.
5. Explain the importance of the essay's final sentence and word.

Writing

1. **Exposition** — Recreate a childhood memory that prominently involves the acquisition or preparation of food. As you write about the event from your memory, illuminate the meaning of the experience for your audience.
2. **Analysis** — Write an essay in which you identify Fisher's purpose and analyze how she uses the resources of language to achieve it.

Ruth Reichl
The Queen of Mold

The writer is editor in chief of *Gourmet* magazine, a former restaurant critic for *The New York Times*, and the culinary editor for the Modern Library. Her 1998 memoir *Tender at the Bone* focuses on the central role of food in her life. This passage opens the first chapter of that book. Reichl illustrates that food can "be a way of making sense of the world."

This is a true story.

Imagine a New York City apartment at six in the morning. It is a modest apartment in Greenwich Village. Coffee is bubbling in an electric percola-
5   tor. On the table is a basket of rye bread, an entire coffee cake, a few cheeses, a platter of cold cuts. My mother has been making breakfast—a major meal in our house, one where we sit down to fresh orange juice every morning, clink our glasses as if
10   they held wine, and toast each other with "Chee-rio. Have a nice day."

Right now she is the only one awake, but she is getting impatient for the day to begin and she cranks WQXR up a little louder on the radio, hop-
15   ing that the noise will rouse everyone else. But Dad and I are good sleepers, and when the sounds of martial music have no effect she barges into the bedroom and shakes my father awake.

"Darling," she says, "I need you. Get up and
20   come into the kitchen."

My father, a sweet and accommodating person, shuffles sleepily down the hall. He is wearing loose pajamas, and the strand of hair he combs over his bald spot stands straight up. He leans against the
25   sink, holding on to it a little, and obediently opens his mouth when my mother says, "Try this."

Later, when he told the story, he attempted to convey the awfulness of what she had given him. The first time he said that it tasted like cat toes
30   and rotted barley, but over the years the descrip-tion got better. Two years later it had turned into pigs' snouts and mud and five years later he had refined the flavor into a mixture of antique ancho-vies and moldy chocolate.

35   Whatever it tasted like, he said it was the worst thing he had ever had in his mouth, so ter-rible that it was impossible to swallow, so terrible that he leaned over and spit it into the sink and then grabbed the coffeepot, put the spout into his
40   mouth, and tried to eradicate the flavor.

My mother stood there watching all this. When my father finally put the coffeepot down she smiled and said, "Just as I thought. Spoiled!"

And then she threw the mess into the garbage
45   can and sat down to drink her orange juice.

• • •

For the longest time I thought I had made this story up. But my brother insists that my father told it often, and with a certain amount of pride. As far
50   as I know, my mother was never embarrassed by the telling, never even knew that she should have been. It was just the way she was.

Which was taste-blind and unafraid of rot. "Oh, it's just a little mold," I can remember her saying
55   on the many occasions she scraped the fuzzy blue stuff off some concoction before serving what was left for dinner. She had an iron stomach and was incapable of understanding that other people did not.

60   This taught me many things. The first was that food could be dangerous, especially to those who loved it. I took this very seriously. My parents en-tertained a great deal, and before I was ten I had appointed myself guardian of the guests. My mis-
65   sion was to keep Mom from killing anybody who came to dinner.

Her friends seemed surprisingly unaware that they took their lives in their hands each time they ate with us. They chalked their ailments up to
70   the weather, the flu, or one of my mother's more unusual dishes. "No more sea urchins for me," I imagined Burt Langner saying to his wife, Ruth, after a dinner at our house, "they just don't agree with me." Little did he know that it was not the
75   sea urchins that had made him ill, but that bargain beef my mother had found so irresistible.

"I can make a meal out of anything," Mom told her friends proudly. She liked to brag about "Everything Stew," a dish invented while she was
80   concocting a casserole out of a two-week-old tur-key carcass. (The very fact that my mother con-fessed to cooking with two-week-old turkey says a lot about her.) She put the turkey and a half can of mushroom soup into the pot. Then she began
85   rummaging around in the refrigerator. She found some leftover broccoli and added that. A few car-

rots went in, and then a half carton of sour cream. In a hurry, as usual, she added green beans and cranberry sauce. And then, somehow, half an
90 apple pie slipped into the dish. Mom looked momentarily horrified. Then she shrugged and said, "Who knows? Maybe it will be good." And she began throwing everything in the refrigerator in along with it—leftover pate, some cheese ends, a
95 few squishy tomatoes.

That night I set up camp in the dining room. I was particularly worried about the big eaters, and I stared at my favorite people as they approached the buffet, willing them away from the casserole. I
100 actually stood directly in front of Burt Langner so he couldn't reach the turkey disaster. I loved him, and I knew that he loved food.

Unknowingly I had started sorting people by their tastes. Like a hearing child born to deaf
105 parents, I was shaped by my mother's handicap, discovering that food could be a way of making sense of the world.

At first I paid attention only to taste, storing away the knowledge that my father preferred salt
110 to sugar and my mother had a sweet tooth. Later I also began to note how people ate, and where. My brother liked fancy food in fine surroundings, my father only cared about the company, and Mom would eat anything so long as the location
115 was exotic. I was slowly discovering that if you watched people as they ate, you could find out who they were.

Then I began listening to the way people talked about food, looking for clues to their personalities.
120 "What is she really saying?" I asked myself when Mom bragged about the invention of her famous corned beef ham.

"I was giving a party," she'd begin, "and as usual I left everything for the last minute." Here she'd
125 look at her audience, laughing softly at herself. "I asked Ernst to do the shopping, but you know how absentminded he is! Instead of picking up a ham he brought me corned beef." She'd look pointedly at Dad, who would look properly sheepish.

130 "What could I do?" Mom asked. "I had people coming in a couple of hours. I had no choice. I simply pretended it was a ham." With that Dad would look admiringly at my mother, pick up his carving knife, and start serving the masterpiece.

First Reading

1. How does the title suggest the subject of this text?
2. What is the implication of the opening sentence of the passage?
3. How would you characterize the diction of Reichl's essay? How does her diction shape the essay's overall tone? Cite particular words that convey the tone.
4. What structural features are evident in this passage? What content distinguishes its various segments?
5. What makes anecdote such an important feature of this text?

Second Reading

1. How does Reichl arrange the representation of her father in the passage? How does her presentation of her father relate to how she represents her mother?
2. What would be the effect of flipping the position of paragraph 5 (lines 21–26) with paragraph 6 (lines 27–34)? What is the impact of the published arrangement?
3. What is the impact of following the last sentence of paragraph 10 (line 52) ("It was just the way she was") with "Which was taste-blind and unafraid of rot"?
4. Reichl peppers her essay with direct quotations. After accounting for the quotations, explain how they help reveal her purpose.
5. How does Reichl purposefully use the resources of language in the "Everything Stew" vignette (lines 77–102)?
6. Why does Reichl's simile "Like a hearing child born to deaf parents…" (lines 104–105) appear later on in the passage rather than at its beginning?

1. **Analysis/Comparison** — In their texts, both M.F.K. Fisher and Ruth Reichl revel in childhood experiences involving food. However, these texts differ in significant ways. Write an essay in which you account for their important differences. In planning your essay, reflect upon the different reading experiences that the two texts provide.

2. **Research** — In the context of this text, Ruth Reichl makes a somewhat humorous observation: "food could be dangerous." Outside the context of Reichl's essay, the statement might be taken quite seriously. Write a researched essay in which you identify a controversial incident that raised public concern about a matter involving food safety. Note the source of the controversy and the responses of members of the public and of regulatory, political, and/or business officials. After noting and evaluating conflicting viewpoints, explain your own stance on the controversy.

The painting is oil on canvas, 38" × 50". The artist holds a Master of Fine Arts from Cranbrook Academy of Art. She painted "Cake Walk" in 2002.

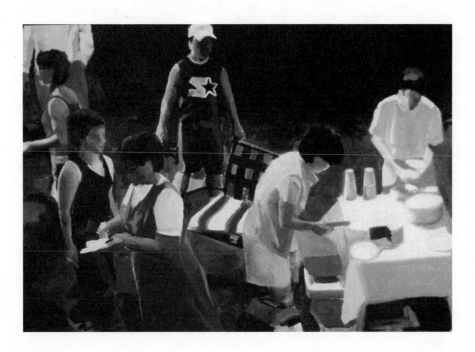

Artist's Statement

During the time when I painted this piece, I used my extended family members in the midst of social gatherings as my subject matter. I was interested in reflecting an interactive disconnect experienced by individuals within ritual group gatherings. *Cake Walk* depicts members of my stepfamily either walking to pick up or walking away with a piece of the cake that rests upon a table in the right third of the painting. The figures in the work seem to be bound in a choreographed routine, central to which is the cake table. None of the figures have defined features or marked characteristics; they appear to act out of habit or instinct, initially drawn to the cake table and then, once a piece of cake is procured, completely absorbed with the food. There is no visible interaction between any of the figures, only the figures and the cake.

First Reading

1. How does the title represent the argument of the painting?
2. What objects allow for an appreciation of the painting's context?
3. How does the phrase "choreographed routine" take shape in the painting? What are the implications of the phrase as used by the artist?

Second Reading

1. Seven human "figures" are represented in the image. What patterns are evident in their arrangement?
2. What does the absence of recognizable facial expressions suggest?
3. What is the role and importance of "ritual" in connection with food? In what sense are food rituals positive? Negative?

Writing

1. **Analysis** — Observe patterns of behavior around food in a public setting. Consider, for example, such locations as your school's cafeteria, the food court in a busy mall, or a local restaurant. In light of the patterns you discern, develop a brief commentary on how people eat.

2. **Synthesis** — Each of the preceding three texts concerns food and family. In a prepared essay of 5–7 pages that refers to each of the texts and at least two others for support, respond to the following prompt.

   In *The Gospel of Food* (2007), Barry Glassner writes, "We Americans romanticize in our own way. We're saps for phrases that begin with 'family.' Attach that word to a noun, and poof! It becomes charmed, as witness the mileage Republicans have gotten from 'family values' over the past quarter century, food companies get from 'family farms,' and journalists and advocacy groups get from 'family meals.'"

In light of Glassner's comment, write an essay that, first, characterizes the relationship between food and family in contemporary North American culture and then argues the extent to which that relationship is suitable and healthy. Draw upon your reading of the sources (both the supplied texts and those you locate on your own), observation, and personal experience to support your argument. Properly cite and account for sources used in your essay.

Samuel L. Johnson
Coriatachan in Sky[1]

On a journey to Scotland and its remote Western Islands in 1773, 18th-century English author Samuel Johnson observed and experienced local customs associated with food, including its procurement, preparation, presentation, and ingestion. He wrote this essay in 1775 about a visit to a house on the Isle of Skye. Johnson traveled with James Boswell, his eventual biographer, who produced his own account of their trip in 1786.

It need not, I suppose, be mentioned, that in countries so little frequented as the Islands, there are no houses where travellers are entertained for money. He that wanders about these wilds, either
5 procures recommendations to those whose habitations lie near his way, or, when night and weariness come upon him, takes the chance of general hospitality. If he finds only a cottage, he can expect little more than shelter; for the cottagers have
10 little more for themselves: but if his good fortune brings him to the residence of a gentleman, he will be glad of a storm to prolong his stay. There is, however, one inn by the sea-side at Sconsor, in Sky, where the post-office is kept.
15   At the tables where a stranger is received, neither plenty nor delicacy is wanting. A tract of land so thinly inhabited, must have much wild-fowl; and I scarcely remember to have seen a dinner without them. The moorgame is every
20 where to be had. That the sea abounds with fish, needs not be told, for it supplies a great part of Europe. The Isle of Sky has stags and roebucks, but no hares. They sell very numerous droves of oxen yearly to England, and therefore cannot be
25 supposed to want beef at home. Sheep and goats are in great numbers, and they have the common domestick fowls.
    But as here is nothing to be bought, every family must kill its own meat, and roast part of it some-
30 what sooner than Apicius would prescribe. Every kind of flesh is undoubtedly excelled by the variety and emulation of English markets; but that which is not best may be yet very far from bad, and he that shall complain of his fare in the Hebrides, has
35 improved his delicacy more than his manhood.
    Their fowls are not like those plumped for sale by the poulterers of London, but they are as good as other places commonly afford, except that the geese, by feeding in the sea, have universally a
40 fishy rankness.

These geese seem to be of a middle race, between the wild and domestick kinds. They are so tame as to own a home, and so wild as sometimes to fly quite away.
45   Their native bread is made of oats, or barley. Of oatmeal they spread very thin cakes, coarse and hard, to which unaccustomed palates are not easily reconciled. The barley cakes are thicker and softer; I began to eat them without unwillingness;
50 the blackness of their colour raises some dislike, but the taste is not disagreeable. In most houses there is wheat flower, with which we were sure to be treated, if we staid long enough to have it kneaded and baked. As neither yeast nor leaven
55 are used among them, their bread of every kind is unfermented. They make only cakes, and never mould a loaf.
    A man of the Hebrides, for of the women's diet I can give no account, as soon as he appears
60 in the morning, swallows a glass of whisky; yet they are not a drunken race, at least I never was present at much intemperance; but no man is so abstemious as to refuse the morning dram, which they call a skalk.
65   The word whisky signifies water, and is applied by way of eminence to strong water, or distilled liquor. The spirit drunk in the North is drawn from barley. I never tasted it, except once for experiment at the inn in Inverary, when I thought it preferable
70 to any English malt brandy. It was strong, but not pungent, and was free from the empyreumatick[2] taste or smell. What was the process I had no opportunity of inquiring, nor do I wish to improve the art of making poison pleasant.
75   Not long after the dram, may be expected the breakfast, a meal in which the Scots, whether of the lowlands or mountains, must be confessed to excel us. The tea and coffee are accompanied not only with butter, but with honey, conserves,
80 and marmalades. If an epicure could remove by a

---

1 **Sky:** Today spelled Skye.

2 **Empyreumatick:** Arising from the distilling of decomposing animal or vegetable matter at high heat.

wish, in quest of sensual gratifications, wherever he had supped he would breakfast in Scotland.

In the islands however, they do what I found it not very easy to endure. They pollute the tea-table by plates piled with large slices of cheshire cheese, which mingles its less grateful odours with the fragrance of the tea.

Where many questions are to be asked, some will be omitted. I forgot to inquire how they were supplied with so much exotic luxury. Perhaps the French may bring them wine for wool, and the Dutch give them tea and coffee at the fishing season, in exchange for fresh provision. Their trade is unconstrained; they pay no customs, for there is no officer to demand them; whatever therefore is made dear only by impost, is obtained here at an easy rate.

A dinner in the Western Islands differs very little from a dinner in England, except that in the place of tarts, there are always set different preparations of milk. This part of their diet will admit some improvement. Though they have milk, and eggs, and sugar, few of them know how to compound them in a custard. Their gardens afford them no great variety, but they have always some vegetables on the table. Potatoes at least are never wanting, which, though they have not known them long, are now one of the principal parts of their food. They are not of the mealy, but the viscous kind.

Their more elaborate cookery, or made dishes, an Englishman at the first taste is not likely to approve, but the culinary compositions of every country are often such as become grateful to other nations only by degrees; though I have read a French author, who, in the elation of his heart, says, that French cookery pleases all foreigners, but foreign cookery never satisfies a Frenchman.

Their suppers are, like their dinners, various and plentiful. The table is always covered with elegant linen. Their plates for common use are often of that kind of manufacture which is called cream coloured, or queen's ware. They use silver on all occasions where it is common in England, nor did I ever find the spoon of horn, but in one house.

The knives are not often either very bright, or very sharp. They are indeed instruments of which the Highlanders have not been long acquainted with the general use. They were not regularly laid on the table, before the prohibition of arms, and the change of dress.[3] Thirty years ago the Highlander wore his knife as a companion to his dirk or dagger, and when the company sat down to meat, the men who had knives, cut the flesh into small pieces for the women, who with their fingers conveyed it to their mouths.

There was perhaps never any change of national manners so quick, so great, and so general, as that which has operated in the Highlands, by the last conquest, and the subsequent laws. We came thither too late to see what we expected, a people of peculiar appearance, and a system of antiquated life. The clans retain little now of their original character, their ferocity of temper is softened, their military ardour is extinguished, their dignity of independence is depressed, their contempt of government subdued, and the reverence for their chiefs abated. Of what they had before the late conquest of their country, there remain only their language and their poverty. Their language is attacked on every side. Schools are erected, in which English only is taught, and there were lately some who thought it reasonable to refuse them a version of the holy scriptures, that they might have no monument of their mother-tongue.

That their poverty is gradually abated, cannot be mentioned among the unpleasing consequences of subjection. They are now acquainted with money, and the possibility of gain will by degrees make them industrious. Such is the effect of the late regulations, that a longer journey than to the Highlands must be taken by him whose curiosity pants for savage virtues and barbarous grandeur.

First Reading

1. Complete an analysis of the content (what the language *says*) and function (what the language *does*) of each paragraph of this 17-paragraph excerpt. Account for the content and function of *each* paragraph in the passage.

2. Account for the structure of the excerpt by considering the relationship between the paragraphs.

---

3 **Change of dress:** In 1745, the British government banned the wearing of the kilt and tartan. The ban was lifted in 1782.

Second Reading

Review your says/does analysis from First Reading question 1 on page 172. Then answer these reading comprehension questions. After each one, explain what the question asked you to do or know, and why you answered as you did.

1. The main point Johnson makes in the excerpt is that the Highland Scots

   (A) are poised to resume hostilities with the English.
   (B) are fully functional despite abstemious tendencies.
   (C) have moved beyond the presumed limits of their culture.
   (D) have been frustrated in attempts to develop gourmet fare.
   (E) have grown more mindful of the economic importance of hospitality.

2. The overall function of paragraph 3 (lines 28–35) is to

   (A) criticize previous accounts.
   (B) enumerate multiple shortcomings.
   (C) expand upon prevailing conditions.
   (D) compare epicurean accomplishments.
   (E) allude to venerated prescriptions.

3. In paragraph 5 (lines 41–44), the author makes use of each of the following EXCEPT

   (A) definitive statement.
   (B) personification.
   (C) parallel structure.
   (D) direct comparison.
   (E) gentle assertion.

4. The overall thrust and character of paragraph 6 (lines 45–57) is best described as

   (A) anecdotal.
   (B) judgmental.
   (C) speculative.
   (D) informational.
   (E) censorious.

5. The function of the final sentence of paragraph 9 (lines 80–82) is to

   (A) emphasize already stated praise.
   (B) reinforce lamentable stereotypes .
   (C) provide concrete support for an assertion.
   (D) contradict the details of the previous sentence.
   (E) anticipate pending objections.

6. The relationship between the second and third sentences of paragraph 11 (lines 89–93) is best described as

   (A) a claim followed by compelling support.
   (B) an ironic observation followed by two related claims.
   (C) a defensive statement followed by a fanciful assertion.
   (D) an inquiry followed by dismissive examples.
   (E) an admission followed by reasoned speculation.

7. The main purpose of paragraph 13 (lines 110–117) is to

   (A) rebuke English tastes.
   (B) satirize with scorn.
   (C) characterize with condescension.
   (D) mock French attitudes.
   (E) inform with humor.

8. The diction in the passage as a whole might best be characterized as

   (A) abstract and unconventional.
   (B) condescending and satiric.
   (C) allusive and scholarly.
   (D) oratorical and inflated.
   (E) precise and definitive.

Writing

Exposition — Recall an occasion when you and family or friends dined at the home of a relative or friend for the first time, or in a restaurant that was new to you. Then write an essay that chronicles the experience with particular attention to and emphasis on the place and the food. Be sure to observe beyond your own person. For example, do not limit your details to the experience of your own particular meal.

The writer is an attorney in New Orleans and president of the Southern Food and Beverage Museum. This essay appeared in *Gastronomica: The Journal of Food and Culture* in 2006. In addition to gluttony, the traditional seven deadly sins of early Christian teaching include lust, greed, sloth, anger, envy, and pride.

In the early nineteenth century French intellectuals considered an appreciation of fine food and the development of the palette a subject worthy of philosophical discourse. The most famous instance is *The Physiology of Taste*, written in 1826 by the erudite gentleman lawyer Jean-Anthelme Brillat-Savarin. In counterpoint to Brillat-Savarin's physical and philosophical enjoyment of food was the Roman Catholic Church's prescription against the sixth deadly sin, gluttony. One could savor, but not to excess. And, unlike those who indulge in the other sins, people who regularly committed gluttony wore the evidence for all to see. (King Louis XVI seems to have paid the ultimate temporal price for his self-indulgence.)[1] Yet even though gluttony was considered a deadly sin, most of the faithful never had the luxury of enough food to face that particular temptation.

Issues of food and its relationship to the body found particularly fertile intellectual ground in United States, where numerous food fads rose during the nineteenth century. Will Keith Kellogg's belief in the social need for clear bowels and vegetarianism led to the development and popularization of corn flakes, a food that revolutionized the American breakfast. Kellogg founded the W. K. Kellogg Company in Battle Creek, Michigan, in the pursuit of health, both mental and spiritual, that could be attained by eating right. A bowl of breakfast cereal became a catalyst for social change, based on consumer response to its perceived health benefits.[2]

Today, there are still plenty of health food gurus who promote various panaceas to American excess at the table, but increasingly it is lawyers who are shaping the way our society thinks about food. These lawyers are not as sympathetic as Brillat-Savarin, however. Rather than celebrate food, they choose to punish it through damaging lawsuits. We also have a Congress and state legislatures that scramble to limit such lawsuits by passing laws in knee-jerk reaction to them.[3] Restaurants, food and beverage manufacturers, and others are being forced to find a balance between two basic American values—seeking redress in the courts and the freedom to make personal choices.

The Next New Enemy

Obesity has emerged as the primary domestic health problem of the new millennium, displacing smoking. Before smoking was seen as an enemy to public health, diseases, rather than activities, were considered the causes of sickness. Even the demon of the temperance movement, alcohol, generated arguments about morality and religion, not about health. It took years to establish smoking as an enemy to public health.

Almost twenty years have elapsed since 1988, when Surgeon General C. Everett Koop made his first remarks about nicotine. Cigarette advertisements on television were soon banned, and eventually, laws were enacted that prohibited smoking in government buildings, office buildings, and restaurants. Over the past few decades smoking

---

1 In what is likely an apocryphal story, Louis XVI was said to be so gluttonous that he had to stop to eat while escaping from revolutionary forces and so was captured at the table, later to be executed.

2 Seven decades later, Dr. Robert Atkins similarly convinced people that if they eliminated carbohydrates from their diets, they could easily lose weight and acquire the health benefits of being thin. The Atkins diet became extremely popular. Fanatical adherence to it changed the way people ate to the extent that the economic viability of the grain industry was threatened. The true social changes resulting from his diet—which is simply a present-day example of the social connection between food and health—are too recent, however, for a complete assessment.

3 For updated charts of states that have enacted legislation to limit food-related lawsuits, visit www.restaurant.org. This chart also contains the status of pending legislation in other states and Congress.

has been transformed from a habit that was seen
65 as cool and sophisticated to one that is vilified. Today, if smokers become sick from smoking, they're
just as likely to suffer a "What did you expect" as
to receive a sympathetic "I'm so sorry."

A small backlash has developed against the
70 crackdown on smoking. Smokers' advocates argue that those who smoke have the right to do so.
This argument is countered by nonsmokers, who
complain that they are forced to endure second-
hand smoke, a by-product of the smokers' habits.
75 These countervailing positions illustrate the conflict between exercising personal freedom and not
infringing on the rights of others.

When in 1954 smokers first sued tobacco companies for compensation for injuries to their
80 health caused by smoking, the tobacco industry
argued that the plaintiffs chose to smoke their
legally-produced products despite health warnings on the label. These early suits were dismissed because the courts found that (1) there
85 was no causal relationship between smoking and
cancer; and (2) smoking was volitional, therefore even if there was a causal relationship, the
plaintiff had chosen to smoke. The downfall of
the tobacco industry came only with the discov-
90 ery that the tobacco companies had intentionally
increased the level of nicotine in cigarettes.[4] Addicted to the nicotine, people bought more cigarettes and the companies enjoyed larger profits.
The companies also publicly denied what they
95 were doing. When the truth came out, the public perception of smoking changed dramatically,
as did the behavior of the tobacco industry. This
new approach eliminated the enemy. A void was
created. A new enemy was needed.
100   The new enemy, it appears to me, is obesity.
Obesity brings with it the plethora of health problems necessary to qualify as a public enemy—diabetes, high blood pressure, heart disease, stroke,
and more. It is a disease that could exact a very
105 high public health and social cost. It appears to
be a public sin caused by eating too much, denot-
ing a lack of self-control that in turn engenders
embarrassment and feelings of self-loathing. This
disease is complicated by the contemporary soci-
110 etal standard of beauty, which is defined as thin,

leaving the obese to suffer consequences that are
not only physical but also psychological.

We can make analogies is in this case to the
path taken against smoking and the tobacco
115 companies. Those who benefited from lawsuits
against tobacco companies can similarly attempt
to find the culprits behind obesity and bring them
to their knees in court. They can claim lots of
money to fight obesity and restore public health
120 (and become wealthy in the process). If America
indeed has a weight problem, it must be somebody's fault. And that somebody had better have
deep pockets.

The Legal Argument
125   I am starting from the proposition that we
in the United States have defined public policy
through law. Alexis de Tocqueville described this
phenomenon in his book *Democracy in America*,
which was based on his observations of the United
130 States in early nineteenth century. Everyone has
the opportunity to get into the act: the executive
branch through executive orders and regulation;
the legislative branch through enacting laws; the
judicial branch through its rulings and interpreta-
135 tion of laws; and the public, directly by bringing
lawsuits and indirectly by influencing legislation
and regulation. To watch the debate over the new
enemy, we need only observe what is happening
in the legal process. But first we must review legal
140 arguments involve and the matters than have to
be proved.

Let us begin with John F. Banzhaf III. Banzhaf
is the self-proclaimed ringleader of the anti-
tobacco company lawsuits and a professor at
145 George Washington University Law School. He
makes no bones about his desire to bring the fast-
food restaurant industry to its knees. On his web
site, www.banzhaf.net, he has posted his mani-
festo. Unlike Brillat-Savarin, who appreciated
150 the complexity of the conditions that can lead
to the enjoyment of food, Banzhaf presents his
legal arguments brusquely, without subtlety. He
clearly draws the analogy between fast food and
tobacco and attempts to rally the forces around
155 this position, claiming to be a proponent of consumer protection.

---

4 During a 1988 trial it was revealed that a 1972 report entitled "Motive and Incentives in Cigarette
Smoking" by Philip Morris Research Center characterized cigarettes as very efficient nicotine dispensers.
Up until that time the tobacco companies had maintained that cigarettes were not addictive and that
therefore smoking was volitional. This report proved that the industry knew that nicotine was addictive
and that they used it to keep people smoking. This report did much to remove the volitional argument
from the playbook of the tobacco companies. Because all of the companies knew of the report and its
findings, the court found that the three big tobacco companies were in a conspiracy to hide their business
plan to create addiction. By this time the link between smoking and cancer had been scientifically
established, but the defense was still that it was a volitional act, i.e., the choice of the smoker. This report
removed the "choice of the smoker" argument.

The legal argument in the tobacco cases was simple: (1) smoking tobacco was the direct cause of illness of the plaintiffs; (2) the tobacco companies sold tobacco; and (3) the tobacco companies ensured that the act of smoking was not volitional by knowingly manipulating the nicotine level in tobacco to make it addictive. This argument essentially made the tobacco companies directly responsible for the illness of the plaintiff, in a manner similar to the person who causes injury while driving a car.

But does the legal argument against fast foods follow the same simple paradigm?

Defining the New Enemy

It is easy to say that obesity as a national problem. One can find statistics to support the mental and physical health risks associated with obesity, although, on the other side, the latest scientific evidence indicates that the obesity problem is not as widespread as has been believed.[5] Social and economic problems are associated with obesity. Airlines, for example, have recalculated the average weight of passengers, a change that affects both the size of the seats (and hence the profitability of each flight) and the cost of fuel needed to support the increased weight load.

But, unlike the case with tobacco, obesity is not accompanied by a simple solution. The solution to preventing the health problems associated this smoking is to stop smoking. One can live without smoking. It is a choice. But there is no similar univalent solution to obesity, which is caused by multiple factors. And one cannot live without eating. It's easy enough to recite the cause of obesity: we eat too many calories for the number of calories that we burn. Excess calories are stored in the form of fat. In other words, we eat too much and exercise too little.

Lawyers who bring what can collectively be called obesity lawsuits must establish a direct link between the obesity suffered by the plaintiff and the illness that the person has contracted (the obesity is the *probable cause* of the malady); that the defendant (read "culprit") was a source of the obesity; that the food eaten in excess was somehow nonvolitional and the fault of the defendant, not the choice of the plaintiff. And unspoken, but nevertheless important, is the need for the culprit to have deep pockets. Call me naïve, but I am still trying to figure out what can be gained should there be a successful plaintiff in an obesity lawsuit. The money judgment will not cure a plaintiff's obesity. That person is still eating too much and exercising too little. And I can hardly see how, in legal terms, one could sustain the burden of proof. There are simply too many questions. Does merely being obese without health problems entitle a person to compensation? That is, are the social issues alone sufficient to trigger a fault/responsibility response in a lawsuit?

The Direct Link

If we analyze the legal dots that have to be connected to establish a legally viable case, it becomes clear that the problem is vast. Let's start with the cause of obesity: overeating. To establish that a particular food is at fault, the plaintiffs would have to demonstrate that that particular food caused the obesity. The lawsuit filed in 2002 by Caesar Barber, plaintiff, named McDonald's, Burger King, Kentucky Fried Chicken, and Wendy's as defendants. It would have been Barber's burden to establish that each of those defendants had caused his obesity. He withdrew the lawsuit. Since that time, new suits have focused on child plaintiffs. By using children as plaintiffs, the attorneys representing them can avoid the defense that eating the product is volitional, claiming that parents, not children, are responsible for their offsprings' diet.[6]

How does a plaintiff's attorney choose the next defendant? Coke or Pepsi? Oreo or Little Debbie? Burger King or McDonald's? Unless a person eats only one company's food to the exclusion of all others, it will be hard to trace the path of any particular calories to a final resting place on the plaintiff's hips. Certainly, eating too much foie gras, too much peanut butter, even too much "health" food could cause obesity. Are these other pockets simply too shallow for the plaintiffs to pursue? The sandwich shop Subway seems to have evaded the problem that has faced

---

5 The Centers for Disease Control in Atlanta promulgated statistics from a study in 2004 that projected 400,000 deaths annually in the United States that were related to obesity and overweight. By contrast, in April 2005 researchers from the National Institutes of Health and the same Centers for Disease Control published an article in the *Journal of the American Medical Association* in which they claim that fewer than 26,000 deaths annually in the United States are due to obesity related causes. See Mokdat et al. "Actual Causes of Death in the United States, 2000," *JAMA* 291 (2004):1238–1245; and Flegal et al. "Excess Deaths Associated with Underweight, Overweight, and Obesity," *JAMA* 293 (2005):1861–1867,

6 One indirect result of these lawsuits and the social impact of the debate surrounding them is the movie *Supersize Me* (2004). This documentary fuels the position that food from McDonald's is unhealthy. Written and directed by Morgan Spurlock, it tells a story of his experience eating food exclusively from McDonald's.

other fast-food chains by touting the weight loss benefits of eating Subway sandwiches. I am waiting for someone who doesn't lose weight eating as Jared Fogle did (Fogle is Subway's spokesman) to sue for false claims.[7]

What about the other side of the equation, the expenditure of calories? Perhaps, limiting ourselves to children for the moment, we can examine latchkey kids who stay inside because their parents have to work and live in areas where the streets aren't safe. They eat junk food at home and don't get enough exercise. Should they sue their parents for not giving them a better life? Should they sue the municipal government for not keeping the streets safer? Should they sue Kraft for making tasty snacks? Can we sue school systems for limiting or eliminating physical education? Can we sue Nintendo, computer manufacturers, television manufacturers and producers, the auto industry, or the federal government for building a highway system that keeps us from walking enough?

Those Pesky Deadly Sins

There are people who are obese because they eat too much. Some people eat too much even when they don't eat junk food. We live in a land of plenty where food is abundant and cheap, and where, when one can ride, it is not considered acceptable to walk. It is not cool to get off the sofa to use the television buttons instead of a remote control. Why would anyone use a crank can opener when an electric one is available? We have changed from a country whose wealth has made people grow taller and be healthier to one whose very wealth and sense of plenty have become the problem. All of the self-checking mechanisms of society have been eliminated, and ease is available to just about all of us. Now we must try to impose balance on ourselves, and this is no mean trick.

Whom can we blame for a society that has become so rich that gluttony is a real sin, not a theoretical one? Perhaps it is only the devil finally getting his due. After roasting all those scrawny sinners, maybe he needed a few fat ones who would be tender and self-baste.

First Reading

1. What is the overall tone of Williams's essay? Identify the sections of the text that exemplify her attitude.

2. In paragraph 3 (lines 33–46), Williams identifies what she says are two "basic American values" and suggests that the "balance" between them is at issue: "seeking redress in the courts and the freedom to make personal choices." How does she illustrate the importance of each value?

3. Where in the essay does Williams explicitly address the need for "balance"? Does she offer explicit solutions?

4. Where in the essay does Williams appeal to logic?

5. Where in the essay does Williams vary her syntax in order to emphasize important points?

6. Where in the essay does Williams use comparison/contrast to develop her argument?

---

7 Jared S. Fogle, a spokesman for Subway, claims to have lost 245 pounds eating Subway sandwiches. Subway advertises the lean benefits of eating its sandwiches.

Annotate the essay, carefully noting the function of the footnotes and other text elements. Then answer these reading comprehension questions. After each one, explain what the question asked you to know or do, and why you answered as you did.

1. The primary function of note 1 in paragraph 1 is to

   (A) elaborate on an allusion.
   (B) offer a contradictory viewpoint.
   (C) limit a definition.
   (D) examine a historical prediction.
   (E) cite a questionable source.

2. Taken together, paragraph 2 and note 2 do each of the following EXCEPT

   I. narrow the focus of the essay.
   II. illuminate the central point of paragraph 1.
   III. illustrate and elaborate upon a claim.

   (A) I only
   (B) I and II only
   (C) I and III only
   (D) II and III only
   (E) I, II, and III

3. The purpose of footnote 2 (line 32) is to provide the reader with

   (A) evidence that doctors Kellogg and Atkins championed social change.
   (B) further insight into the economic consequences of fanaticism.
   (C) information that casts doubts upon Brillat-Savarin's work.
   (D) an analogy that offers additional support for a claim.
   (E) an introduction to contemporary dietary science.

4. In light of current discussions of public policy related to food, the first three sentences of paragraph 3 (lines 33–40) indicate that the author views "lawyers" as

   (A) more influential than health food gurus.
   (B) lamentably potent in shaping public attitudes.
   (C) major players in setting a course for change.
   (D) reluctant to celebrate food.
   (E) indispensable allies against reactive legislation.

5. In the sentence "This new approach eliminated the enemy" (lines 97–98), "this" refers to

   (A) establishment of a link between smoking and cancer.
   (B) policies balancing freedom of choice with public health concerns.
   (C) court rulings upholding volitional activity.
   (D) revelations affecting public perception of tobacco companies.
   (E) increased prominence of health warnings.

6. In paragraph 8 (lines 100–112), a primary rhetorical strategy of the author is to

   (A) arouse the interest of the audience, then cite compelling statistics.
   (B) present competing definitions that prove to lack substance.
   (C) make an assertion and support it with commonly held views.
   (D) buttress her own position by denouncing views of competing authorities.
   (E) qualify previous statements with additional information.

7. The structure of paragraph 11 (lines 142–156) can best be described as

   (A) an exordium accompanied by neutral commentary.
   (B) a review of activities punctuated by explicit denunciation.
   (C) a series of references followed by presentation of credentials.
   (D) an introduction followed by characterizing details.
   (E) an *ad hominem* attack extended by a comparative assertion.

8. The purpose of footnote 5 (line 176) is to deepen the reader's

   (A) understanding of the author's subsequent assertion.
   (B) awareness of competing medical claims.
   (C) appreciation of recent revelations.
   (D) confidence in scientific research.
   (E) concern about continuing legal actions.

9. Paragraph 15 (lines 183–194) includes

   I. the use of personal voice
   II. the use of rhetorical questions
   III. the use of parallelism

   (A) I only
   (B) I and II only
   (C) I and III only
   (D) II and III only
   (E) I, II, and III

10. The footnotes collectively suggest that the author believes it is important to

    (A) relate personal experience to historical and scientific trends.
    (B) value Web sites as a source of statistical information.
    (C) present current statistics that affirm her views.
    (D) comment upon a variety of apt contemporary and historical developments.
    (E) offer conflicting viewpoints on controversial issues.

Writing

1. **Analysis** — Write an essay in which you define the central argument of Williams's essay, then analyze the rhetorical strategies she uses to present and support it.

2. **Argument** — Write an essay in which you support, refute, or qualify Williams's argument. Use appropriate evidence to develop your position, conducting your own research in service of your own argument. Properly cite and account for sources used in your essay.

Peter Singer and Jim Mason

Food is an Ethical Issue—But You Don't Have to Be Fanatical About It

The ethics of choices around human eating are the subject of the 2006 book *The Way We Eat: Why Our Food Choices Matter*, co-authored by a prominent ethicist and an attorney with a family background in agriculture. The passage that follows is excerpted from the book's final chapter.

Sometimes the very success of the ethical consumer movement and the proliferation of consumer concerns it has spawned seems to threaten the entire ethical consumption project. When one ethical concern is heaped upon another and we struggle to be sure that our purchases do not contribute to slave labor, animal exploitation, land degradation, wetland pollution, rural depopulation, unfair trade practices, global warming, and the destruction of rainforests, it may all seem so complicated that we could be tempted to forget about everything except eating what we like and can afford.

When we feel overwhelmed, it is important to avoid the mistake of thinking that if you have ethical reasons for doing something, you have to do it all that time, no matter what. Some religions, like Orthodox Judaism, Islam, and Hinduism, have strict rules against eating particular foods, and their adherents are supposed to follow these rules all the time. If they break them they may feel polluted, or disobedient to their God. But this rule-based view isn't the only possible approach to ethics, nor the best one, in our view. Ethical thinking can be sensitive to circumstances.

Suppose that your elderly uncle Bob lives in a town two hundred miles from where you live, and you are his only living relative. Is it wrong not to go to see him on his birthday? The answer might well depend on how much he would enjoy seeing you, whether you have a car, or, if not, whether you can get there by bus, whether you can easily afford the bus fare, what else you could do with your time, and so on. In thinking about these things, you are paying attention to the consequences of what you are doing. How much of a difference will my visit make to Bob? How much of a sacrifice, for me or others, does it require? Similarly, a sound ethical approach to food will ask: what difference does it make, if I eat this food? How do my food choices affect myself and others? It's not wrong, in answering that question, to give some weight to your own interests and even your own convenience, as long as you don't do it to a degree that outweighs the major interests of others affected by your choices. You can be ethical without being fanatical.

Amanda Paulson, writing in the *Christian Science Monitor* about one woman's quest to enjoy her dinner without guilt, describes the ethics of Daren Firestone, a Chicago law student who won't buy meat, but will eat the remnants of a big Thanksgiving dinner before they get tossed out. Whether or not you agree with that view—don't eat meat unless it will otherwise be wasted—there's nothing that disqualifies it as an ethical principle. Yale philosophy professor Shelly Kagan takes the same view about airline meals. A vegetarian in his everyday life, he orders meatless meals when he flies. Airlines, however, sometimes fail to deliver on such requests. If that happens, and he is offered a meat meal that he knows will be thrown out if he doesn't eat it, he'll eat it. In these circumstances—in contrast to buying meat at the supermarket—his consumption of meat seems to make no difference to the demand for it. (It's like dumpster diving without getting your clothes dirty.) Nevertheless, by not making a fuss, Kagan is sending the airlines a message that failing to provide a vegetarian meal is not a serious problem. He might also be missing an opportunity to start a conversation with the passenger next to him about why he is a vegetarian.

We are not too concerned about trivial infractions of the ethical guidelines we have suggested. We think intensive dairy production is unethical. Because dairy products are in so many foods, avoiding them entirely can make life difficult. But remember, eating ethically doesn't have to be like keeping kosher. You can take into account how difficult it is to avoid factory-farmed dairy products, and how much support you would be giving to the dairy industry if you were to buy an energy bar that includes a trace of skim milk powder. Personal purity isn't really the issue. Not supporting animal abuse—and persuading others not to support it—is. Giving people the impression that it is virtually impossible to be vegan doesn't help animals at all.

How relaxed can we be? Firestone's dietary rules also include what she calls the "Paris exemption:" if she is lucky enough to find yourself in a fine restaurant in Paris—or, very occasionally, in a truly outstanding restaurant elsewhere— she allows herself to eat whatever she likes.[1] We wondered whether she believes that on these rare occasions, the pleasure that she gets from eating meat outweighs the contribution her meal makes to animal suffering. When we contacted her, however, she readily admitted that her "Paris exemption is more self-indulgence than utilitarian calculus." But that doesn't mean that her general opposition to eating meat is not ethical. It is, but she gives more weight to what she wants to do than she would if she were acting on strictly ethical principles all that time. Very few of us are in any position to criticize that, and most of those who do criticize it are deceiving themselves about their choices when their own desires are at stake. A little self-indulgence, if you can keep it under firm control, doesn't make you a moral monster, and it certainly doesn't mean that you might as well abandon your principles entirely. In fact, Firestone believes that by allowing herself to satisfy her occasional cravings—maybe once every three months—she has been able to be faithful to her principles for many years, while other vegetarians she knows have given up the whole practice because one day they could not resist the smell of bacon frying.

At the opposite end to the "Paris exemption" is the "hardship exemption." Factory farming and other unethical methods of producing food have spread because they lead to food that sells for less than food produced by more traditional methods. Replacing these foods with organically produced food generally means paying more for your food. In recommending foods that are more expensive, we are not saying that people who can comfortably afford organic food and humanely-raised meat are more ethical than those who cannot. As with your visit to uncle Bob, circumstances matter. If Bob would very much like to see you, but the bus fare will make such a dent in your budget that your children will go to bed hungry, no one will blame you for not going. But few families in industrialized nations are as poor as that. In the United States, families that consider themselves poor often drink sodas rather than water. Shopping at Wal-Mart, Jake bought a lot of prepared, packaged foods like corn dogs, steak fingers, and breaded fish fillets. Unfortunately, these products delivered poor value for money in terms of their nutritional content. Food that is both more ethical and more economical is available in every supermarket. Buying organic food without incurring extra expense, on the other hand, is usually not possible. Taking that into account, and considering that there are more powerful grounds for avoiding factory-farm products than for buying only organic food, it is reasonable to limit the obligation to buy organic food to what one can afford without undue hardship, while seeing the obligation to avoid factory farm products as more stringent.

No other human activity has had as great an impact on our planet as agriculture. When we buy food we are taking part in a vast global industry. Americans spend more than a trillion dollars on food every year. That's more than double what they spend on motor vehicles, and also more than double what the government spends on defense. We are all consumers of food, and we are all affected to some degree by the pollution that the food industry produces. In addition to its impact on over six billion humans, the food industry also directly affects more than fifty billion nonhuman land animals a year.[2] For many of them, it controls almost every aspect of their lives, causing them to be brought into existence, reared in totally artificial, factory-style production units and then slaughtered. Additional billions of fish and other sea creatures are swept up out of the sea and killed so we can eat them. Through the chemicals and hormones it put into the rivers and seas and the spread the diseases like avian influenza, agriculture indirectly affects all living creatures. All of this happens because of our choices about what we eat. We can make better choices.

First Reading

1. Prepare a *says/does analysis* for each paragraph.
2. What assumptions do Singer and Mason appear to make about the reader?

1 Amanda Paulson, "One woman's quest to enjoy her dinner without guilt," Christian Science Monitor, October 27, 2004, http://csmonitor.com/2004/1027/p15s02-lifo.htm.
2 According to figures for 2003 from the Food and Agriculture Organisation of the United Nations.

3. What is the thesis of this passage? Where does it become manifest?
4. The authors raise many questions in paragraph 2. How is it that the hypothetical example featured in the paragraph invites such an array of questions, while the "real-life" examples (e.g., Daren Firestone and Shelly Kagan) featured in other paragraphs do not?

Second Reading

1. Paragraphs 2 and 3 (lines 14–47) both end with assertions. What do these assertions accomplish?
2. Why are Singer and Mason mildly critical of Shelly Kagan at the end of paragraph 4 (lines 48–73)?
3. Paragraph 6 (lines 89–119) begins with a question. What does the implied answer suggest about the authors' attitude concerning "strict ethical principles" when it comes to matters of dietary choices?
4. Where do the authors most prominently appeal to logic?
5. Which paragraph in the essay would you cite as most pivotal? Why?
6. How does the final paragraph shift the focus of the text?

Writing

1. **Analysis** — Singer and Mason argue that ethical reasoning should not result in behaviors that require strict adherence to an ideal. After carefully rereading the essay, analyze how the authors present and develop their stance. You might consider such elements as structure, tone, and use of examples and appeals.
2. **Argument** — In their book *The Way We Eat: Why Our Food Choices Matter,* Peter Singer and Jim Mason argue that as responsible global inhabitants and as food consumers we ought to pay closer attention to the consequences of what we are doing and make better food choices. They argue that, although individual food choices may seem insignificant, the collective ramifications of such choices are immense; the "major interests of others" are affected by responsible individual choices. In effect, they argue that the needs of the many outweigh the needs of the one.

   In a carefully prepared essay with at least one writing conference, defend, challenge, or qualify the assertion that *collective* needs are always more important than individual needs. Support your position with appropriate evidence drawn from research, reading, observation, and experience.

Synthesis Essay

Directions

Reading Time: 3 evenings of preparation

Writing Time: 2 full class periods: one for writing a rough draft, one for producing a final version

This task asks you to synthesize the text and visual sources provided on the following pages into a thoughtful and well-written essay of your own. Refer to the sources in support of your own argument. Do not merely summarize the sources, as *your own* argument is vital. Use the sources so that they are integrated into your essay in support of *your* argument.

Make certain that you attribute both direct and indirect citations.

Activities   In preparation for writing, carefully read and annotate each source text, and then complete the discourse activities that immediately follow. Do not, however, limit your observations and analysis to the discourse activities. You should read each source more than once as you build your initial understanding and then deepen your analysis of the various sources. Try to see sources in light of both each other and the assignment. After you have concluded your discourse with the sources, take stock of your deliberations and state your own position. Use the Planning Your Synthesis Essay activity on page 190, following the last source text.

Introduction   Trans fat is partially hydrogenated vegetable oil, the result of a process that adds hydrogen to liquid vegetable oil, making it thicker. Used in food manufacturing and preparation, trans fat (which is sometimes referred to as "trans fatty acids") reduces the amount of grease in the oil and extends the shelf life of products that contain it. Trans fat provides an economical option not only for manufacturers of convenience and snack foods such as pastries, microwave popcorn, and crackers, but also for sellers of "fast" foods such as fried chicken, French fries, and donuts. However, while trans fat has been in use for years, recent studies have linked the product with heart disease and related serious health problems.

Assignment   Read the following five sources, as well as accompanying contextual information, thoughtfully. In light of efforts by some citizens in your locality to ban the use of trans fat in local restaurants, write an essay in which you propose a course of action to your community leaders. Synthesize at least three of the sources for support.

In your essay, refer to the sources either as Source A, Source B, and so on, or by the designations below in parentheses.

Source A   (HHS/USDA)

Source B   (Tucker)

Source C   (Beato)

Source D   (Rogers)

Source E   (Miller)

Source A

United States Department of Health and Human Services and United States Department of Agriculture. *Dietary Guidelines for Americans 2005: Key Recommendations for the General Population*. 11 Jan. 2005. 16 Feb. 2007.
http://www.health.gov/dietaryguidelines/dga2005/recommendations.htm.

Dietary Guidelines for Americans is a joint publication of the Department of Health and Human Services (HHS) and the Department of Agriculture (USDA). Published every five years, their recommendations serve as the basis for the food and nutrition education programs of the United States Government.

Adequate Nutrients within Calorie Needs
- Consume a variety of nutrient-dense foods and beverages within and among the basic food groups while choosing foods that limit the intake of saturated and *trans* fats, cholesterol, added sugars, salt, and alcohol.
5
- Meet recommended intakes within energy needs by adopting a balanced eating pattern, such as the U.S. Department of Agriculture (USDA) Food Guide or the Dietary Approaches to Stop Hypertension (DASH) Eating Plan....

Food Groups to Encourage
- Consume a sufficient amount of fruits and vegetables while staying within ener-
10 gy needs. Two cups of fruit and 2½ cups of vegetables per day are recommended for a reference 2,000-calorie intake, with higher or lower amounts depending on the calorie level.
- Choose a variety of fruits and vegetables each day. In particular, select from all five vegetable subgroups (dark green, orange, legumes, starchy vegetables, and
15 other vegetables) several times a week.
- Consume 3 or more ounce-equivalents of whole-grain products per day, with the rest of the recommended grains coming from enriched or whole-grain products. In general, at least half the grains should come from whole grains.
- Consume 3 cups per day of fat-free or low-fat milk or equivalent milk products.

20 *Fats*
- Consume less than 10 percent of calories from saturated fatty acids and less than 300 mg/day of cholesterol, and keep *trans* fatty acid consumption as low as possible.
- Keep total fat intake between 20 to 35 percent of calories, with most fats coming
25 from sources of polyunsaturated and monounsaturated fatty acids, such as fish, nuts, and vegetable oils.
- When selecting and preparing meat, poultry, dry beans, and milk or milk products, make choices that are lean, low-fat, or fat-free.
- Limit intake of fats and oils high in saturated and/or *trans* fatty acids, and choose
30 products low in such fats and oils.

Carbohydrates
- Choose fiber-rich fruits, vegetables, and whole grains often.
- Choose and prepare foods and beverages with little added sugars or caloric sweeteners, such as amounts suggested by the USDA Food Guide and the DASH
35 Eating Plan.
- Reduce the incidence of dental caries by practicing good oral hygiene and consuming sugar- and starch-containing foods and beverages less frequently.

Sodium and Potassium
- Consume less than 2,300 mg (approximately 1 teaspoon of salt) of sodium per day.
40
- Choose and prepare foods with little salt. At the same time, consume potassium-rich foods, such as fruits and vegetables.

Alcoholic Beverages
- Those who choose to drink alcoholic beverages should do so sensibly and in moderation—defined as the consumption of up to one drink per day for women
45 and up to two drinks per day for men.
- Alcoholic beverages should not be consumed by some individuals, including those who cannot restrict their alcohol intake, women of childbearing age who may become pregnant, pregnant and lactating women, children and adolescents, individuals taking medications that can interact with alcohol, and those with spe-
50 cific medical conditions.
- Alcoholic beverages should be avoided by individuals engaging in activities that require attention, skill, or coordination, such as driving or operating machinery.

Food Safety
To avoid microbial foodborne illness:
55
- Clean hands, food contact surfaces, and fruits and vegetables. Meat and poultry should not be washed or rinsed.
- Separate raw, cooked, and ready-to-eat foods while shopping, preparing, or storing foods.
- Cook foods to a safe temperature to kill microorganisms.
60
- Chill (refrigerate) perishable food promptly and defrost foods properly.
- Avoid raw (unpasteurized) milk or any products made from unpasteurized milk, raw or partially cooked eggs or foods containing raw eggs, raw or undercooked meat and poultry, unpasteurized juices, and raw sprouts.

Discourse Activity

1. What is the importance of the authority behind these guidelines? What assumptions about audience are evident?
2. Like other statements that comprise the guidelines, statements about trans fat and trans fatty acids are presented with negligible commentary. How does the absence of such information affect the tone of the document?
3. Which features of the guidelines are open to question?
4. How explicitly do the guidelines warn about particular health risks?
5. How would those who regularly cook and dine for pleasure view the guidelines?
6. Which features mark the guidelines as informative? As persuasive?

Source B

Tucker, Cynthia. "Broad-based Effort Needed to Attack Americans' Obesity."
Portland Press Herald 30 Dec. 2006: A9.

An award-winning journalist, Cynthia Tucker writes a syndicated column on national issues.

There are many Americans whose politics remain deeply skeptical of government involvement in affairs of personal health—whether laws regulating seat-belt use or bans on smok-

5 ing in public places. But the data are clear: When government starts a crusade to improve habits of personal health, from seat-belt use to breast cancer screening, lives are saved and disabilities avoided.

10 It's high time, then, for government to use its powers of persuasion—and coercion—to confront the obesity crisis and its impact on public health. While we're all aware of the damage done by those added pounds, few of us have the discipline

15 to get rid of them. That might change if federal and state governments used all the levers at their disposal to push us in the right direction.

Think of the four-decade effort to curb smoking. In 1964, U.S. Surgeon General Luther Terry

20 issued a report linking cigarettes to lung cancer. Back then, about 68 percent of American men (and an unknown percentage of American women) smoked, and cigarettes were synonymous with glamour. Now, only about 20 percent of American

25 adults—23 percent of men, 18 percent of women—report that they smoke regularly.

It wasn't easy to change such an inbred habit. It took a variety of initiatives—from public awareness campaigns, to laws banning smoking, to

30 civil lawsuits against tobacco companies. But that broad-based war on smoking worked.

Something similar—equally far-reaching and long-term—will be required to curb obesity and its clear consequences, notably the increase in dia-

35 betes. The number of diabetics has increased 80 percent over the last decade, according to the *New York Times*.

Perhaps the most alarming news about diabetes is the sharp increase in Type 2, usually asso-

40 ciated with lifestyle factors, in children. As kids have grown fatter, a disease that had been largely associated with middle-aged adults has turned up increasingly in youngsters. While many careful diabetics live normal lives, others are stricken by

45 kidney failure, blindness and amputation due to poor circulation. The increase in diabetes in children has led some public health experts to predict that this generation of American children may be the first whose average life span is shorter than

50 that of their parents.

So what should the government do, ban fatty foods? Interestingly, The New York City Board of Health recently instituted a ban on the use of most artificial trans fats in restaurants in that city. While

55 that experiment will be useful to watch, it will likely be decades—if ever—before other locales, especially those in the Deep South, are willing to go that far.

Medicaid and Medicare, both government-

60 funded health insurances programs, have only recently begun to offer physicians incentives to keep their patients healthy. Research has found that overweight patients who are treated to a broad range of practical interventions—includ-

65 ing, in some cases, nutritionists who visit their homes and rummage through their refrigerators and pantries—are able to adhere to changes in diet and exercise more readily than patients who are not similarly nagged.

70 Of course, those interventions are costly up front. But they save money, both for insurance companies and for the national budget, over the long haul. A patient who loses weight and exercises is less likely to end up severely incapacitated

75 by heart disease, diabetes or other ills.

Meanwhile, there's no reason to wait for your insurance company to send a nutritionist to overhaul your kitchen. You can make some relatively simple changes to your lifestyle that will pay off

80 in years to come. Forget about the radical New Year's resolutions that you know you won't keep. Instead, resolve to cut your trips to Mickey D's in half. That's a start.

An aunt of mine, a 69-year-old diabetic, lost 70

85 pounds over 2½ years after she took a part-time job as secretary at her church. The church has no soda machines, and she doesn't like to leave the phones untended to fetch lunch from a fast-food restaurant. So she's forced to eat her packed

90 lunch, which is usually fruit. (I'm proud of you, Aunt Mittie!) Her success came without nutritionists, personal trainers or those weird machines sold on infomercials.

Yours can, too.

1. Where does Tucker's intent become clear?
2. What tactics does Tucker employ in order to emphasize her views?
3. Where in her essay does Tucker acknowledge perspectives that contrast with hers? How does she address them?
4. What features distinguish the content of Tucker's commentary from the HHS/USDA Guidelines?
5. What is the impact of Tucker's closing anecdote?
6. What are the implications of Tucker's essay for community leaders?

Source C

Beato, Greg. "How Big Nutrition Destroys Your Will to Fatness."
Reason Dec. 2006: 19.

The author is a writer based in San Francisco.

In yet another expose of the scrumptiousness epidemic, Robert Lustig, a professor of clinical pediatrics at UCSF Children's Hospital, explains in the August *Nature Clinical Practice Endocrinology & Metabolism* that "Big Food" is creating a "toxic environment" that stacks the (high-fat) chips against us. The reason for our scale-denting corpulence, Lustig postulates, is that supermarkets and fast food outlets push fructose-laden, low-fiber, processed fare on us, which in turn causes excess insulin production. Apparently the extra insulin makes our brains think we're still hungry even as our bellies are engorged with a sweet mush of Big Macs and milk shakes.

"It will take a grassroots effort of doctors, community leaders and consumers to force the government and the food industry to get those sugary foods out of mainstream American diets" Lustig told the *San Francisco Chronicle*. "Everyone's assuming you have a choice, but when your brain is starving, you don't have a choice…. Congress says you can't sue McDonald's for obesity because it's your fault. Except the thing is, when you don't have a choice, it's not your fault."

If Lustig lived in, say, a French fry vat at Hamburger University, his argument might be convincing. Instead he lives, or at least works, in San Francisco, where starving brains are routinely exposed to an endless buffet of raw food cafes, vegetarian grocery stores, sustainable-agriculture farmers' markets, and locally grown produce delivery services. Organic apples are so abundant here that I can only assume they grow on trees—but just try to find a McDonald's fried apple pie. (In 1992 most McDonald's outlets replaced their beloved fried apple pies with a merely tolerated baked version.

Out of the 28 McDonald's franchises in San Francisco, just one still serves the fried dessert.)

And it's not as if San Francisco is the country's one exception to fructose hegemony. You can get veggie burgers at Wal-Mart now—or, for that matter, at Burger King. Even if, somehow, you don't live near a Wal-Mart or a Burger King, just log onto DiamondOrganics.com. Your organic sea lettuce will be at your door the next day.

While it's easy to get fat in a world where $10 can buy you approximately five pounds of burrito at Taco Bell, it also has never been easier to get thin. Long after most KFCs have retired their deep fryers for the night, you can still do half-squats at 24-Hour Fitness. FitTV broadcasts hours of exercise programs to some 35 million U.S. households each day. Online tools like MyFoodDiary.com make it a cinch to track every calorie you consume. Infomercial Adonises pitch elliptical trainers and recumbent cycles far more vigorously than Ronald McDonald pitches McNuggets. Add it all up, and you have an epidemic of fitness with no historical precedent.

So forget "starving brains" and the notion that we have "no choice" in the ultimate destiny of our waistlines. If there's anything to blame for our increasing heft, it's the dizzying array of choices that tempt us in every McDonald's and in every Whole Foods Market. Some of the choices available to us are good for our health, some are bad, and every day plenty of people somehow escape the tyranny of their insulin-duped noggins and choose the former.

You can even argue that without Subway's 12-inch Chicken & Bacon Ranch sandwich (1,080 calories) or Hardee's Monster Thickburger (1,420

calories), millions of Americans might not be so healthy: The ubiquity of such tasty slop has created a great demand for more nourishing alternatives, and that great demand has led to increased availabil-
75 ity and better value. Without the scourge of Burger King's onion rings, would Wal-Mart be making low-priced organic food accessible to the masses? Would Target have an entire aisle devoted to yoga products? Now more than ever, we really can have
80 it our way, whatever that way happens to be.

Discourse Activity

1. State Beato's argument in your own words.
2. How would Beato respond to the HHS/USDA Dietary Guidelines?
3. What are the most prominent organizational features of Beato's essay, and how do they contribute to his argument?
4. Where are the sharpest points of disagreement between the views of Beato and those of Tucker? Are there areas of agreement?
5. What issues does Beato raise that Tucker ignores? What do you think Tucker would have to say about those issues?
6. What issues does Tucker raise that Beato ignores? What do you think Beato would have to say about those issues?

Source D

Rogers, Rob. "Trans Fat." Cartoon. *Pittsburgh Post-Gazette* 13 July 2003. 10 Nov. 2006 http://www.post-gazette.com/robrogers/.

Discourse Activity

1. What points does the cartoon make about trans fat? About food and health? About commerce? About behavior?
2. What words contribute to the argument of this text?
3. What visual elements contribute to its argument?
4. What features make this text entertaining?
5. What would Beato say after encountering this cartoon? What would Tucker say?

Source E

Miller, Alan. "A Transitional Phase." *Spiked* 27 Oct. 2006. 11 Nov. 2006
http://www.spiked-online.com/index.php?/site/article/2035/.

Alan Miller is director of the NY Salon, an organization that seeks to engage citizen-participants in substantive debates on matters of principle.

Hardly a day goes by without another major story on what is bad for us in the contemporary diet.[1] This is as true in Europe as it is in the US. For instance, a casual glance at the last few weeks' reporting could leave us confused and worried just trying to unpick what we should digest or not. Cholesterol, for instance, the concern of so many in the western world, is coming under further scrutiny, with some researchers arguing that the latest health guidelines on cutting cholesterol levels actually go too far.[2]

The latest dietary villain appears to be trans fats. This is what the Food and Drug Administration (FDA) says about trans fats: 'Trans fat is made when manufacturers add hydrogen to vegetable oil, a process called hydrogenation. Hydrogenation increases the shelf life and flavor stability of foods containing these fats...Trans fat, like saturated fat and dietary cholesterol, raises the LDL cholesterol that increases your risk for coronary heart disease.'

New York City's Board of Health voted unanimously recently to proceed with plans to ban the majority of trans fats from restaurants in the city.[3] Bureaucratic-minded politicians and legislators increasingly want to interfere in matters that once were considered up to the discretion of us as autonomous and rational citizens. There is increasing skepticism that ordinary people can be trusted to be discerning and make the 'right' decisions for themselves.

There seems to be a new climate of morality that is being pursued that seeks to re-create notions of 'deserving' and 'undeserving' people in a modern setting. Quite aside from the fact there are competing scientific views as to what extent trans fats cause heart disease,[4] there is a broader concern here it seems to me. Once, the debate about health was to do with how we could provide more and better resources for society, improve technology and provision for all sections in the community—and the best way to organise such a task. With the low horizons of modern political life, however, we seem to be headed toward a situation where we can play out a morality tale of 'good' and 'bad' people—based on how they eat, drink, smoke, shop, and have sex in an age where we don't seem to agree upon very much else.

So what? A large part of where one stands on this debate depends on how we view people. If we think that they are all addiction-prone dim-wits that just want to eat rubbish (and live rubbish lifestyles) then perhaps banning certain things would be a good idea. Many have argued for bans and other interventions based on a cost-benefit analysis of healthcare, arguing that the 'nasty corporates' are preying on us and our kids.[5]

It does indeed take the sugar-coated biscuit, when Bill Clinton, a 'self-confessed overeater' tells us that we all need to slim down and pundits make comments like 'It's not our dependence on foreign oil that's killing us. It's our dependence on vegetable oil.'[6]

This debate has come to represent our low regard for the decision-making faculties of adults, as well as the low point of political discourse. It is far easier to create a bit of a moral panic around food and encourage us to engage in anxiety-ridden label-reading while we shop than discuss the impasse we seem to be at politically in society.

1 *New York Times* editorial, 19 October 2006

2 Value of Cholesterol Targets is Disputed, *New York Times*, 17 Oct 2006

3 New York City plans limits on restaurants' use of trans fats, *New York Times*, 27 Sep 2006

4 For example, read Elizabeth Whelan, ASCH.org and Denise Mann, Web MD.

5 Sponge Bob Square Pants Health Risk, *Nation*, 31 Jan 2006

6 Goodbye, war on smoking, Hello war on Fat, *Slate*, 15 April 2006

75 We end up being somewhat predisposed to think of ourselves as 'at risk' from all quarters. But are we a Fast Food Nation gulping obsessively too many calories or is the problem, as the *New York Times Magazine* put it recently that we have a 'Veg-
80 etable-Industrial Complex'? Or are we just slightly overwhelmed with all this competing and somewhat banal information that is being discussed in shrill voices? This constant preoccupation with what we ingest is only mildly less infuriating than
85 the fact that we are being treated like children by those that would know best.[7]

And nowhere can the emotions be manipulated and heightened more than on the subject of children. There is increasing pressure on com-
90 panies not to co-brand and market their characters with certain food and drinks. Disney is now promising to take the lead in promoting their merchandise 'responsibly', which means no more licensing their characters on waffles and pop tarts
95 or burgers.[8]

100 However, while we had a raging debate about political correctness, the food correctness 'debate' looks as though it is being accepted with only limited critical consideration. Anyone that questions it is presumed to have some corporate interest or ulterior motives. In the spirit of our age, a public confession here: I remember a period I went through while at school when I enjoyed a lunch-time diet of two chocolate bars, a bag of crisps
105 and a can of coke. Silly teenage years perhaps. But it was, as adults used to like to tell us in the days that they believed they knew better, just a phase.

However, far more silly—and worrying—is that in an age where we find so little to agree
110 about, in terms of who we are as a society, where we are going, that the big vision future should be a culture of clamping down, bans and legislating behaviour—all promoted in the name of making us healthier subjects. It is enough to
115 make you sick.

Discourse Activity

1. What distinguishes paragraph 4 (lines 33–50) from the first three paragraphs?
2. What words and phrases mark the tone of this essay? Would such a tone be appropriate if used by a local official in articulating public policy?
3. Miller mentions "competing scientific views" about trans fat (line 37), but does not specifically cite them. Does this matter?
4. Respond to the thrust of paragraph 5 (lines 51–60). How would Tucker, Whelan, and Rogers respond to it?
5. In light of paragraph 9 (lines 87–95), how would Miller characterize Tucker's "Aunt Mittie" anecdote? (See Source B, lines 84–93.)
6. What is the implication of the word "subjects" in the final paragraph?

Activity: Planning Your Synthesis Essay

After completing all Discourse Activities that follow the preceding five sources, review your responses. Then perform these planning steps:

- Explain the issue that is before the community.
- Consider the range of possible actions suggested by the sources.
- Address the pros and cons of various approaches.
- Make a proposal, giving reasons for the course of action you propose.

Finally, refer back to the Synthesis Essay directions and assignment on page 183.

---

7 Ban Trans Fats? That Takes the Cake, *LA Times*, 3 Oct 2006
8 Disney says it will link marketing to nutrition, *New York Times*, 17 Oct 2006

Chapter 10

Wit

Background

Laughter makes us feel better, both physically and emotionally. Contemporary society seems to relish humorous films, books, television programs, and cartoons, and we laugh at funny song lyrics. Why do some artists seek laughter as appreciation for their creativity? We might consider that the desired effect could be that the artists ask us to look amusingly at ourselves as individuals and as a society. Humor seems to have healing powers, with laughter and thoughtful consideration the primary desired effects for the individual and for some groups. Satire has a broader purpose in that it points out a specific failing of a social institution. The primary goal of satire is to seek change by ridiculing the failing of the institution under attack. Consider these variations of humor and satire as means to attain an end: burlesque, caricature, hyperbole, irony, lampoon, parody, *reductio ad absurdum*, sarcasm, and solecism. This is not an exhaustive list but one to offer ideas about methods of approach to analyze humor and satire.

Humorists and satirists ask us to laugh in response to their creative efforts, to laugh at conduct as a means of sharing sentiment about a situation, to laugh at our own conduct and to consider correcting it, and to inspire a sense of outrage about a situation by exposing and ridiculing conduct we consider wrong because of shared values, and by exposing and ridiculing to inspire change.

Readings

Samuel Clemens
Letter to William Dean Howells

J. B. Lee, Jr.
Letter to the Honorable Ed Foreman

Benjamin Franklin
Letter of Recommendation

E. B. White
Letter to Gas Company

Groucho Marx
Letter to Warner Brothers

Ellen Goodman
Breaking the Hungry Teen Code

The Onion
Girl Moved To Tears By *Of Mice And Men* Cliffs Notes

Herblock
Read me what it says, Dad

Samuel Clemens
Advice to Youth

Jonathan Swift
A Meditation Upon a Broom-Stick

Samuel Clemens
Letter to William Dean Howells

Samuel Clemens, who wrote as Mark Twain, and William Dean Howells, who was a novelist and critic, were lifelong friends.

18 May 1880

Friend Howells—

Could you tell me how I could get a copy of your portrait as published in Hearth & Home? I hear so much about it as being among the finest works of art which have yet appeared
5   in the journal, that I feel a strong desire to see it. It is suitable for framing? I have written the publishers of H&H time and again, but they say that the demand for the portrait immediately exhausted the edition & now a copy cannot be had, even for the European demand, which has now begun. Bret Harte[1] has been here, & says his family would not be without that portrait for any consideration. He says his children get up in the night & yell
10   for it. I would give anything for a copy of that portrait to put up in my parlor. I have Oliver Wendell Holmes's & Bret Harte's, as published in Every Saturday, & of all the swarms that come every day to gaze upon them none go away that are not softened & humbled & made more resigned to the will of God. If I had yours to put up alongside of them, I believe the combination would bring more souls to earnest reflection & ultimate conviction of
15   their lost condition, than any other kind of warning would. Where in the nation *can* I get that portrait? Here are heaps of people that want it, —that *need* it. There is my uncle. *He* wants a copy. He is lying at the point of death. He has *been* lying at the point of death for two years. He wants a copy—& I want him to *have* a copy. And I want you to send a copy to the man that shot my dog. I want to see if he is dead to Every human instinct.
20   Now you send me that portrait. I am sending you mine, in this letter' & am glad to do it, for it has been greatly admired, People who are judges of art, find in the execution a grandeur which has not been equaled in this country, & an expression which has not been approached in *any*.

Ys Truly

25   S. L. Clemens

P.S.—62,000 copies of *Roughing It* sold & delivered in 4 months.

First Reading

1. Mark each example of humor that you find in the letter, and make notes about what makes each one humorous.
2. In the letter, identify examples of irony, understatement, hyperbole, absurdity, and anecdote. You will probably include items you have noted and possibly others.
3. Explain what you consider to be Clemens's intended effect in each example you noted.
4. Write a statement that you believe describes Clemens's purpose in this letter.
5. Reread lines 20–23. What is Clemens suggesting about the portrait?

---

1   Bret Harte was an author and a friendly rival of Clemens', and in this letter Clemens included a bad picture of himself.

Second Reading

Reread the passage and annotate the letter, carefully noting the effect of words, phrases, and details that enhance your understanding of the irony of Clemens's letter. Then answer the following reading comprehension questions. For each question, explain why you answered as you did.

1. In the statement "I hear so much about it as being among the finest works of art which have yet appeared in that journal" (lines 4–5), Clemens employs which of the following devices?

   (A) paradox
   (B) hyperbole
   (C) sarcasm
   (D) parody
   (E) euphemism

2. In the statement "of all the swarms that come every day to gaze upon them none go away that are not softened & humbled & made more resigned to the will of God" (lines 11–13), Clemens employs which of the following strategies?

   (A) an appeal to logic
   (B) an appeal to ethics
   (C) an appeal to authority
   (D) an argument of fact
   (E) an argument by analogy

3. In the following reference to his uncle, "He has *been* lying at the point of death for two years" (lines 17–18), Clemens's intention can best be inferred to mean which of the following?

   (A) His uncle is seriously ill.
   (B) His uncle is a hypochondriac.
   (C) His uncle requires much attention.
   (D) His uncle may not be ill.
   (E) His uncle is being very tiresome.

4. In his statement, "I want to see if he is dead to Every human instinct" (line 19), which of the following best describes Twain's attitude?

   (A) profound anger
   (B) ambivalent objectivity
   (C) condescending humor
   (D) reasoned subjectivity
   (E) qualified fierceness

5. Which of the following is the most prominent object of Clemens's ridicule in this letter?

   (A) *Hearth & Home* magazine
   (B) W. D. Howells
   (C) himself
   (D) Bret Harte
   (E) European journals

Writing

1. **Analysis** — Write an essay in which you identify the elements of humor in Clemens's letter to Howells. Analyze how his rhetorical choices support his ironic and humorous purpose.
2. **Imitation/Tone** — Imagine that you are writing a letter of congratulations to someone who has won some honor that you consider dubious. In a light, teasing, and humorous tone, ironically belittle the accomplishment and the award. Model your letter after Clemens's.

J. B. Lee, Jr.
Letter to the Honorable Ed Foreman

The following letter was written to a Texas member of the United States Congress. The subject of the letter is U.S. farm subsidies.

March 20, 1963

The Honorable Ed Foreman
House of Representatives
Congressional District #16
5 Washington 25, D.C.

Dear Sir:

My friend over in Terebone Parish received a $1,000 check from the government this year for not raising hogs. So I am going into the not-raising hogs business next year.

What I want to know is, in your opinion, what is the best kind of farm not to raise
10 hogs on and the best kind of hogs not to raise? I would prefer not to raise Razorbacks, but if that is not a good breed not to raise, I will just as gladly not raise any Berkshires or Durocs.

The hardest work in this business is going to be in keeping an inventory of how many hogs I haven't raised.

15 My friend is very joyful about the future of his business. He has been raising hogs for more than 20 years and the best he ever made was $400, until this year when he got $1,000 for not raising hogs.

If I can get $1,000 for not raising 50 hogs, then will I get $2000 for not raising 100 hogs? I plan to operate on a small scale at first, holding myself down to 4,000 hogs,
20 which means I will have $80,000 coming from the government.

Now, another thing: these hogs I will not raise will not eat 100,000 bushels of corn. I understand that you also pay farmers for not raising corn. So will you pay me anything for not raising 100,000 bushels of corn not to feed the hogs that I am not raising?

I want to get started as soon as possible as this seems to be a good time of the year
25 for not raising hogs.

One thing more, can I raise 10 or 12 hogs on the side while I am in the not-raising-hog-business just enough to get a few sides of bacon to eat?

Very truly yours,
J. B. Lee, Jr.
30 Potential Hog Raiser

First Reading

1. Mark each action Lee suggests he intends not to take.
2. Consider how Lee's if/then reasons escalate to the absurd.
3. Circle each concrete or abstract noun that suggests the serious issues.
4. Write a statement that you consider explains Lee's purpose in writing the letter.

Second Reading

1. What is the logical argument Lee sets out?

2. Trace the numbers to which Lee refers and explain how they, along with other concrete details, suggest the seriousness of the issues he addresses, despite the humor.

3. Consider these elements of satire: the institution attacked by the satire, the failing of the institution, the methods of ridicule, and the hoped-for change. Explain how Lee addresses these elements. Would you classify this letter as satiric or simply ironic? Explain your reasoning.

Writing

1. **Analysis** — Write an essay in which you identify the elements of humor and irony in Lee's letter, and analyze how his rhetorical choices convey his view of the absurdity of the government's action.

2. **Argument/Imitation** — Write your own humorous and ironic letter to a government official. Consider your choices of concrete nouns and details to create absurdities, and consider how you can address the following elements of satire: institution addressed, failing under attack, methods of ridicule, and hoped-for change.

Benjamin Franklin
Letter of Recommendation

The statesman and philosopher Benjamin Franklin may also have been America's first humorist. Franklin represented the American colonies as a diplomat in Paris during the American Revolution. Very likely he received many requests for letters of recommendation.

Paris, April 2, 1777

Sir,

The Bearer of this who is going to America, presses me to give him a Letter of Recommendation, tho' I know nothing of him, not even his Name. This may seem extraordinary, but I assure you it is not uncommon here. Sometimes indeed one unknown Person brings me another equally unknown, to recommend him; and sometimes they recommend one another! As to this Gentleman, I must refer you to himself for his Character and Merits, with which he is certainly better acquainted than I can possibly be; I recommend him however to those Civilities which every Stranger, of whom one knows no Harm, has a Right to, and I request you will do him all the good Offices and show him all the Favour that on further Acquaintance you shall find him to deserve. I have the honour to be, &C.

Benjamin Franklin

First Reading

1. Mark each word that tells you information Franklin does not know about the Bearer.
2. What does Franklin suggest about the Bearer to the letter's recipient?

Second Reading

1. What do you learn about the Bearer from the information Franklin indicates he does NOT have about him?
2. What information can you discern about the place from which Franklin writes?

Writing

1. **Imitation/Tone** — Imagine that someone you do not know has asked you to write a letter of introduction for him or her to a prospective employer. Model your letter after Franklin's, and create two drafts, one that models Franklin's tone and one that you change to a tone that is morose or whimsical.
2. **Exposition** — Write the letter that might recap Franklin's conversation with a friend about the subject of his letter.

E. B. White
Letter to Gas Company

E. B. White was an essayist for *The New Yorker*. At the time the letter was written, Consolidated Edison distributed both gas and electricity.

December 21, 1951

Dear Mr. Aiken:

I am a stockholder in the Consolidated Edison Company, and I rent an apartment at 229 East 48 Street in which there is a gas refrigerator. So I have a double interest in your
5 letter of December 19. It seems to me a very odd letter indeed.

You say that my refrigerator, even if it seems to be operating properly, may be producing poison gas, and you suggest that I open a window. I do not want to open a window. It would be a very unpopular move with the cook. Furthermore, I haven't the slightest intention of living under the same roof with a machine that discharges poison
10 gas. Your recommendation is that I get plenty of fresh air—enough to counteract the effect of the gas. But I cannot believe that you are serious.

Will you be good enough to let me know what sort of poison gas is generated by a Servel gas refrigerator, and in what quantity, and how discharged? I know that there is a vent at the top of the machine and that some sort of warm air flows from the vent. I
15 have always assumed it was hot air. Is it something else?

I also know that a gas refrigerator poses a carbon problem, and I ask the landlord to remove the carbon about once a year, which he does. But your letter makes me think that the matter is not so simple and I am anxious to be enlightened.

If gas refrigerators are, as your letter suggests, discharging poison gases into people's
20 homes I don't want to own a gas refrigerator and I shall certainly sell my stock.

E. B. White

First Reading

1. List specific details that you can discern about the writer, audience, and message.
2. Note each instance of White's shifts in point of view.

Second Reading

1. Consider the rhetorical triangle, and explain with specific evidence from the letter how White establishes his argument.
   a. Would you consider the writer trustworthy? Explain using references to the text.
   b. To what does the writer appeal? Explain using references to the text.
   c. What inconsistencies does the writer point out? On what assumptions and on what evidence are they based?
2. Using the Toulmin model, write a thesis sentence for the letter as though you were E. B. White.

Writing

1. **Argument/Imitation** — Write your own description of a similar incident, but focus on another aspect of a product that might be unsafe. Arrange your essay using the White letter as a guide. Establish your plan of argument using the rhetorical triangle.
2. **Analysis** — Write an essay in which you identify White's values and analyze how White's rhetorical strategies convey those values.

Groucho Marx
Letter to Warner Brothers

Groucho Marx was a comedian and one of the famous Marx Brothers. Marx starred in the film *A Night in Casablanca*, released in 1946. The Warner Brothers film, *Casablanca* (1942), starred Ingrid Bergman and Humphrey Bogart. This letter was written in 1946.

Dear Warner Brothers:

Apparently there is more than one way of conquering a city and holding it as your own. For example, up to the time that we contemplated making this picture, I had no idea that the city of Casablanca belonged exclusively to Warner Brothers. However, it was only a

5 few days after our announcement appeared that we received your long, ominous legal document warning us not to use the name Casablanca.

It seems that in 1471, Ferdinand Balboa Warner, your great-great-grandfather, while looking for a shortcut to the city of Burbank, had stumbled on the shores of Africa and, raising his alpenstock (which he later turned in for a hundred shares of the common),

10 named it Casablanca.

I just don't understand your attitude. Even if you plan on re-releasing your picture, I am sure that the average movie fan could learn in time to distinguish between Ingrid Bergman and Harpo. I don't know whether I could, but I certainly would like to try.

You claim you own Casablanca and that no one else can use that name without your

15 permission. What about "Warner Brothers"? Do you own that, too? You probably have the right to use the name Warner, but what about Brothers? Professionally, we were brothers long before you were. We were touring the sticks as The Marx Brothers when Vitaphone was still a gleam in the inventor's eye, and even before us there had been other brothers— the Smith Brothers; the Brothers Karamazov; Dan Brothers, an outfielder with Detroit;

20 and "Brother, Can You Spare a Dime?" (This was originally "Brothers, Can You Spare a Dime?" but this was spreading a dime pretty thin, so they threw out one brother, gave all the money to the other one and whittled it down to, "Brother, Can You Spare a Dime?")

Now Jack, how about you? Do you maintain that yours is an original name? Well, it's not. It was used long before you were born. Offhand, I can think of two Jacks—there was

25 Jack of "Jack and the Beanstalk," and Jack the Ripper, who cut quite a figure in his day.

As for you, Harry, you probably sign your checks, sure in the belief that you are the first Harry of all time and that all other Harrys are imposters. I can think of two Harrys that preceded you. There was Lighthouse Harry of Revolutionary fame and a Harry Appelbaum who lived on the corner of 93rd Street and Lexington Avenue. Unfortunately,

30 Appelbaum wasn't too well known. The last I heard of him, he was selling neckties at Weber and Heilbroner.

Now about the Burbank studio. I believe this is what you brothers call your place. Old man Burbank is gone. Perhaps you remember him. He was a great man in a garden. His wife often said Luther had ten green thumbs. What a witty woman she must have

35 been! Burbank was the wizard who crossed all those fruits and vegetables until he had the poor plants in such a confused and jittery condition that they could never decide whether to enter the dining room on the meat platter or the dessert dish.

This is pure conjecture, of course, but who knows—perhaps Burbank's survivors aren't too happy with the fact that a plant that grinds out pictures on a quota settled in their town,

40 appropriated Burbank's name, and uses it as a front for their films. It is even possible that the Burbank family is prouder of the potato produced by the old man than they are of the fact that from your studio emerged "Casablanca" or even "Gold Diggers of 1931."

This all seems to add up to a pretty bitter tirade, but I assure you it's not meant to. I love Warners. Some of my best friends are Warner Brothers. It is even possible that I am

45 doing you an injustice and that you, yourselves, know nothing at all about this dog-in-

the-Wanger attitude. It wouldn't surprise me at all to discover that the heads of your legal department are unaware of this absurd dispute, for I am acquainted with many of them and they are fine fellows with curly black hair, double-breasted suits and a love of their fellow man that out-Saroyans Saroyan.

50   I have a hunch that this attempt to prevent us from using the title is the brainchild of some ferret-faced shyster, serving a brief apprenticeship in your legal department. I know the type well—hot out of law school, hungry for success and too ambitious to follow the natural laws of promotion. This bar sinister probably needled your attorneys, most of whom are fine fellows with curly black hair, double-breasted suits, etc., into

55   attempting to enjoin us. Well, he won't get away with it! We'll fight him to the highest court! No pasty-faced legal adventurer is going to cause bad blood between the Warners and the Marxes. We are all brothers under the skin and we'll remain friends till the last reel of "A Night in Casablanca" goes tumbling over the spool.

                                                              Sincerely,
60   Groucho Marx

First Reading

1. Mark each detail in Groucho's letter, and trace the elements of the actual message that is couched in the asides that add to the humor.
2. Based on your reading, describe what you can discern about the writer.
3. Based on your reading, describe what you can discern about the audience.

Second Reading

1. Mark each allusion, identify it as historical or literary, and explain how the allusion affects the argument.
2. Mark each pun, and briefly explain how it contributes to the humor.
3. Find more than one mixed metaphor, and briefly explain how each contributes to the humor.
4. Find paragraphs that contain lists of absurdities, and explain how each builds on a detail that contributes to the humor.
5. Explain how the writer addresses a possible counter-argument in the last two paragraphs.

Writing

1. **Analysis** — Write an essay in which you analyze the rhetorical strategies Marx uses to establish his position about the ownership of names.
2. **Argument** — Write an essay in which you support, refute, or qualify Marx's claim that names cannot be owned. Use appropriate evidence to develop your argument.

Ellen Goodman
Breaking the Hungry Teen Code

Ellen Goodman is a Pulitzer Prize-winning columnist for *The Boston Globe*. Her syndicated column appears in newspapers in the United States. This essay was written in 1987.

As a parent who works with words for a living, I have prided my self over many years for a certain skill in breaking the codes of childspeak. I began by interpreting babytalk, moved on to more sophisticated challenges like "chill out" and graduated with "wicked good."

One phrase, however, always stumped me. I was unable to crack the meaning of the common cry echoing through most middle-class American households: "There's Nothing to Eat in This House!"

This exclamation becomes a constant refrain during the summer months when children who have been released from the schoolhouse door grow attached to the refrigerator door. It is during the summer when the average taxpayer realized the true cost-effectiveness of school: It keeps kids out of the kitchen for roughly seven hours a day. A feat no parent is able to match.

At first, like so many others, I assumed that "NETH!" (as in "Nothing to Eat in This House") was a straightforward description of reality. If there was NETH, it was because the children had eaten it all. After all, an empty larder is something you come to expect when you live through the locust phase of adolescence.

I have one friend with three teenage sons who swears that she doesn't even have to unload her groceries anymore. Her children feed directly from the bags, rather like ponies. I have other friends who only buy ingredients for supper on the way home so that supper doesn't turn into lunch.

Over the years, I have considered color-coding food with red, yellow and green stickers. Green for eat. Yellow for eat only if you are starving. Red for "touch this and you die."

However, I discovered that these same locusts can stand in front of a relatively full refrigerator while bleating the same pathetic choruses of "NETH! NETH!" By carefully observing my research subjects, I discovered that the demand of "NETH!" has little to do with supply.

What then does the average underage eater mean when he or she bleats of "NETH! NETH!" You will be glad to know that I have finally broken the code for the "nothing" in NETH and offer herewith my translation.

NETH includes:
1. Any food that must be cooked, especially in a pan or by convectional heat. This covers boiling, frying or baking. Toasting is acceptable under dire conditions.
2. Any food that is in a frozen state with the single exception of ice cream. A frozen pizza may be considered "something to eat" only if there is a microwave oven on hand.
3. Any food that must be assembled before eaten. This means tuna that is still in a can. It may also mean a banana that has to be peeled, but only in extreme cases. Peanut butter and jelly are exempt from this rule as long as they are on the same shelf beside the bread.
4. Leftovers. Particularly if they must be reheated. (See 1)
5. Plain yogurt or anything else that might have been left as a nutrition trap.
6. Food that must be put on a plate, or cut with a knife and fork, as opposed to ripped with teeth while watching videos.
7. Anything that is not stored precisely at eye level. This includes:
8. Any item on a high cupboard shelf, unless it is a box of cookies and:
9. Any edible in the back of the refrigerator, especially on the middle shelf.

While divining the nine meanings of "NETH!" I should also tell you that I developed an anthropological theory about the eating patterns of young Americans. For the most part, I am convinced, Americans below the age of 20 have arrested their development at the food-gathering stage.

They are intrinsically nomadic. Traveling in packs, they engage in nothing more sophisticated than hand-to-mouth dining. They are, in effect, strip eaters who devour the ripest food from one home, and move on to another.

Someday, I am sure they will learn about the use of fire, not to mention forks. Someday, they will be cured of the shelf-blindness, the inability to imagine anything hidden behind a large milk carton. But for now, then can only graze. All the rest is NETH-ing.

First Reading

1. Describe the writer and her audience.
2. Note each incongruity and explain its humorous effect.

Second Reading

1. Find examples of the following rhetorical choices: oxymoron, hyperbole, irony, and absurdity. Explain the meaning and effect of each.
2. Trace the elements of animal imagery. Refer to several examples and explain how each contributes to the humorous qualities of the essay.
3. Explain how the writer uses parody of anthropological study to enhance the humor of her writing.

Writing

1. **Analysis** — Carefully consider the implications of the following definition from the *Merriam-Webster Online Dictionary* as it applies to Ellen Goodman's essay. Then write an essay in which you analyze how Goodman's essay illustrates specific elements of the definition of humor.

    humor a: that quality which appeals to a sense of the ludicrous or absurdly incongruous **b:** the mental faculty of discovering, expressing, or appreciating the ludicrous or absurdly incongruous **c:** something that is or is designed to be comical or amusing. Humor implies an ability to perceive the ludicrous, the comical, and the absurd in human life and to express these usually without bitterness.

2. **Argument/Imitation** — Write an essay in which you create a humorous tone to support, refute, or qualify Goodman's claim that teenagers are hungry locusts, "strip eaters who devour the ripest food from one home and move on to another." Use appropriate evidence to develop your argument.

The Onion
Girl Moved To Tears By *Of Mice And Men* Cliffs Notes

The satiric newspaper *The Onion* parodies traditional newspaper features such as editorials and national and international news. Its layout and design also parody traditional newspaper formats. This essay was published in a 2006 issue of *The Onion*.

CHARLOTTESVILLE, VA—In what she described as "the most emotional moment" of her academic life, University of Virginia sophomore communications major Grace Weaver sobbed openly upon concluding Steinbeck's seminal work of American fiction *Of Mice And Men's* Cliffs Notes early last week.

"This book has changed me in a way that only great literature summaries can," said Weaver, who was so shaken by the experience that she requested an extension on her English 229 essay. "The humanity displayed in the Character Flowchart really stirred something in me. And Lennie's childlike innocence was beautifully captured through the simple, ranch-hand slang words like 'mentally handicapped' and 'retarded.'"

Added Weaver: "I never wanted the synopsis to end."

Weaver, who formed an "instant connection" with Lennie's character-description paragraph, said she began to suspect the novel might end tragically after reading the fourth sentence which suggested the gentle giant's strength and fascination with soft things would "lead to his untimely demise."

"I was amazed at how attached to him I had become just from the critical commentary," said Weaver, still clutching the yellow-and-black-striped study guide. "When I got to the last sentence—'George shoots Lennie in the head,'—it seemed so abrupt. But I found out later that the 'ephemeral nature of life' is a major theme of the novel."

Weaver was assigned *Of Mice And Men*—a novel scholars have called "a masterpiece of austere prose" and "the most skillful example of American naturalism under 110 pages"—as part of her early twentieth-century fiction course, and purchased the Cliffs Notes from a cardboard rack at her local Barnes & Noble. John Whittier-Ferguson, her professor for the class, told reporters this was not the first time one of his students has expressed interest in the novel's plot summary.

"It's one of those universal American stories," said Ferguson after being informed of Weaver's choice to read the Cliffs Notes instead of the pocket-sized novel. "I look forward to skimming her essay on the importance of following your dreams and randomly assigning it a grade."

Though she completed the two-page brief synopsis in one sitting, Weaver said she felt strangely drawn into the plot overview and continued on, exploring the more fleshed-out chapter summaries.

"There's something to be said for putting in that extra time with a good story," Weaver said. "You just get more out of it. I'm also going to try to find that book about rabbits that George was always reading to Lennie, so that I can really understand that important allusion."

Within an hour of completing the cliffs notes, Weaver was already telling friends and classmates that Steinbeck was her favorite author, as well as reciting select quotations from the "Important Quotations" section for their benefit.

"When I read those quotes, found out which characters they were attributed to, and inferred their context from the chapter outlines to piece together their significance, I was just blown away," said a teary-eyed Weaver. "And the way Steinbeck wove the theme of hands all the way through the section entitled 'Hands'—he definitely deserved to win that Nobel Prize."

Weaver's roommate, Giulia Crenshaw, has already borrowed the dog-eared, highlighted summary of the classic Depression-era saga, and is expecting to enjoy reading what Weaver described as "a really sad story about two brothers who love to farm."

"I loved this book so much, I'm going to read all of Steinbeck's Cliffs Notes," said Weaver. "But first I'm going to go to the library to check out the original version *Of Mice And Men* starring John Malkovich and Gary Sinise."

First Reading

1. Describe everything you can discern about the writer and audience.
2. Note each incongruity and explain its humorous effect.
3. Explain how these incongruities humorously reflect an element of contemporary society.

Second Reading

1. Does this essay attack vice or folly? Explain.
2. How does this essay address conventional morality?
3. What would generate a harmonious resolution to the failing of the element of society addressed?

Writing

1. **Analysis** — Write an essay in which you analyze the strategies used in the essay to satirize how some students approach reading assignments.
2. **Argument** — Write an essay in which you evaluate the pros and cons of the statement that follows.

   Indignation and outrage in response to injustice or absurdity can initiate social change.

   Use appropriate evidence as you evaluate each side and indicate which position you fine more persuasive.

Herblock
Read me what it says, Dad

Herb Block, who signed his work Herblock, was a longtime editorial cartoonist for *The Washington Post*. This cartoon was published in 1977.

Reading

1. What does the cartoonist's attitude seem to be toward the subject? Explain your answer with references to elements of the text.
2. Consider the written text in concert with the drawing. What might be the intended effects of this cartoon?
3. What aspect of contemporary society does the cartoonist address? Consider the following: the institution, the failing, the method of ridicule, and the hoped-for change.
4. Based on your observations, would you consider the cartoon satiric? Explain your reasoning.

Writing

Comparison/Argument — Compare the humor in Herblock's cartoon and *The Onion* essay. Then write an essay in which you analyze the humorous elements of each text and explain which text offers the more persuasive argument that some students do not read.

Samuel Clemens, writing as Mark Twain, was a master of satire. The original audience and occasion for this lecture remain unknown, but the talk was probably delivered in 1882.

Being told I would be expected to talk here, I inquired what sort of a talk I ought to make. They said it should be something suitable to youth—something didactic, instructive, or something in the nature of good advice. Very well. I have a few things in my mind, which I have often longed to say for the instruction of the young; for it is in one's tender early years that such things will best take root and be enduring and most valuable.

First, then, I will say to you, my young friends—and I say it beseechingly, urgingly—

Always obey your parents, when they are present. This is the best policy in the long run, because if you don't they will make you. Most parents think they know better than you do, and you can generally make more by humoring that superstition than you can by acting on your own better judgment.

Be respectful to your superiors, if you have any, also to strangers, and sometimes to others. If a person offend you, and you are in doubt as to whether it was intentional or not, do not resort to extreme measures; simply watch your chance and hit him with a brick. That will be sufficient. If you shall find that he had not intended any offense, come out frankly and confess yourself in the wrong when you struck him; acknowledge it like a man and say you didn't mean to. Yes, always avoid violence; in this age of charity and kindliness, the time has gone by for such things. Leave dynamite to the low and unrefined.

Go to bed early, get up early—this is wise. Some authorities say get up with the sun; some others say to get up with one thing, some with another. But a lark is really the best thing to get up with. It gives you a splendid reputation with everybody to know that you get up with the lark; and if you get the right kind of lark, and work at him right, you can easily train him to get up at half past nine, every time—it is no trick at all.

Now as to the matter of lying. You want to be very careful about lying; otherwise you are nearly sure to get caught. Once caught, you can never again be, in the eyes of the good and pure, what you were before. Many a young person has injured himself permanently through a single clumsy and ill finished lie, the result of carelessness born of incomplete training. Some authorities hold that the young ought not to lie at all. That, of course, is putting it rather stronger than necessary; still, I cannot go quite so far as that, I do maintain, and I believe I am right, that the young ought to be temperate in the use of this great art until practice and experience shall give them that confidence, elegance, and precision which alone can make the accomplishment graceful and profitable. Patience, diligence, painstaking attention to detail—these are the requirements; these, in time, will make the student perfect; upon these, and upon these only, may he rely as the sure foundation for the future eminence. Think what tedious years of study, thought, practice, experience, went to the equipment of that peerless old master who was able to impose upon the whole world the lofty and sounding maxim that "truth is mighty and will prevail"—the most majestic compound fracture of fact which any woman born has yet achieved. For the history of our race, and each individual's experience, are sown thick with evidence that a truth is not hard to kill and that a lie told well is immortal. There is in Boston a monument of the man who discovered anesthesia; many people are aware, in these latter days, that that man didn't discover it at all, but stole the discovery from another man. Is this truth mighty, and will it prevail? Ah no, my hearers, the monument is made of hardy material, but the lie is a thing which ought to make it your unceasing study to avoid; such a lie as that has no more real permanence than an average truth. Why, you might as well tell the truth at once and be done with it. A feeble, stupid, preposterous lie will not live two years—except it be a slander upon somebody. It is indestructible, then, of course, but that is no merit of yours. A final word: begin your practice of this gracious and beautiful art early—begin now. If I had begun earlier, I could have learned how.

Never handle firearms carelessly. The sorrow and suffering that have been caused though the innocent but heedless handling of firearms by the young! Only four days ago, right in the next farmhouse to the one where I am spending the summer,

a grandmother, old and gray and sweet, one of the loveliest spirits in the land, was sitting at her work,
95 when her young grandson crept in and got down an old, battered, rusty gun which had not been touched for many years and was supposed not to be loaded, and pointed it at her, laughing and threatening to shot. In her fright she ran screaming
100 and pleading toward the door on the other side of the room; but as she passed him he placed the gun almost against her very breast and pulled the trigger! He had supposed it was not loaded. And he was right—it wasn't. So there wasn't any harm
105 done. It is the only case of that kind I ever heard of. Therefore, just the same, don't you meddle with old unloaded firearms; they are the most deadly and unerring things that have ever been created by man. You don't have to take any pains at all with
110 them; you don't have to take aim, even. No, you just pick out a relative and bang away, and you are sure to get him. A youth who can't hit a cathedral at thirty yards with a Gatling gun in three-quarters
115 of an hour, can take up an old empty musket and bag his grandmother every time, at a hundred. Think what Waterloo would have been if one of the armies had been composed of their female relations. The very thought of it makes one shudder.

There are many sorts of books; but good ones
120 are the sort for the young to read. Remember that. They are great, an inestimable, an unspeakable means of improvement. Therefore be careful in your selection, my young friends; be very careful; confine yourselves exclusively to Robertson's *Ser-*
125 *mons*, Baxter's *Saint's Rest*, *The Innocents Abroad*, and works of that kind.

But I have said enough. I hope you will treasure up the instructions, which I have given you, and make them a guide to your feet and light to your
130 understanding. Build your character thoughtfully and painstakingly upon this precept, and by and by, when you have got it built, you will be surprised and gratified to see how nicely and sharply it resembles everybody else's.

First Reading

1. What can you determine about the speaker from your reading of this talk? What can you determine about the audience?
2. Note each incongruity that produces humor. Mark these incongruities as hyperbole, pun, absurdity, or irony; also note which of these elements can be classified as images or anecdote.

Second Reading

1. Jonathan Swift observed, "Satire is like a mirror in which people see everyone's face except their own." More than one group is addressed in this essay. Explain.
2. Explain how Clemens attempts through humor to inspire a remodeling of behavior.

Writing

1. **Argument/Imitation** — Write an essay entitled "Advice to Adults" or "Advice to Parents." Imitate Clemens's organization of ideas and examples within each paragraph. Also, imitate the strategies that produce humor.
2. **Argument** — Create a photo essay with captions or other form of written text to accompany your imitation of Clemens's advice.

Jonathan Swift
A Meditation Upon a Broom-Stick

Jonathan Swift, a satirist and essayist, wrote this short work in 1710 as a parody of a religious work of the time.

The single stick, which you now behold ingloriously lying in that neglected corner, I once knew in a flourishing state in forest; it was full of sap, full of leaves, and full of boughs; but now, in vain does the busy art of man pretend to vie with nature, by tying that withered bundle of twigs to its sapless trunk; 'tis now at best but the reverse of what
5   it was, a tree turned upside down, the branches on the earth, and the root in the air; 'tis now handled by every dirty wench, condemned to do her drudgery, and by a capricious kind of fate, destined to make other things clean, and be nasty itself: at length, worn to the stumps in the service of the maids, 'tis either thrown out of doors, or condemned to its last use, of kindling a fire. When I beheld this I sighed, and said within myself, Surely
10 mortal man is a Broomstick! Nature sent him into the world strong and lusty, in a thriving condition, wearing his own hair on his head, the proper branches of this reasoning vegetable, till the axe of intemperance has lopped off his green boughs, and left him a withered trunk: he then flies to art, and puts on a periwig, valuing himself upon an unnatural bundle of hairs, all covered with powder, that never grew on his head; but now
15 should this our broomstick pretend to enter the scene, proud of those birchen spoils it never bore, and all covered with dust, though the sweepings of the finest lady's chamber, we should be apt to ridicule and despise its vanity. Partial judges that we are of our own excellencies, and other men's defaults!

   But a broomstick, perhaps you will say, is an emblem of a tree standing on its head; and
20 pray what is man, but a topsy-turvy creature, his animal faculties perpetually mounted on his rational, his head where his heels should be, groveling on the earth! And yet with all his faults, he sets up to be an universal reformer and corrector of abuses, a remover of grievances, rakes into every slut's corner of Nature, bringing hidden corruptions to the light, and raises a mighty dust where there was none before; sharing deeply all the
25 while in the very same pollutions he pretends to sweep away. His last days are spent in slavery to women, and generally the least deserving, till, worn out to the stumps, like his brother besom, he is either kicked out of doors, or made use of to kindle flames for others to warm themselves by.

First Reading

1. At the beginning of paragraph one, how does the repetition, "full of sap, full of leaves, full of boughs" create the emphasis for "in vain"?

2. What is it that is "in vain"? Explain what Swift means by "the busy art of man."

3. How does Swift emphasize incongruities in "a tree turned upside down, the branches on the earth, and the root in the air; 'tis now handled by every dirty wench, condemned to do her drudgery, and by a capricious kind of fate, destined to make other things clean, and be nasty itself"? How is the statement ironic, and how does it serve Swift's satiric purpose in this statement?

4. How does Swift explain his metaphor, "Surely mortal man is a Broomstick"? Paraphrase your answer. What is "the axe of intemperance"? What are "those birchen spoils it never bore"?

5. What is the meaning of the fragment that ends the first paragraph? Why does Swift use a fragment instead of a complete sentence here?

6. How does Swift compete the analogy in the second paragraph? What is Swift's satirical purpose in this analogy?

7. How does Swift's arrangement of comparisons lead us to expect the irony of the concluding sentence?

Second Reading

1. Draw and label all the images Swift includes.

2. With a partner or in a small group, rewrite Swift's essay in your own words. You might consider assigning parts for the rewriting; then collaborate to determine the correctness of the rewrite.

Writing

1. **Analysis** — Examine the satiric qualities of Swift's essay. Then write your own essay that analyzes the rhetorical strategies Swift uses to suggest that "modern man" is turned upside down.

2. **Argument/Imitation** — Write your own essay about modern teenagers. Imitate Swift's strategies, but create your own writer's voice.

3. **Synthesis**

Directions   The following task requires the integration of at least two texts from this chapter along with at least two additional texts, chosen after extended thinking and research. Integrate references to the texts into your essay in support of your own argument. Do not merely summarize the sources. You must attribute both direct and indirect quotations.

Introduction   Carefully consider the following comments by Bruce Michelson in *Literary Wit*. "Wit needs to be appreciated not as verbal joust but as a strategy for interpreting the complexities of the world. It is a way to integrate thinking about the seriousness and the worries and challenges of life." And "Wit is not simply an end to itself, a classification for verbal play, a comedic interlude, a joke; it is a means to find and to understand what is important in and about our lives." How does your view of wit resemble or differ from Michelson's?

Assignment Options   Choose one of the following writing assignments.

Write an essay in which you offer an extended definition of wit that explains the range of human responses to it and its value in forming our views of the world. Illustrate your definition by combining at least two of the sources you read in this chapter and at least two other sources. Prepare a draft for a teacher or peer conference; then write and submit a final version.

Write an essay in which you develop a position on the value of wit as a means of "interpreting the complexities of the world." Synthesize at least two of the sources you read in this chapter and at least two other sources in support of your documented argument. Prepare a draft for a teacher or peer conference, and then submit a final version.

Glossary
of Rhetorical Terms

alliteration   the repetition of initial sounds in successive words

anaphora   the use of repeated words at the beginnings of phrases, clauses, and sentences

antithesis   the juxtaposition of opposites, often in parallel structure

arrangement   the order in which ideas are presented in a speech or essay

artistic proofs   the proofs that are within the control of the speaker or writer; identified by Aristotle as ethos, logos, and pathos

backing   in the Toulmin scheme, support for the warrant; the unstated assumption behind the argument

claim   a statement of a position; a stand or thesis

conditions of rebuttal   in the Toulmin scheme, the anticipation and addressing of counter-arguments

confirmatio   the arguments supporting the proposition; the evidence propping up the argument

enthymeme   a statement that omits a premise that is understood by the audience; a shortened syllogism that serves as a practical and more expedient way to argue

ethos   the character or credibility of the speaker or writer

exordium   the introduction that gains the audience's attention

grounds   in the Toulmin scheme, the actual evidence in support of the reasons

hyperbole   an exaggeration to achieve a heightened effect

invention   the process of formulating and ordering ideas for speaking and writing

irony   a figure of speech in which the actual meaning of the words is expressed as the literal opposite

logos   the content of the written or spoken message

metaphor   a comparison between unlike things

narratio   background information; the facts of the case

pathos   the emotional appeal to the audience by the speaker or writer

partitio   the main headings or topics under which a topic will be discussed

periodic sentence   a very long sentence that delays the predicate until the end, or both the subject and the predicate, until the end

peroratio	conclusion; summary of arguments, calling for a specific response and making a final emotional appeal
propositio	the main idea or thesis
qualifier	in the Toulmin scheme, a limit on the claim
reasons	in the Toulmin scheme, supports for a claim
refutatio	the counter-arguments
rhetorical context	background or situation to which a persuasive message is addressed
rhetorical triangle	traditionally, a figure representing the writer, audience, and message as the three points of the triangle; in the modern version, a figure consisting of five elements: writer, audience, message, purpose, and rhetorical context
Rogerian argument	a modern method of argumentation that tries to find mutually agreeable solutions to problems by seeking common ground, building trust, and reducing threat
says/does analysis	a method for close reading and rhetorical analysis of a text, using summary of the content of the text (what the text says) and description of the construction, organization, and form of the text (what the text does)
style	the way in which the writer or speaker expresses ideas
syllogism	a chain of logical reasoning moving from general, universal principles to specific instances
Toulmin scheme	a model of informal logic commonly used in argumentation
visual rhetoric	the incorporation of visual elements (such as photographs, charts, or Web sites) into an argument, and the rhetorical impact of those images on an audience
warrant	in the Toulmin scheme, the unstated assumption behind an argument

Acknowledgements

Peoples Education, Inc. has made every effort to obtain permission for the reprinting of all selections contained herein. If any owner of copyrighted material is not acknowledged herein, please contact the publisher for proper acknowledgement in all future editions or reprintings of this book.

excerpts from "Letter from Birmingham Jail" by Martin Luther King, Jr. Reprinted by arrangement with The Heirs to the Estate of Martin Luther King Jr., c/o Writers House as agent for the proprietor New York, NY. Copyright © 1963 Martin Luther King Jr., copyright renewed 1991 Coretta Scott King; p. 20, "The Stranger in the Photo is Me." *The Boston Globe*, 1991. Copyright © 1991 by Donald M. Murray. Reprinted by permission of The Rosenberg Group on behalf of author's estate; pgs. 20, 22, photographs of Donald Murray, Courtesy of Anne Murray. Reprinted by permission; p. 25, "Woman Waiting to Take a Photograph" by Dave Eggers, from *The Education of a Photographer* edited by Charles H. Traub, Steven Heller and Adam B. Bell. Published by Allworth Press, New York. Reprinted by permission; p. 27, excerpt from "Photography and the Art of Seeing: A Visual Perception Workshop for Film and Digital Photography" by Freeman Patterson, published by Key Porter Books, 2004. Reprinted with permission of Key Porter Books. Copyright: © 1985, 1989, 2004 by Freeman Patterson; p. 30, Foreword by N. Scott Momaday from Sacred Legacy: Edward S. Curtis and the North American Indian, Copyright © 2005 Verve Editions Ltd. And Cardozo Fine Art, Inc. Reprinted by permission; p. 31, photograph (left) National Archives, photograph (right) Slow Bull – Ogalala by Edward S. Curtis. From the collection of Christopher Cardozo. Reprinted by permission; p. 32, "The Power of Pictures" from LIFE Special Issue: *150 Years of Photography: Pictures That Made a Difference*, Fall 1998. Copyright 1998 Life Inc. Reprinted with permission. All rights reserved; p. 33, photograph, NASA; p. 34, excerpt from "ON PHOTOGRAPHY" by Susan Sontag. Copyright © 1977 by Susan Sontag. Reprinted by permission of Farrar, Straus and Giroux, LLC.; p. 35, excerpt from "Photojournalism: A Blend of Artifice and Actuality" by Andy Grundberg, published in the *New York Times*, January 10, 1998. Reprinted in *Crisis of the Real: Writings of Photography Since 1974* by Andy Grundberg, Copyright © 1999 by Andy Grundberg. Published by the Aperture Foundation, Inc.; p. 38, excerpt from "On Duties" by Marcus Tullius Cicero. Published by the Press Syndicate of the University of Cambridge, Cambridge University Press 1991; p. 39, excerpt from "Message to Invasion Troops" by Dwight D. Eisenhower; p. 41, "Into the Jaws of Death," photograph from Franklin D. Roosevelt Library; p. 43, excerpt from Catiline's Speech To His Army Before His Defeat in Battle; p. 45, excerpt from "On War" by James Boswell; p. 50, "Farewell Address to the Nation" by Dwight D. Eisenhower; p. 53, "Commencement Address" by Douglas MacArthur. This work originally appeared in *Centennial Review*, Volume 5, 1961, published by Michigan State University Press; p. 56, Stockholm International Peace Research Institute, "Patterns of Major Armed Conflicts 1990-2005" by Mikael Eriksson and Peter Wallensteen. Source: Uppsala Conflict Data Program. Published in SIPRI Yearbook, 2004; p. 58, excerpt from "Warfare: An Invention – Not a Biological Necessity" by Margaret Mead, *Asia*, Vol. 40, No. 8, 1940, Institute for Intercultural Studies. Reprinted by permission; p. 62, "Mary Ewald to Iraqi President Saddam Hussein" from *Letters of a Nation: A Collection of Extraordinary American Letters*, edited by Andrew Carroll. Published by Broadway Books, an imprint of Random House. Copyright © 1997 by Andrew Carroll. All rights reserved; p. 64, photographs (left), Marilyn Monroe, AP/Wide World Photos, (right), "Swahili Women" by A.C. Gomes, 1910; p. 66, "Why I Wear Purple Lipstick" by Jean Godfrey-June, from *What is Beauty?* by Dorothy Schefer, p. 131. Copyright © 1997, Universe Publishing. A division of Rizzoli International Publications, Inc. Reprinted by permission; p. 68, excerpt from SURVIVAL OF THE PRETTIEST by Nancy Etcoff, copyright © 1999 by Nancy Etcoff. Used by permission of Doubleday, a division of Random House, Inc.; p. 71, excerpt from "HOPE IN A JAR: The Making of America's Beauty Culture" by Kathy Peiss. Copyright 1998 by Kathy Peiss. Reprinted by permission of Henry Holt and Company; p. 74, excerpt from THE BEAUTY JUNKIES INSIDE OUR $15 BILIION OBSESSION WITH COSMETIC SURGERY by Alex Kuczynski, copyright © 2006 by Alex Kuczynski. Used by permission of Doubleday, a division of Random House, Inc.; p. 77, "The Democratization of Beauty" by Christine Rosen, published by *The New Atlantis*, Copyright © 2004. Reprinted by permission; p. 84, "The Truth About Beauty" by Virginia Postrel, from *"The Atlantic Monthly,"* March 2007, Volume 299. Copyright © Virginia Postrel 2007; p. 88, Pages 61-63 from "The Fixed" from PILGRIM AT TINKER CREEK by ANNIE DILLARD. Copyright © 1974 by Annie Dillard. Reprinted by permission of HarperCollins Publishers; p. 90, excerpt from "Brute Neighbors," from *Walden* by Henry David Thoreau; p. 92, "Letter to Fellow-Naturalist in Another Part of England," 1777, by Gilbert White; p. 94, "The Lives of a Cell," copyright © 1971 by the Massachusetts Medical Society, from THE LIVES OF A CELL by Lewis Thomas. Used by permission of Viking Penguin, a division of Penguin Group (USA) Inc.; p. 96, "The Round Walls of Home" by Diane Ackerman. Copyright © 1990 by Diane Ackerman. Reprinted by permission of William Morris Agency, LLC on behalf of the Author; p. 98, photograph, Earth from Apollo 17, October 26, 1997. NASA; p. 100, "Respect" by Suquamish, Chief Seattle; p. 103, "The Slow Awakening" from THE WEATHER MAKERS by Tim Flannery. Copyright © 2005